Intel® Xeon Phi™ Coprocessor Architecture and Tools

The Guide for Application Developers

Rezaur Rahman

Intel® Xeon Phi™ Coprocessor Architecture and Tools: The Guide for Application Developers

Rezaur Rahman

ISBN 978-1-4302-5926-8

ISBN 978-1-4302-5927-5 (eBook)

Trademarked names, logos, and images may appear in this book. Rather than use a trademark symbol with every occurrence of a trademarked name, logo, or image we use the names, logos, and images only in an editorial fashion and to the benefit of the trademark owner, with no intention of infringement of the trademark.

The use in this publication of trade names, trademarks, service marks, and similar terms, even if they are not identified as such, is not to be taken as an expression of opinion as to whether or not they are subject to proprietary rights.

While the advice and information in this book are believed to be true and accurate at the date of publication, neither the authors nor the editors nor the publisher can accept any legal responsibility for any errors or omissions that may be made. The publisher makes no warranty, express or implied, with respect to the material contained herein.

President and Publisher: Paul Manning
Lead Editors: Jeffrey Pepper (Apress); Patrick Hauke (Intel)
Development Editor: Robert Hutchinson
Coordinating Editor: Anamika Panchoo
Cover Designer: Anna Ishchenko

Distributed to the book trade worldwide by Springer Science+Business Media New York, 233 Spring Street, 6th Floor, New York, NY 10013. Phone 1-800-SPRINGER, fax (201) 348-4505, e-mail orders-ny@springer-sbm.com, or visit www.springeronline.com.

For information on translations, please e-mail rights@apress.com, or visit www.apress.com.

About ApressOpen

What Is ApressOpen?

- ApressOpen is an open access book program that publishes high-quality technical and business information.

- ApressOpen eBooks are available for global, free, noncommercial use.

- ApressOpen eBooks are available in PDF, ePub, and Mobi formats.

- The user friendly ApressOpen free eBook license is presented on the copyright page of this book.

To my mother, who has always been so proud of me and wanted for me to be my best, and to my mother-in-law, who has eagerly been waiting for this book to be published

Contents at a Glance

Contents

About the Author

Rezaur Rahman is a Senior Staff Engineer in the Intel Software and Services Group. He played a key role in the inception and development of the Xeon Phi coprocessor for technical computing applications by demonstrating the viability of applying Intel's manycore graphics processor codenamed Larrabee to solving technical computing problems. He led the worldwide technical enabling team for Intel Xeon Phi products, focused on porting and optimizing applications on the Xeon Phi coprocessor for hundreds of technical computing customers. He has worked internally with hardware architects and Intel compiler and tools teams to optimize and add features to improve the performance of Intel Many Integrated Core (MIC) and Xeon Phi software and hardware components. With 25 years experience in computer architecture and software design, Rahman contributes his expertise in technical code optimization, performance tuning, and hardware microarchitectural analysis in the HPC domain to various industry standardization groups such as the World Wide Web Consortium (W3C). Rahman holds a master's degree in computer science from Texas A&M University and a bachelor's in electrical engineering from Bangladesh University of Engineering and Technology.

About the Technical Reviewer

Leonardo Borges is a Senior Staff Engineer in the Intel Software and Services Group. He realizes system and software design and optimization with a primary focus on the energy vertical. Borges has specialized in applying his background in numerical analysis and parallel numerical mathematics libraries development in the HPC domain for the past two decades. He joined the Intel Many Integrated Core (MIC) program at its early stages. Borges holds a master's degree in applied mathematics and a PhD in computer science from Texas A&M.

Acknowledgments

I appreciate all the support and encouragement I received while writing the book from my wife Farzana, my daughters Fariha and Ridwana, and my father.

My sincere thanks go to the ApressOpen publishing team—Robert Hutchinson, Anamika Panchoo, and others—and to the technical reviewer, Leo Borges, for helping me get through the tough job of completing the book by editing the presentation and helping to refine the content. Thanks to Patrick Hauke and Stuart Douglas from Intel Press for encouraging me to take on the project and providing the necessary support to get it published.

Finally, I appreciate the unstinting help from my engineering colleagues at Intel who have helped me understand and improve my knowledge of the architecture and optimization techniques for the Intel Xeon Phi coprocessor.

Introduction

This book provides a comprehensive introduction to Intel Xeon Phi architecture and the tools necessary for software engineers and scientists to develop optimized code for systems using Intel Xeon Phi coprocessors. It presents the in-depth knowledge of the Xeon Phi coprocessor architecture that developers need to have to utilize the power of Xeon Phi. My book presupposes prior knowledge of modern cache-based processor architecture, but it begins with a review of the general architectural history, concepts, and nomenclature that I assume my readers bring.

Because this book is intended for practitioners rather than theoreticians, I have filled it with code examples chosen to illuminate features of Xeon Phi architecture in the light of code optimization. The book is divided into three parts corresponding to the areas engineers and scientists need to know to develop and optimize code on Xeon Phi for high-performance technical computing:

> Part 1—"Hardware Foundation: Intel Xeon Phi Architecture"—sketches the salient features of modern cache-based architecture with reference to some of the history behind the development of Xeon Phi architecture that I was personally engaged in. It then walks the reader through the functional details of Xeon Phi architecture, using code samples to disclose the performance metrics and behavioral characteristics of the processor.

> Part 2—"Software Foundation: Intel Xeon Phi System Software and Tools"—describes the system software and tools necessary to build and run applications on the Xeon Phi system. I drill into the details of the software layers involved in coordinating communication and computations between the host processor and a Xeon Phi coprocessor.

> Part 3—"Applications: Technical Computing Software Development on Intel Xeon Phi"—discusses the characteristics of algorithms and data structures that are well tuned for the Xeon Phi coprocessor. I use C-like pseudo-algorithms to illustrate most instructively the various kinds of algorithms that are optimized for the Xeon Phi coprocessor. Although this final part of the book makes no pretensions to being comprehensive, it is rich with practical pointers for developing and optimizing your own code on the Xeon Phi coprocessor.

Although each of the three parts of the book is relatively self-contained, allowing readers to go directly to the topics that are of most interest to them, I strongly recommend that you read Part 1 for the architectural foundation to understand the discussion of algorithms in Part 3. These algorithms are mainly of practical interest to the Xeon Phi community for optimizing their code for this architecture.

Hardware Foundation: Intel Xeon Phi Architecture

PART 7

Hardware Foundation: Intel Xeon Phi Architecture

CHAPTER 1

■ ■ ■

Introduction to Xeon Phi Architecture

Technical computing can be defined as the application of mathematical and computational principles to solve engineering and scientific problems. It has become an integral part of the research and development of new technologies in modern civilization. It is universally relied upon in all sectors of industry and all disciplines of academia for such disparate tasks as prototyping new products, forecasting weather, enhancing geosciences exploration, performing financial modeling, and simulating car crashes and the propagation of electromagnetic field from mobile phones.

Computer technology has made substantial progress over the past couple of decades by introducing superscalar processors with pipelined vector architecture. We have also seen the rise of parallel processing in the lowest computational segment, such as handheld devices. Today one can buy as much computational power as earlier supercomputers for less than a thousand dollars.

Current computational power still is not enough, however, for the type of research needed to push the edge of understanding of the physical and analytical processes addressed by technical computing applications. Massively parallel processors such as the Intel Xeon Phi product family have been developed to increase the computational power to remove these research barriers. Careful design of algorithm and data structures is needed to exploit the Intel *Many Integrated Core* (MIC) architecture of coprocessors capable of providing teraflops (trillions of mathematical operations per second) of double-precision floating-point performance. This book provides an in-depth look at the Intel Xeon Phi coprocessor architecture and the corresponding parallel data structure and algorithms used in the various technical computing applications for which it is suitable. It also examines the source code-level optimizations that can be performed to exploit features of the processor.

Processor microarchitecture describes the arrangements and relationship between different components to perform the computation. With the advent of semiconductor technologies, hardware companies were able to put many processing cores on a die and interconnect them intelligently to allow massive computing power in the modern range of teraflops of double-precision arithmetic. This type of computing power was achieved first by the supercomputer *Accelerated Strategic Computing Initiative* (ASCI) Red in the not-so-distant past in 1996.

This chapter will help you develop an understanding of the design decisions behind the Intel Xeon Phi coprocessor microarchitecture and how it complements the Intel Xeon product line. To that end, it provides a brief refresher of modern computer architecture and describes various aspects of the Intel Xeon Phi architecture at a high level. You will develop an understanding of Intel MIC architecture and how it addresses the massively parallel one-chip computational challenge. This chapter summarizes the capabilities and limitations of the Intel Xeon Phi coprocessor, as well as key impact points for software and hardware evaluators who are considering this platform for technical computing, and sets the stage for the deeper discussions in following chapters.

History of Intel Xeon Phi Development

Intel Xeon Phi started its gestation in 2004 when Intel processor architecture teams began looking for a solution to reduce the power consumption of the Intel Xeon family of processors developed around 2001. We ultimately determined in 2010 that the simple low-frequency Intel MIC architecture with appropriate software support would be able to produce better performance and watt efficiency. This solution required a new microarchitectural design. The question was: Could we use the x86 cores for it? The answer was yes, because the *instruction set architecture* (ISA) needed for x86 compatibility dictates a small percentage of power consumption, whereas the hardware implementation and circuit complexity drive most of the power dissipation in a general-purpose processor.

The architecture team experimented on a simulator with various architecture features—removing out-of-order execution, hardware multithreading, long vectors, and so forth—to develop a new architecture that could be applied to throughput-oriented workloads. A graphics workload fits throughput-oriented work nicely, as many threads can work in parallel to compute the final solution.

The design team focused on the in-order core, x86 ISA, a smaller pipeline, and wider *single instruction multiple data*(SIMD)a nd *symmetric multithreading* (SMT) units. So they started with Pentium 5 cores connected through a ring interface and added fixed-function units such as a texture sampler to help with graphics. The design goal was to create architecture with the proper balance between chip-level multiprocessing with thread and data-level parallelism. A simulator was used to anticipate various performance bottlenecks and tune the core and uncore designs (discussed in the next section).

In addition to understanding the use of such technology in graphics, Intel also recognized that scientific and engineering applications that are highly compute-intensive and thread- and process-scalable can benefit from manycore architecture. During this time period the high-performance computing (HPC) industry also started playing around with using graphics cards for general-purpose computation. It was obvious that there was promise to such technology.

Working with some folks at Intel Labs in 2009, I was able to demonstrate theoretically to our management and executive team that one could make some key computational kernels that would speed up quite a bit with such a low-frequency, highly-parallel architecture, such that overall application performance would improve even in a coprocessor model. This demonstration resulted in the funding of the project that led to Intel Xeon Phi development. The first work had started in 2005 on Larrabee 1 (Figure 1-1) as a graphics processor. The work proceeded in 2010 as a proof-of-concept prototype HPC coprocessor project code-named *Knights Ferry*. The visual computing product team within Intel started developing software for technical computing applications. Although the hardware did not change, their early drivers were based on graphics software needs and catered to graphics application programming interface (API) needs, which were mainly Windows-based at that point.

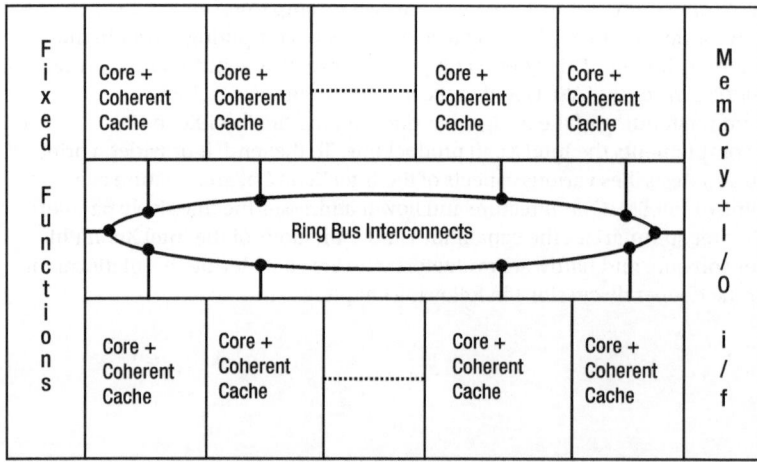

Figure 1-1. *Larrabee 1 silicon block diagram*

The first thing the software architects recognized was that a lot of technical and scientific computing is done on the Linux platform. So the first step was to create software support for Linux. We also needed to develop a programming language that could leverage the existing skills of the software developers to create multithreaded applications using Message Passing Interface (MPI) and OpenMP with the C, C++, and Fortran languages. The Intel compiler team went to the drawing board to define language extensions that would allow users to write applications that could run on coprocessors and host at the same time, leveraging the compute power of both. Other Intel teams went back to the design board to make tools and libraries—such as cluster tools (MPI), Debugger, Amplifier XE, Math Kernel Library, and Numeric—to support the new coprocessor architecture.

As the hardware consisted of x86 cores, the device driver team ported a modular microkernel that was based on standard Linux kernel source. The goal of the first phase of development was to prove and hash out the usability of the tools and language extensions that Intel was making. The goal was to come out with a hardware and software solution that could fill the needs of technical computing applications. The hardware roadmap included a new hardware architecture code-named *Knights Corner* (KNC) which could provide 1 teraflop of double-precision performance with the reliability and power management features required by such computations. This hardware was later marketed as *Intel® Xeon Phi™*—thes ubjecto ft hisb ook.

Evolution from Von Neumann Architecture to Cache Subsystem Architecture

There are various functional units in modern-day computer architecture that need to be carefully designed and developed to achieve target power and performance. The center of these functional units is a generic programmable processor that works in combination with other components such as memory, peripherals, and other coprocessors to perform its tasks. It is important to understand the basic computer architecture to get the grasp of Intel Xeon Phi architecture, since in essence the latter is a specialized architecture with many of the components used in designing am odernp arallelc omputer.

Basic computer architecture is known as Von Neumann architecture. In this fundamental design, the processor is responsible for arithmetic and logic operations and gets its data and instructions from the memory (Figure 1-2). It fetches instructions from memory pointed to by an instruction pointer and executes the instruction. If the instruction needs data, it collects the data from the memory location pointed to by instruction and executes on them.

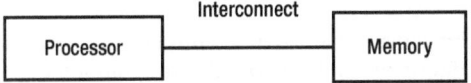

Figure 1-2. Von Neumann architecture

Over the past few decades, computer architecture has evolved from this basic Von Neumann architecture to accommodate physical necessities such as the need for faster data access to implement cache subsystems. Depending on the computational tasks at hand, demands are increasingly made upon various other elements of computer architecture. This book's focus is on Xeon Phi architecture in the context of scientific computing.

Modern scientific computing often depends on fast access to the data it needs. High-level processors are now designed with two distinct but important components known as the *core* and *uncore*. The core components consist of engines that do the computations. These include vector units in many of the modern processors. The uncore components includes cache, memory, and peripheral components. A couple of decades ago, the core was assumed to be the most important component of computer architecture and was subject to a lot of research and development. But in modern computers the uncore components play a more fundamental role in scientific application performance and often consume more power and silicon chip area than the core components.

General computer architecture with a cache subsystem is designed to reduce the memory bandwidth/latency bottleneck encountered in the Von Neumann architecture. A cache memory is a high-speed memory with low latency and a high-bandwidth connection to the core to supply data to instructions executing in the core. A subset of data currently being worked on by a computer program is saved in the cache to speed up instruction execution based on generally observed temporal and spatial locality of data accessed by computer programs. The general architecture of such a computer (Figure 1-3) entails the addition of a cache to the processor core and its communication through a memory controller (MC) with the main memory. The MC on modern chips is often fabricated on a die to reduce the memorya ccessl atency.

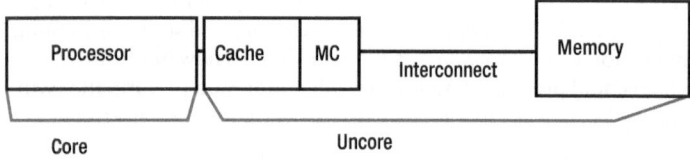

Figure 1-3. *Computer architecture with cache memory. The memory controller is responsible for managing data movement to and from the processor*

One common cache architecture design progression is to introduce and vary multiple levels of caches between the core and the main memory to reduce the access latency and interconnect bandwidth. Cache design continues to evolve in tandem with processor technology to mitigate memory bottlenecks. New memory technologies and semiconductor processes are allowing processor designers to play with various cache configurations as the architecture evolves.

The cache subsystem plays an extremely important role in application performance on a given computer architecture. In addition, the introduction of cache to speed-up applications causes a cache coherency problem in a manycore system. This problem results from the fact that the data updated in the cache may not reflect the data in the memory for the same variable. The coherency problem gets even more complex when the processor implements a multilevel cache.

There are various protocols designed to ensure that the data in the cache of each core of a multicore processor remain consistent when they are modified to maintain application correctness. One such protocol implemented in Intel Xeon Phi is described in Chapter 5.

During the development of the cache subsystem, the computer architecture remained inherently single-threaded from the hardware perspective, although clever time-sharing processes developed and supported in the computer operating systems gave the users the illusion of multiple processes being run by the computer simultaneously. I will explain in subsequent sections in this chapter how each of the components of the basic computer architecture shown in Figure 1-3—memory, interconnect, cache, and processor cores—has evolved in functionality to achieve the current version of Xeon Phi coprocessor architecture.

Improvements in the Core and Memory

To improve the single-threaded performance of programs, computer architects started looking at various mechanisms to reduce the amount of time it takes to execute each instruction, increase instruction throughput, and perform more work per instruction. These developments are described in this section.

Instruction-Level Parallelism

With the development of better semiconductor process technologies, computer architects were able to execute more and more instructions in a parallel and pipelined fashion, implementing what is known as *instruction-level parallelism*—the process of executing more than one instruction in parallel.

The instructions executed in a processor core go through several stages as they flow through logic circuits in sync with core clock pulses. At each clock pulse a part of the instruction is executed. It is possible, however, to stagger multiple instructions so that the various stages of multiple instructions can be executed in the same cycle. This is the principle behind pipelined executions.

All computer instructions based on Von Neumann architecture go through certain high-level basic stages. The first stage performs *instruction fetches* (IF), by which the next instruction to be executed by the core is accessed. The instructions usually reside in the instruction cache or are fetched from the main memory and cache hierarchy at this stage. Note that each stage will take a minimum of one cycle but may extend to further cycles if it gets blocked on some resource issue. For example, if the instructions to be executed are not in the cache, they have to be fetched from memory and, in the worst case, from a nonvolatile storage area such as a hard disk, solid state disk, or even flash memory.

Once the instructions have been fetched, they have to be decoded to understand how to execute the instructions. Now the instructions usually work on some sort of data, which might be in a processor register (the fastest memory nearest to the core), in a cache, or in a memory location. The semantics of the instructions are well defined by a set of rules and a behavioral model—namely, the instruction set architecture.[1]

A decoded instruction next moves to the execution (E) stage, where all necessary memory or cache access happens. The execution completes when all the necessary data are available. Otherwise, a pipeline stall might happen while waiting for data to come from the memory. Once the E stage completes, the data are written back (WB) to the memory/register or flags are updated to change the processor state.

Instruction Pipelining

The execution stage itself may take multiple cycles to accommodate the complexity of the semantics of that instruction. The fundamental pipelining described in the preceding section is shown in Figure 1-4. Note that this is a very simplified representation compared with the complex execution stages for the Xeon Phi processor that will be described in this book. Nonetheless, today's complex execution stages recapitulate the high-level classical instruction stagess howni nF igure 1-4.

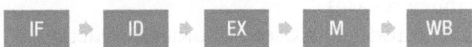

Figure 1-4. *Pipeline stages for an instruction execution. IF = instruction fetch; ID = instruction decode; EX = instruction execution; M = memory fetch; WB = write back, whereby the output of the instruction execution is written back to main memory*

Figure 1-5 shows how the pipelining process helps the respective stages of two different instructions to overlap, thus providing instruction-level parallelism. In this figure, the first instruction (inst1), after being fetched from memory, enters the instruction-decodes stage. Since these stages are executed in different hardware components, the second instruction fetch can happen while the first instruction is in the decode stage. So in clock (clk) tick 2, the first instruction is decoded and the second instruction is fetched, thus overlapping the execution of two instructions.

---

[1]How ISAs affect the overall performance and productivity of software systems developed for particular lines of computer hardware is an important research area but beyond the scope of this book.

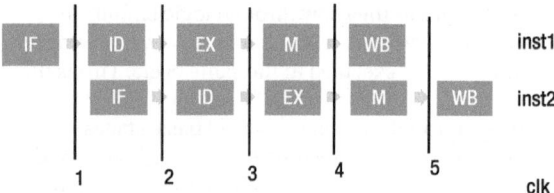

Figure 1-5. *Instruction pipeline showing two instructions executing at the same clock cycle but at different stages*

Processor engineers were, however, looking for more parallelism to satisfy the demand of computer users wanting to execute faster and more complex applications on these pieces of hardware. To further improve processor architecture, the architects designed the cores such that they could execute multiple instructions in parallel in the same cycle. In this case, some of the hardware functions were replicated so that, in addition to the pipelining shown in Figure 1-5, two independent instructions could be executed in two different pipelines. Thus they could both be in the execution stage at the same clock cycle. This architecture is known as *superscalar architecture.*O nes uch architecture which was in wide use in early 1990s was Intel P5 architecture. The Intel Xeon Phi core is based on such architecture and contains two independent pipelines arbitrarily known as the *U* and *V* pipelines. Chapter 4 details how instructions are dispatched to these two pipelines, as well as some of the limitations of superscalar architecture.

Engineers kept increasing processor execution speed by increasing core clock frequencies. Increased clock rate required, however, that each of the stages described above be broken into several substages to be able to execute with each clock tick. Eventually the number of stages increased from the five basic stages shown in Figure 1-5 to over 30 stages to accommodate faster processor clock rate.[2] This increase resulted in faster and faster processors that could execute a single thread of instructions at a speed that was improving with clock rate improvement in each subsequent processor generation. The Intel Pentium 4 processors could run at 3.7GHz at 90nm technology during the 2004 launch date.[3] Given the technology limitations of that time, this was a great achievement.

But progress hit the "power wall": the increased clock rate was resulting in too much wasted energy in the form of heat. So engineers went back to the design board. Intel Xeon Phi instructions go through fewer stages (5 stages for best case execution) than the Pentium 4 families of processors (20 stages for the best case).

Another way to improve instruction-level parallelism was through the introduction of out-of-order instruction processing. In general the processor executes the code in the order generated by the compiler based on the source code provided by the programmer. If the instructions are independent in the instruction stream that is fed to the processor, however, it is possible to execute the instructions out of order—that is, the instruction that comes later in the compiler-generated code may be executed earlier than the instruction before it in the same code stream.

In out-of-order instruction execution, the hardware can detect independent instructions and execute them in any order that speeds up the instruction execution. This meant that the order of the instructions given in the source code by the programmer was not maintained by the execution unit. This was all right from the program-correctness perspective, since the instructions were executed in parallel or even earlier than the following instruction in the program order, independently of each other. This feat was achieved by increasing resources in the various stages of the processor—primarily in the dispatch and execution units of the pipeline. The processor was able to execute them out of order and, in many cases, in speculative fashion. For example, if there were a branch in the code stream, the processor could go ahead and execute both sides of the branch even though one of the branches were later thrown out, as that branch did not meet the actual branch criterion when it reached that point. To maintain the consistency semantics of program execution, which requires that the processor state should be in the order that the programmer desired in the original code, the WB stage was nevertheless maintained in the program order.

---

[2]Intel Pentium 4 Processors with Netburst Architecture (Codenamed Prescott) had a 31-stage pipeline (http://people.apache.org/~xli/presentations/history_Intel_CPU.pdf).
[3]http://ark.intel.com/products/27492/Pentium-4-Processor-Extreme-Edition-supporting-HT-Technology-3_73-GHz-2M-Cache-1066-MHz-FSB

Single Instruction Multiple Data

In order to increase parallelization within the hardware, the architects implemented a new hardware that allows you to work on multiple data items in parallel with a single instruction. Suppose, for example, that you have image-processing software in which you want to increase the brightness of every pixel by a certain amount. The computation involves working on consecutive bytes of data to be incremented by a certain value. Before the introduction of the *single instruction multiple data* (SIMD) feature, the hardware had to read one byte at a time and add the constant and write the data back. With the introduction of the *SIMD unit*, also commonly dubbed the *vector unit*, the hardware can now work on many bytes in the same cycle by one instruction.

As you will learn in Chapter 3, the vector unit in Intel Xeon Phi can work on 16 single-precision floating point values at the same time. This provided a big performance gain in applications that are *data-parallel*—meaningt hat the dataset being processed by the application has no dependencies among the data and can be processed at the samet ime.

Multithreading

As processor frequency was coming down to reduce the power dissipation resulting from high-speed switching, the engineers turned to hardware multithreading to increase parallelism. In this strategy, many processor resources are replicated in hardware, so that applications can indicate to the operating system that it can execute multiple instruction streams in parallel through high-level parallelism constructs such as OpenMP and Posix thread.

To the operating system, this looked like multiple processors working together to achieve the performance it wants. In the Intel Xeon Phi processor, there are four hardware threads sharing the same core as though there were four processors connected to a shared cache subsystem. Figure 1-6 shows the multithreading support in the core is displayed as logical processors, as they still share some resources among themselves.

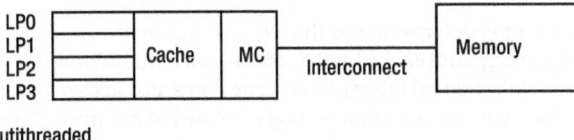

Figure 1-6. *Multithreaded processor cores with superscalar execution units. LP0–3 in the diagram indicate logical processors. MC indicates the memory controller controlling data flow to or from the logical processors*

Multicore and Manycore Architecture

A logical design evolution from multithreading's sharing of some of the resources needed for instruction execution was the cloning of the whole core multiple times to allow multiple threads of execution to happen in parallel. As a first step, architects cloned the big cores used in single-core processors multiple times to create *multicore processors*. These cores started life with a lower frequency than an equivalent single-core processor to limit the total power consumption of the chip. If the applications are properly parallelized, however, parallel processing provided a much bigger gain than the loss due to core frequency reduction. But big-core cloning is limited to a certain number of cores owing to the power envelope imposed by the physical process technology. In order to gain more parallelism, the architects needed to create simpler core running at even lower frequencies but numbered in the hundreds. This architecture is known as *manycore architecture* and the cores are often designated *small cores* as contrasted with the *big cores* used in manycore architecture. This massive level of parallelism of manycore architecture can be exploited only by the codes designed to run on such architecture. This type of manycore architecture, in which all cores are similar, is known as *homogeneous manycore architecture.* (There are other possibilities, such as *heterogeneous manycore architecture*, where all the cores in the processor may not be identical.)

The evolution to manycore architecture allowed applications to improve performance without increasing the clock frequencies. But this advance shifted the burden of achieving application performance improvement from hardware engineers toward software engineers. Software engineers and computer scientists leveraged years of experience in developing parallel applications used in technical computing and HPC applications to start exploiting the manycore architecture. Although the parallel constructs to exploit such machines are still in their infancy, there are sufficient tools to start developing for these machines. Figure 1-7 shows the initial thinking on architectures in which more than one core is made part of a processor, such that the processor cores P0–Pn are connected to a common interconnect known as a *bus* through the cache subsystem (C) and share the bus bandwidth with each other.

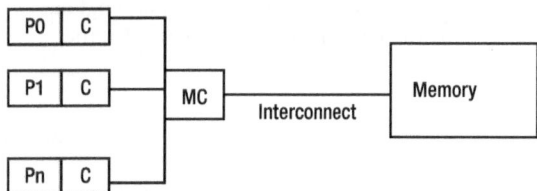

Figure 1-7. *Architecture evolving toward a manycore processor-based computer. C = cache; MC = memory controller; Px = processor cores*

Interconnect and Cache Improvements

In using multiple cores to create a processor, it was soon discovered that single shared-interconnect architectures, such as the bus used in some early processor designs, were a bottleneck for extracting parallel application performance.

The interconnect topology selected for a manycore processor is determined by the latency, bandwidth, and cost of implementing such technology. The interconnect technology chosen for Intel Xeon Phi is a bidirectional ring topology. Here all the cores talk to one another through a bidirectional interconnect. The cores also access the data and code residing in the main memory through the interconnect ring connecting the cores to memory controller. Chapter 5 examines the interconnect technology implemented in Xeon Phi. As new designs come out, the interconnect technology will also evolve to provide a low-latency/high-bandwidth network.

Figure 1-8 shows the evolution of the manycore processor depicted in Figure 1-7 so that the cores are connected in a ring network, which allows memory to be connected to the network through a memory controller responsible for getting data to the cores as requested. There may be one or more memory controllers to improve the memory bandwidth.

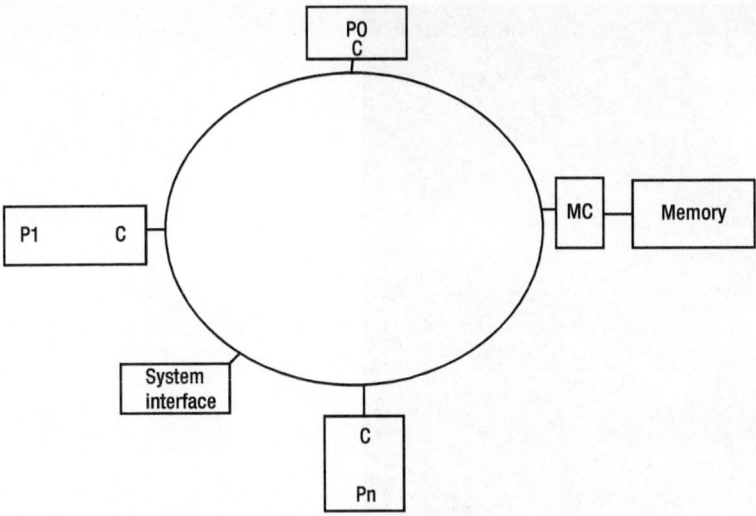

Figure 1-8. *Manycore processor architecture with cores connected through a ring bus. P0–Pn = cores; C = cache; MC = memory controller*

System Interconnect

In addition to talking to memory through memory interconnects, coprocessors such as Intel Xeon Phi are also often placed on *Peripheral Component Interconnect Express* (PCIe) slots to work with the host processors, such as Intel Xeon processors. This is done by incorporating a system interface logic that can support a standard *input/output*(I /O) protocol such as PCIe to communicate with the host. In Figure 1-8, the system interface controller is shown as another box connected to the ring.

Figure 1-9 shows a system-level view of Xeon Phi coprocessor working with a host processor over a PCIe interface. Note that the data movement between the host memory and Xeon Phi memory can happen through *direct memory access* (DMA) without host processor intervention in certain cases, which will be covered in Chapter 6. It is possible to connect multiple Intel Xeon Phi cards to the host system to increase computational power.

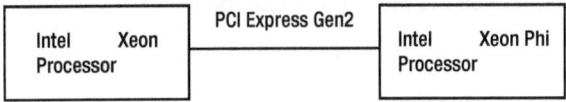

Figure 1-9. *System with the Intel Xeon Phi coprocessor*

Figure 1-10 shows the Intel Xeon Phi coprocessor packaged as a PCIe gen2-based card. The card with the fan is known as the *active-cooled* version, whereas the other is *passively cooled*. The passively cooled version of the card needs to be placed in a special server where the host system needs to provide sufficient cooling for the card. These cards can be placed on a validated server or workstation platforms in various configurations to complement the parallelp rocessingpo werof hos tpr ocessors.

Figure 1-10. *Intel Xeon Phi coprocessors in actively-cooled and passively-cooled versions. (Source: http://newsroom.intel.com/docs/DOC-3126#multimedia)*

Intel Xeon Phi Coprocessor Chip Architecture

This section describes the various functional components of the Intel Xeon Phi coprocessor and explains why they are designed thew ayt heya re.

Figure 1-11 is a simple diagram of the logical layout of some of the critical chip components of the Intel Xeon Phi coprocessor architecture, which include the following:

- *coprocessor cores*: These are based on P54c (Intel Pentium from 1995) cores with major modifications including Intel 64 ISA, 4-way SMT, new vector instructions, and increased cache sizes.[4]

- *VPU*: The *vector processing units* are part of the core and capable of performing 512-bit vector operations on 16 single-precision or 8 double-precision floating-point arithmetic operations as well as integer operations.

- *L2 Cache*: The L2 cache and uncore interface.

- *tag directories* (TD): Components used to look up cache data distributed among the cores.

- *ring interconnect*: The interconnect between the cores and the rest of the coprocessor's components—memory controllers, PCI interface chip, and so on.

- *memory controller (MC)*: Interface between the ring and the *graphics double data rate* (GDDR) memory.

- *PCIe interface*:T oc onnectw ithP CIeb us.

---

[4]Various other features in the coprocessor such as the debug features required to validate and debug the hardware will not be covered in this book.

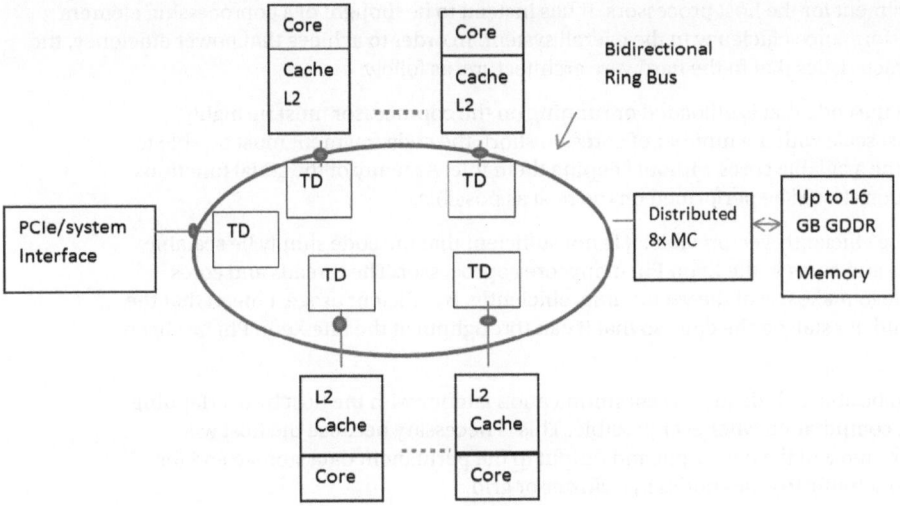

Figure 1-11. *Logical layouts of functional components*

Intel Xeon Phi consists of up to 61 Intel-architecture cores. For so many cores and functional units to access and communicate with each other, carefully designed interconnects are needed to hold the memory/data/control traffic between the cores and various parts of the chip. Figure 1-11 shows the logical layout of the Intel Xeon Phi coprocessor; the actual physical layout of the individual functional units may be vastly different from the depiction in the figure. For example, the eight memory controllers represented as "distributed 8x MC" in the figure are physically distributed on the ring for optimal memory access latency. The L2 caches are fully coherent with each other. Coherency is maintained by the globally owned and locally shared (GOALS) coherency protocols, described in Chapter 5. The functional units communicate with one another by on-die bidirectional interconnects.

For eight memory controllers with two GDDR5 channels running at 5.5 GT/s, one can compute the theoretical memory bandwidth as follows:

```
aggregate memory bandwidth = 8 memory controllers × 2 channels × 5.5 (GT/s) × 4
(bytes/transfer) = 352 GB/s
```

The system interface of the chip supports PCIe2 × 16 protocols with 256-byte packets.

The chip also provides reliability features useful in a technical computing environment. These include parity support in the L1 cache, *error correction code* (ECC) on L2 and memory transactions, *cyclic redundancy code*(CR C), and *command-address parity* on the memory I/O. Chapter 6 will provide further details on these.

Applicability of the Intel Xeon Phi Coprocessor

As seen in the preceding section, Xeon Phi is a manycore processor with up to 61 cores, with each core capable of performing 512-bit vector operations per cycle. The coprocessor card can also host up to 16GB of high-bandwidth memory. The card is, however, in a PCIe card form factor and must incur some overhead transferring data from the host processor or other nodes in a cluster. Another issue is that the cores of Xeon Phi run at about a third the speed of Intel Xeon processors, causing computations to be single-threaded. Hence the question customers often face: In which situations does it make sense to employ the Xeon Phi coprocessor-based model?

The card is not a replacement for the host processors. It has instead to be thought of a coprocessing element providing optimal power performance efficiency to the overall system. In order to achieve that power efficiency, the code must have certain characteristics that fit the hardware architecture, as follow:

- The fragment of the code that is offloaded or running on the coprocessor must be highly parallel and must scale with the number of cores. In short, the code fragment must be able to make use of all the available cores without keeping them idle. As many of the serial functions of the computation should be performed on the host as possible.

- The code must be efficiently vectorizable. It is not sufficient that the code simply be scalable to all the threads and cores in the Xeon Phi manycore coprocessor. The threads and cores must also be able to make use of the vector units efficiently. By efficient usage, I mean that the vector unit should not stall on the data, so that it can throughput at the rate Xeon Phi has been designedf or.

- The code should be able to hide the I/O communication latency with the host by overlapping the I/O with the computation whenever possible. This is necessary because the host will be responsible for most of the data input and output to the permanent data storage and for managing network traffic to other nodes in a cluster or grid.

These three power-efficiency optimization characteristics will be explored in detail in Chapter 9. In my opinion, Xeon Phi's prime value is in providing the best power performance per node in a cluster. The chief benefit to be gained from adding Xeon Phi to your Xeon cluster of nodes is the increase in overall cluster performance resulting from improved performance per watt if you exploit Xeon Phi's architecture and tools in accordance with the programming guidance presented in this book.

Intel Xeon Phi is an architecture designed to enable scientific and technical computing applications in areas as disparate as weather forecasting, medical sciences, energy exploration, manufacturing, financial services, and academic research. All of these technical computing domains rely on applications that are highly parallel. If such applications are deemed a proper fit for the Xeon Phi architecture and if they are programmed properly, Xeon Phi enables a much higher performance and power efficiency than is attainable by host nodes only.

Summary

This chapter reviewed the development of the Intel Xeon Phi coprocessor and examined the thinking behind the evolution of Von Neumann basic architecture into a complex manycore design embedded in the current Xeon Phi architecture. The motive force driving this evolution has been the quest for the ever higher levels of processor performance necessary for executing the computational tasks that today underlie scientific discoveries and new technical applications.

The next chapter will delve into the programming for Xeon Phi.

CHAPTER 2

■ ■ ■

Programming Xeon Phi

Viewing the Intel Xeon Phi as a black box, you can infer its architecture from its responses to the impulses you provide it: namely, the software instructions you execute on the coprocessor. The objective of this book is to introduce you to Intel Xeon Phi architecture in as much as it affects software performance through programming. I believe one of the best ways to understand and learn about a new architecture is to observe its behavior with respect to how it performs in relation to the requests made of it.

This chapter looks at the tools and development environment that are available to developers as they explore and develop software for this coprocessor. The knowledge in this chapter provides the foundation for writing code to evaluate various architectural features implemented on the coprocessor, which will be covered in Chapters 3 through 6.

Intel Xeon Phi Execution Models

Intel Xeon Phi cores are Pentium cores and work as coprocessors to the host processor. Pentium core adoption allowed developers to port many of the tools and much of the development environment from the Intel Xeon-based processor to the Xeon Phi coprocessor. In fact, the software designer opted for running a complete micro OS based on the Linux kernel rather than the driver-based model often used for PCIe-based attached cards, comparable to graphics cards on a system.

There are various execution models that can be used to design and execute an application on the Intel Xeon Phi coprocessor in association with the host processor. The programming models supported for the coprocessor vary between the Windows OS and Linux OS used on the host system. For example, the native programming model is only available on Linux but not on Windows. Intel Xeon Phi supports only Linux and Windows operating environments. The compiler syntax for running on the Windows environment is very close to that for the Linux environment. To simplify the presentation, I focus in this book on the Linux-based platform only.

The most common execution models can be broadly categorized as follows (Figure 2-1):

> *Offload execution mode.* Also known as the *heterogeneous programming mode*, the
> host system in this mode offloads part or all of the computation from one or multiple
> processes or threads running on the host. The application starts execution on the host.
> As the computation proceeds, it can decide to send data to the coprocessor and let the
> coprocessor work on it. The host and the coprocessor may or may not work in parallel in
> the offload execution model. This is the common execution model in other coprocessor
> operating environments. As of this writing, there is an OpenMP 4.0 TR being proposed and
> implemented in Intel Composer XE to provide directives to perform offload computations.
> Composer XE also provides some custom directives to perform offload operations. This
> mode of operation is available on both Linux and Windows.

Coprocessor native execution mode. An Intel Xeon Phi has a Linux micro OS running in it and can appear as another machine connected to the host, like another node in a cluster. This execution environment allows the users to view the coprocessor as another compute node. In order to run natively, an application has to be cross-compiled for the Xeon Phi operating environment. Intel Composer XE provides a simple switch to generate cross-compiledc ode.

Symmetric execution. In this mode the application processes run on both the host and the Intel Xeon Phi coprocessor. They usually communicate through some sort of message-passing interface such as Message Passing Interface (MPI). This execution environment treats the Xeon Phi card as another node in a cluster in a heterogeneous clustere nvironment.

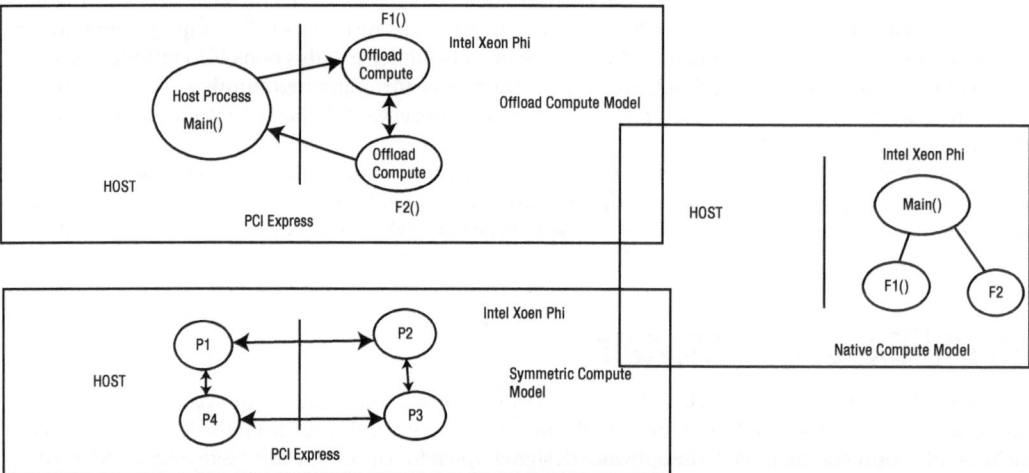

Figure 2-1. *Intel Xeon Phi execution models. Here P indicates processes and F() indicates function calls in various execution modes. The arrows indicate the function invocation, message passing, and data communication directions between the processes and functions*

Development Tools for Intel Xeon Phi Architecture

Various tools (Figure 2-2) developed by Intel ease developing and tuning applications for the Intel Xeon Phi coprocessor. Various excellent tools developed by third-party vendors will not be covered in this section.

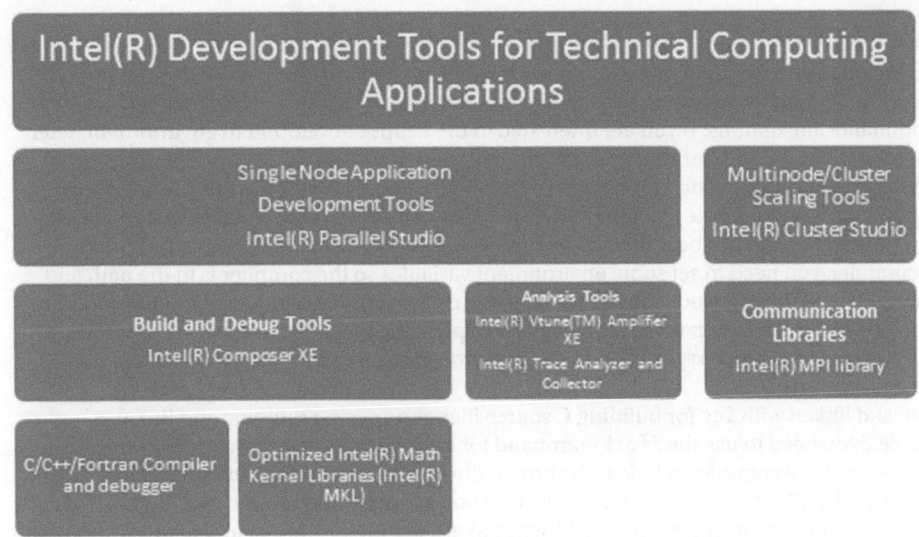

Figure 2-2. *Software development tools for Intel Xeon Phi*

IntelCom poserX E

Intel Composer XE is the key development tool and Software Development Kit (SDK) suite available for developing on Intel Xeon Phi. The suite includes C/C++ and Fortran compiler and related runtime libraries and tools such as OpenMP, threading building block, Cilk Plus, a debugging tool, and the math kernel library (MKL). Together they give you the necessary tools to build your application for Intel Xeon-compatible processors and Intel Xeon Phi coprocessors. You can also use the same compiler for cross-compilation to Intel Xeon Phi.

On the assumption that you have access to an Intel Xeon Phi–based development environment, I will walk you through how you can write a simple application to run on the various execution modes described above. Once you learn to do that, you can progress to Chapter 3 on Xeon Phi architecture to get a better understanding through experimentation.

The present chapter also covers the runtime environment and system-level details to give you a complete understanding of how the software architecture is created to work in conjunction with the host processor to complement its computations.

The C/C++/Fortran tools contained in the Intel Composer XE support various parallel programming models for Intel Xeon Phi, such as Intel Cilk Plus, Intel threading building blocks (TBB), OpenMP, and POSIX threads (pthread). The Composer XE also contains the Intel MKL, which contains common routines for technical and high-performance computing applications, including Basic Linear Algebra Subroutines (BLAS), Fast Fourier Transform (FFT), and standard interfaces for technical computing applications.

Getting the Tools

All of the toolsdescribed in this chapter for developing for Intel Xeon Phi are available from the Intel web site. If you do not have the tools, you can get an evaluation version of the tools from
http://software.intel.com/en-us/intel-software-evaluation-center/.

Using the Compilers

The C++/Fortran compilers included as part of the Intel Composer XE package generate both offload and cross-compiled code for Intel Xeon Phi. The compiler can be used in a command-line or Eclipse development environment. This book will follow the command-line options. If you are interested in the Eclipse development environment, refer to the user's guide provided as part of the compiler documentation.

This book covers Xeon Phi-specific and -related features on 64-bit Redhat Linux 6.3 for the Intel Xeon processor. I will assume "bash" script command syntax in the examples. The compiler contains a lot of features that will not be covered in this book. The command prompt will be indicated by the ➤ symbol.

In order to invoke the compiler, you need to set some environment variables so the compiler is in the path and runtime libraries are available. To do this, you need to invoke a batch file called `compilervars.sh` included with the compiler. If you have installed this in the default path chosen by the compiler, the batch file to set the environment can be found at `/opt/intel/composerxe/bin/compilervars.sh`. To set the path invoke `> source /opt/intel/composerxe/bin/compilervars.sh intel64`.

The compiler is invoked and linked with `icc` for building C source files and `icpc` for building and linking C++ source files. For Fortran sources, you need to use the `ifort` command for both compiler and link. Make sure you link with the appropriate command, as these commands link to the proper libraries to produce the executable.

Of course, you can use the make utility to build multiple objects. If you are porting an application built with GNU C Compiler (gcc) to Xeon Phi, you will need to change the build script to use the Intel compiler and to modify the command line switches appropriately. Because it is hard to remember all the switches, you can always invoke Intel compilers like icc with `>icc -help` to figure out the appropriate options for your compiler builds. In most cases, if not asked specifically for compiling only, an `icc` or `icpc` command will invoke both the compiler and the linker. In fact the commands `icc`, `icpc`, and `ifort` are driver programs that in turn parse the command-line arguments and processes in accordance with the compiler or the linker as necessary. The driver program processes the input file and calls the linker with the object files created, as well as the library files necessary to generate final executables or libraries. That is why it is important to use the proper compiler so that the appropriate libraries can be linked.

The Intel compiler uses file extensions to interpret the type of each input file. The file extension determines whether the file is passed to the compiler or linker. A file with .c, .cc, .CC, .cpp, or .cxx is recognized by the C/C++ compiler. A Fortran compiler recognizes .f90, .for, .f, .fpp .i90, and .ftn extensions. A Fortran compiler assumes that files with .f90 or .i90 extensions are free-form Fortran source files. The compiler assumes .f, .for, and .ftn as fixed-form Fortran files. Files with extensions .a, .so, .o, and .s are passed on to the linker. Table 2-1 describes the action by the compiler depending on the file extensions.

Table 2-1. *File Extensions and Their Interpretation by the Intel Compiler*

Fileexten sions	Interpretation	Execution
.c	Cs ourcef ile	C/C++c ompiler
.C, .CC, .cc, .cpp, .cxx	C++ source file	C++ compiler
.f, .for, .ftn, .i, .fpp, .FPP, .F, .FOR, .FTN	Fixed form Fortran	Fortran compiler
.f90, .i90, .F90	Free form Fortran	Fortran compiler
.a, .so, .o	Library, object files	Linker
.s	Assemblyf ile	assembler

The Intel compiler can be invoked as follows:

```
<compiler name> [options] file1 [file2…]
```

where

      `<compiler name>` is one of the compiler names such as icc, icpc, ifort;

      `[options]` are options that are passed to the compiler and can control code generation, optimization, and output file names, type, and path.

      If no `[options]` are specified, the compiler invokes some default options, such as –O2 for default optimization. If you want to modify the default option for compilation, you will need to modify the corresponding configuration file found in the installed `<compiler install path>bin/intel64_mic` or similar folders and named as `icc.cfg`, `icpc.cfg`, and so forth. Please refer to the compiler manual for details.

      Compiler options play a significant role in tuning Intel MIC architecture, as you can control various aspects of code generation such as loop unrolling and prefetch generation.

      You might find it useful to look at the assembly code generated by the compiler. You can use the –S option to generate the assembly file to see the assembly-coded output of the compiler.

Setting Up an Intel Xeon Phi System

I will assume you have access to a host with one or more Intel Xeon Phi cards installed in it and one of the supported Linux OSs on the host. (For Windows please refer to the corresponding user's guide.) There are two high-level packages: the drivers (also known as the Manycore Platform Software Stack (MPSS) package) and the development tools and libraries packages (distributed as Intel Cluster Studio or a single-node version of Intel Composer XE) from which to build a system and in which you can develop applications for Intel Xeon Phi.

Install the MPSS Stack

Install the MPSS stack by the following steps:

1. Go to the Intel Developer Zone web page (`http://software.intel.com/mic-developer`), go to the tab Tools & Downloads, and select "Intel Many Integrated Core Architecture (Intel MIC Architecture) Platform Software Stack." Download the appropriate version of the MPSS to match your host OS and also download the `readme.txt` from the same location.

2. You will need super-user privilege to install the MPSS stack.

3. Communication with the Linux micro OS running on the Intel Xeon Phi coprocessor is provided by a standard network interface. The interface uses a virtual network driver over the PCIe bus. The Intel Xeon Phi coprocessor's Linux OS supports network access for all users using ssh keys. A valid ssh key is required for you to access the card. Most users will have it on their machine. If you have connected to the other machine from this host through ssh you most probably have it. If you do not have an ssh key, execute the following code to generate the ssh key:

```
user_prompt> ssh-keygen
user_prompt> sudo service mpss stop
user_prompt> sudo micctrl --resetconfig
user_prompt> sudo service mpss start
```

4. Make sure you have downloaded the correct version of the MPSS stack that matches your host operating system where you installed the Intel Xeon Phi card. If not, the MPSS source is provided to build for some of the supported Linux OS versions.

5. These packages are distributed as gzipped Linux tar files with extension .tgz. Untar the *.tgz package and go to untarred location.

6. Install the rpms in the untarred directory with an appropriate rpm install command. For example, on Red Hat Enterprise Linux you can use the following command on the command line as a root user:

```
command prompt> yum install --nopgpcheck --noplugins --disablerepo=* *.rpm
```

7. Resett he driveru sing:

```
command_prompt>micctrl -r
```

8. Update the system flash if necessary. To see whether you need to update, please run `command_prompt>/opt/intel/mic/bin/micinfo`, which will print out the Intel Xeon Phi–related information including the flash file.[1]

   The flash files can be found in the folder `/opt/intel/mic/flash` and should match with those printed out as part of the micinfo. If the installed version is older than the one available with the new MPSS you are installing, update the flash with the micflash utility. Please refer to the `readme.txt` provided with the documentation to select the proper flash file. Once you have determined the proper flash file for the revision of the card on your system, use the following command to flash: `command_prompt>/opt/intel/mic/bin/ micflash -Update /opt/intel/mic/flash/<your flash file name>`

9. Once the flash is updated, reboot the machine for the new flash to take effect. The MPSS is installed as a Linux service and can be started or stopped by `service mpss start|stop|restart`com mands.

10. Note that you need to have the proper driver configuration to get the card started. A mismatched card configuration from a previous install could prevent the card from booting. I would strongly suggest you read up on MPSS configuration and micctrl utility in the `readme.txt` if you encounter any issue starting the card.

Installthe D evelopmentT ools

Install the Intel C/C++ compiler by obtaining the Intel Composer XE package or a superset of this package such as Intel Cluster Studio XE for Linux. Follow the instructions provided in the link in the "Install the MPSS Stack" section on how to get access to the tools and for step-by-step methods to install. Since these steps are the same as for installing the Intel tools on any Intel Xeon processor-based hosts, I am not going to cover them here.

Code Generation for Intel Xeon Phi Architecture

The traditional Intel compiler has been modified to support Intel Xeon Phi code generation. In order to do that, compiler engineers had to make changes at various levels.

The first step was adding new language features that allow you to describe the offload syntax for a code fragment that can be sent to the coprocessor. These language features are introduced by the new OpenMP 4.0 Technical Report as well as the Intel proprietary C/CFortran extensions.

---

[1] The default MPSS install puts most of the Intel Xeon Phi–related drivers, flash, and utilities in the `/opt/intel/mic` and `/usr/sbin` default paths. If your system administrator put it somewhere else, you need to check with that person. I shall assume everything is installed in the default folder.

Second, Intel needed some new compiler options to account for Intel MIC architecture-specific code generations and optimizations. These include providing new intrinsics corresponding to Intel Xeon Phi–specific ISA extensions, as discussed in Chapter 3. These intrinsics will help us explore various architectural features of the hardware. Finally, we need to provide support for the new environment variables and libraries to allow execution of the offload programs on the hardware.

There are two predominant programming models for Intel Xeon Phi. One is the *native execution mode* by which you cross-compile the code written for Intel Xeon processors and run the resulting executable on the Xeon Phi micro OS. The other is the *heterogeneous* or *hybrid mode,* by which you start the main code on the host and the code executes on the coprocessor or both the host and the coprocessor.

NativeE xecutionM ode

Being chiefly concerned with architecture, this book mainly deals with the native execution mode, as this is the simplest way to run something on the Xeon Phi hardware. In native execution mode, you can run any C/C++/Fortran source that can be compiled for Intel Xeon or can be cross-compiled for Intel Xeon Phi architecture. The code is then transferred to the Xeon Phi coprocessor OS environment using familiar networking tools such as *secure copy* (scp) and executed in Xeon Phi's native execution environment.

In this section I shall assume you already have access to a system with an Intel Xeon Phi coprocessor installed in it. I shall also assume you have downloaded the appropriate driver and Composer XE on your machine from the Intel registration center.

Hello World Example

Let's try running a simple "Hello world" application on the Intel Xeon Phi processor in native mode. Say you have a simple code segment as follows in a source file test.c:

```
//Content of test.c
#include <stdio.h>
int main()
{
 printf("Hello world from Intel Xeon Phi\n");
}
```

To build the code you need to compile and link these files with a -mmic switch as follows:

```
command_prompt>icc -mmic test.c -o test.out
```

This will create an output file test.out on the same folder as your source. Now copy the source file to the Intel Xeon Phi mic0 as follows:

```
command_prompt>scp test.out mic0:
```

This will copy the test.out file to your home directory on the coprocessor environment.

At this phase you can log in to the coprocessor using the ssh command as follows:

```
command_prompt>ssh mic0
[command_prompt-mic0]$ ls
test.out
```

The listing now shows the file `test.out` on the native coprocessor environment. If you run it on the card, it will printout:

```
command_prompt-mic0>./test.out
Hello world   //printed from Intel Xeon Phi
command_prompt-mic0>
```

I have also captured a screenshot of this execution, as shown in Figure 2-3.

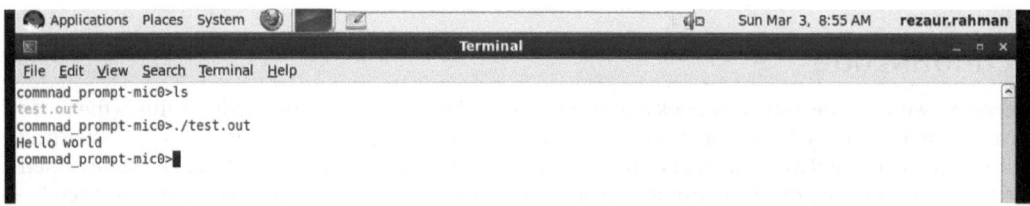

Figure 2-3. *Executing a Hello world program inside Intel Xeon Phi micro OS command prompt. The printout is from the code running on a Xeon Phi coprocessor*

Language Extensions to Support Offload Computation on Intel Xeon Phi

Intel has extended the C/C++ and Fortran language to support programming the Intel Xeon Phi coprocessor. OpenMP 4.0 standard also includes extensions to target similar coprocessor computing models.

Heterogeneous ComputingM odela ndO ffloadP ragmas

There are two supported ways to deal with nonshared memory between an Intel Xeon Phi coprocessor and the host processor. One is *data marshaling*, in which the compiler runtime generates and sends data buffers over to coprocessors by marshaling the parameters provided by the application. The second option is the *virtual shared memory model*, which depends on system-level runtime support to maintain data coherency between the host's and coprocessor's virtual shared memory address space. Because the first model is supported by OpenMP 4.0 specifications and is more prevalent than the second model, the first model will be the working model in all subsequent chapters.

The Intel compiler had proprietary language extensions that were implemented to support the nonshared programming model before the OpenMP 4.0 specifications were published.

In the nonshared virtual memory space programming model, the main program starts on the host and the data and computation can be sent to Intel Xeon Phi through offload pragmas when the data exchange between the host and the coprocessor are bitwise copyable. The bitwise copyable data structures include scalars, arrays, and structures without indirections. Since the coprocessor memory space is separate from the host memory space, the compiler runtime is in charge of copying data back and forth between the host and the coprocessor around the offload block indicated by the pragmas added to the source code.

The data selected for offload may be implicitly copied if used inside the offload code block and provided the variables are in the lexical scope of the code block performing the offload and the variables are listed explicitly as part of the pragmas. The requirement is that the data must have a flat structure. However, the data that are used only within the offload block can be arbitrarily complex with multiple indirections but cannot be passed between host and the coprocessor. If this is needed, you have to marshal the data into a flat data structure or buffer the data to move them back and forth. The Intel compiler does support transparent marshaling of data using shared virtual memory constructs (described in Chapter 8), which can handle more complex data structures.

In order to provide seamless execution so the same code can run on the host processor with or without a coprocessor, the compiler runtime determines whether or not the coprocessor is present on the system. So if the coprocessor is not available or inactive during the offload call, the code fragment inside the offload code block may execute on the host as well.

Language Extensions and Execution Model

In order to understand the new language extensions for nonshared memory programming, we should understand the terminology introduced in OpenMP 4.0 specifications to describe the language support.[2] The treatment of the terminology and directives in this section is not comprehensive but rather covers those parts of the specifications that are relevant to the Intel Xeon Phi offload programming model.

Terminology

device. A *device* may have one or more co-processors with their own memories or a host. A *host device* is the device executing the main thread. A *target device* executes the offloaded code segment.

offload. The process of sending a computation from host to target.

data environment. The variables associated with a given execution environment.

device data environment. A data environment associated with *target data* or a *target construct*.

mapped variable. Either variable when a variable in a data environment is mapped to a variable in a device data environment. The original and corresponding variables may shares torage.

mappable type. A valid *data type*f ora m appedv ariable.

Offload Function and Data Declaration Directives

These directives are used to declare functions and variables so that these are available on the coprocessor.

declare target Directives

declare target directives declare data, functions, and subroutines that should be available in a target (coprocessor) execution environment. They allow the creation of versions of specified function or data that can be used inside a target region executing on the coprocessor.

Syntax
C/C++

```
#pragma omp declare target new-line
 declaration-definition-sequence
#pragma omp end declare target new-line
```

---

[2] http://www.openmp.org/mp-documents/OpenMP_4.0_RC2.pdf

Fortran

!$omp declare target *(list) new-line*

In C/C++/Fortran, variables and function declarations that appear between declare and end declare target or in the list argument are created in the device context and can be used or executed in the target region.

Restrictions

- Threadprivate variables cannot be in a declare targetdir ective.

- Variables declared in a declare target directive must have a mappable type.

- In C/C++ the variables declared in a declare target directive must be at file or namespaces cope.

Function Offload and Execution Constructs

In order to execute on a coprocessor, a target device must be available on the host system running the code. For the nonshared memory model, the host application executes the initial program, which spawns the master execution thread called the *initial device thread*. The OpenMP pragma target and pragma target data provide the capability to offload computations to a coprocessor(s).

Target Data Directive

This directive causes a new device data environment to be created and, encountering the task, executes the target data region.

Syntax

C/C++

```
#pragma omp target data [clause [[,] clause],...] new-line
structured-block
```

Fortran

```
!$omp target [clause[[,] clause],...]
parallel-loop-construct | parallel-sections-construct
!$omp end target
```

Where clauses are:

- device(scalar-integer-expression)

    - The integer expression must be a positive number to differentiate various coprocessors available on a host. If no device is specified, the default device is determined by internal control variable (ICV) named default-device-var(OMP_DEFAULT_DEVICE openmp environment variable). The default data environment is constructed from the enclosing device environment, the data environment of the enclosing task, and the data mapping clausesinthe cons truct.

- map([map-type:]*list*)

  - These are data motion clauses that allow copying and mapping of variables or common block to or from the host scope to the target device scope. The map type:

  - alloc indicates the data are allocated on the device and have an undefined initial value.

  - to declares that on entering the region, each new data in the list will be initialized to original list item value.

  - from declares that the data elements are "out" type and copied from the device data to host data on exit from the region.

  - tofrom(Default) declares that data elements are in or out type and values are copied to and from the data elements in the device corresponding to data elements on the host.

  - If the list is an array element, it must be a contiguous region.

- if(scalar-expr)

  - ift hes calar-expressione valuatest of alse,t hed evicei sa h ost.

Restrictions

- Atm osto ne device clause may appear on the directive. The device expression must evaluate to a positive integer value.

- At most one if clause can appear on the directive.

Target Directive

This directive provides a superset of functionality and restriction of the target data directive, as discussed in the previous subsection.

- A target region begins as a single thread of execution and executes sequentially, as if enclosed in an implicit task region, called the *initial device task region*.

- Whena target construct is encountered, the target region is executed by the implicit devicet ask.

- The task that encounters the target construct waits at the end of the construct until execution of the region completes. If a coprocessor does not exist, is not supported by the implementation, or cannot execute the target construct, then the target region is executed by the host device.

- The data environment is created at the time the construct is encountered, if needed. Whether a construct creates a data environment is defined in the description of the construct.

Syntax
C/C++

```
#pragma omp target [clause[[,] clause],...] new-line
structured-block
```

Fortran

```
!$omp target [clause[[,] clause],...]
structured-block
!$omp end target
```

where clauses are:

- device(scalar-integer-expression)

  - The integer expression must be a positive number to differentiate various coprocessors available on a host. If no device is specified, the default device is determined by the ICV named default-device-var(OMP_DEFAULT_DEVICE openmp environment variable). The default data environment is constructed from the enclosing device environment, the data environment of the enclosing task, and the data mapping clauses in the construct.

- map([map-type:]*list*)

  - These are data motion clauses that allow copying and mapping of variables or common block to or from the host scope to the target device scope. The map type:

  - alloc indicates the data are allocated on the device and have an undefined initial value.

  - to declares that on entering the region, each new data in the list will be initialized to original list item value.

  - from declares that the data elements is "out" type and copied from the device data to the host data on exit from the region.

  - tofrom(Default) declares that data elements are in or out type and values are copied to and from the data elements in the device corresponding to data elements on the host.

  - If the list is an array element, it must be contiguous region.

- if(scalar-expr)

  - ift hes calar-expressione valuatest of alse,t hed evicei sa h ost.

The target directive creates a device data environment and executes the code block on the target device. The target region binds to the enclosing structured block code region. It provides a superset of *target data constructs* and describes data as well as the code block to be executed on the target device. The master task waits for the coprocessor to complete the target region at the end of the constructs.

When an if clause is present and the logical expression inside the if clause evaluates to false, the target region is not executed by the device but executed on the host.

Restrictions

- If a target, target update, or target data construct appears within a target region, then the behavior is undefined.

- The result of an omp_set_default_device, omp_get_default_device,or omp_get_num_devices routine called within a target region is unspecified.

- The effect of access to a threadprivate variable in a target region is unspecified.

- A variable referenced in a target construct that is not declared in the construct is implicitly treated as if it had appeared in a map clause with a *map type* of tofrom.

- A variable referenced in a target region but not declared in the target construct must appear in a **declare target**dir ective.

- *C/C++ specific*: A throw executed inside a target region must cause execution to resume within the same target region, and the same thread that threw the exception must catch it.

The syntax for expressing data transfers between host and coprocessors is expressed by target data and update constructs, as discussed in the next section.

Target Update Directive

Target update directive synchronizes the list items in the device data environment consistent with their corresponding original list items according to the map clause.

Syntax
C/C++

```
#pragma omp target update motion-clause[clause[[,] clause],...] new-line
```

Fortran

```
!$omp target update motion-clause [clause[[,] clause],...]
```

Where motion-clause is one of the following:

```
to(list)
from(list)
```

Each list item in the to or from clause corresponds to a device item and a host list item. The fromc lause corresponds to out data from the device to the host and the to clause corresponds to in data from the host to the device.

Clauses are:

- device(scalar-integer-expression)

  - The integer expression must be a positive number to differentiate the various coprocessors available on a host. If no device is specified, the default device is determined by an ICV named default-device-var.

- if(scalar-expr): If the scalar expression evaluates to false, the updatec lausei si gnored.

RuntimeL ibraryR outines

The OpenMP 4.0 specifications also provide routines to set and get runtime environment settings (referred to as ICVs in the OpenMP specs) and to query the number of available coprocessors using the following APIs:

```
void omp_set_default_device(int device_num),
int omp_get_default_device();
```

Description: Set default device for offload. This gets or sets the ICV default-device-var. The corresponding environment variable is OMP_DEFAULT_DEVICE.

```
int omp_get_num_devices();
```

Description: Query number of coprocessors in the system.

OffloadE xample

Listing 2-1 gives a simple example of how the constructs discussed for OpenMP 4.0 can be used to offload computation to an Intel Xeon Phi coprocessor.

Listing 2-1. Sample Test Code

```
1 // Sample code reduction.cpp
2 // Example showing use of OpenMP 4.0 pragmas for offload calculation
3 // This code was compiled with Intel(R) Composer XE 2013
4
5 #include <stdio.h>
6
7 #define SIZE 1000
8 #pragma omp declare target
9 int reduce(int *inarray)
10 {
11
12 int sum=0;
13 #pragma omp target map(inarray[0:SIZE]) map(sum)
14 {
15  for(int i=0;i<SIZE;i++)
16    sum += inarray[i];
17 }
18 return sum;
19 }
20
21 int main()
22 {
23 int inarray[SIZE], sum, validSum;
24
25 validSum=0;
26 for(int i=0; i<SIZE; i++){
27  inarray[i]=i;
28  validSum+=i;
29 }
30
31 sum=0;
32 sum = reduce(inarray);
33
34 printf("sum reduction = %d, validSum=%d\n",sum, validSum);
35 }
```

On line 13 of the listing, you will notice the offload pragma #pragma omp target map(inarray[0:SIZE]) map(sum), which causes specific code block lines (14 to 17) to be sent to the coprocessor for computing. In this case it is computing the reduction of an array of numbers and returning the computed value through the sum variable to the host. The inarray and the sum are copied in and out of the coprocessor before and after the computation.

The main routine calls the reduce function in line 32 in the code block. The code in turn offloads part of the computation to the Intel Xeon Phi to compute the sum reduction. Once the reduction is done, the results received from the coprocessor are returned to the main function (line 32) and compared against the reduction done on the host to validate the results.

You can compile this code as you would on a Intel Xeon machine using the following command:

```
command_prompt>icpc -openmp reduction.cpp -o test.out
```

And you can run the compiled test.out on the host environment as shown in Listing 2-2 using:

```
command_prompt>./test.out
```

You can see the data movement by the runtime engine if you set OFFLOAD_REPORT=2 in the host environment. The output with OFFLOAD_REPORT set to 2 during runtime is shown in Listing 2-2. Here you see that there were 4012 bytes (1000 integer elements + 4 bytes sum + 8 bytes pointer of the inarray are sent from host to the target). Also because we used the map clause, the same array was sent back from coprocessor to host. Thus you can see in the report that 4004 (1000 integer + sum) bytes are returned.

Listing 2-2.

```
[Offload] [MIC 1] [File]            reduction.cpp
[Offload] [MIC 1] [Line]            13
[Offload] [MIC 1] [Tag]             Tag0
[Offload] [MIC 1] [CPU Time]        0.000000 (seconds)
[Offload] [MIC 1] [CPU->MIC Data]   4012 (bytes)
[Offload] [MIC 1] [MIC Time]        0.000177 (seconds)
[Offload] [MIC 1] [MIC->CPU Data]   4004 (bytes)

sum reduction = 499500, validSum=499500
```

Now suppose you don't want to return the inarray back to the host because it is not modified, thus saving precious bandwidth. You can do so by changing the map clause to map(to:inarray[0:SIZE]) in line 13. The output of such a modification is shown in Listing 2-3 below:

Listing 2-3.

```
[Offload] [MIC 1] [File]            reduction.cpp
[Offload] [MIC 1] [Line]            13
[Offload] [MIC 1] [Tag]             Tag0
[Offload] [MIC 1] [CPU Time]        0.000000 (seconds)
[Offload] [MIC 1] [CPU->MIC Data]   4004 (bytes)
[Offload] [MIC 1] [MIC Time]        0.000156 (seconds)
[Offload] [MIC 1] [MIC->CPU Data]   4 (bytes)
```

Here you can see only 4 bytes are transferred back to host for [MIC->CPU data]v alue.

Summary

This chapter has walked you through the set up of a Xeon Phi processor. You have also looked at programming this processor with OpenMP 4.0 specifications provided for coprocessor programming. You will use this knowledge in the next chapter to explore the Xeon Phi hardware features. Chapter 8 will discuss in depth the other programming languages and tools provided by Intel for developing the Xeon Phi coprocessor.

CHAPTER 3

■ ■ ■

Xeon Phi Vector Architecture and Instruction Set

Two key hardware features that dictate the performance of technical computing applications on Intel Xeon Phi are the vector processing unit and the instruction set implemented in this architecture. The vector processing unit (VPU) in Xeon Phi provides data parallelism at a very fine grain, working on 512 bits of 16 single-precision floats or 32-bit integers at a time. The VPU implements a novel instruction set architecture (ISA), with 218 new instructions compared with those implemented in the Xeon family of SIMD instruction sets.

Xeon Phi Vector Microarchitecture

Physically, the VPU is an extension to the P54C core and communicates with the core to execute the VPU ISA implemented in Xeon Phi. The VPU receives its instructions from the core arithmetic logic unit (ALU) and receives the data from the L1 cache by a dedicated 512-bit bus. The VPU has its own dependency logic and communicates with the core to stall when necessary.

The VPU is fully pipelined and can execute most instructions with four-cycle latency and single-cycle throughput. It can read/write one vector per cycle from/to the vector register file or data cache. Each vector can contain 16 single-precision floats or 32-bit integer elements or eight 64-bit integer or double-precision floating point elements. The VPU can do one load and one operation in the same cycle. The VPU instructions are ternary operands with two sources and a destination (which can also act as a source for fused multiply-and-add instructions). This configuration provides approximately a 20-percent gain in performance over traditional binary-operand SIMD instructions. Owing to the simplified design, the VPU instructions cannot generate exceptions, but they can set MXCSR flags to indicate exception conditions. A VPU instruction is considered retired when the core sends it to the VPU. If an error happens, the VPU sets MXCSR flags for overflow, underflow, or other exceptions. Each VPU underneath consists of eight master ALUs, each containing two single-precision (SP) and one double-precision (DP) ALU with independent pipelines, thus allowing sixteen SP and eight DP vector operations. Each master ALU has access to a *read-only memory* (ROM) containing a lookup table for transcendental lookup, constants that the master ALU needs, and so forth.

Each VPU has 128 entry 512-bit vector registers divided among the threads, thus providing 32 entries per thread. These are hard-partitioned. There are eight 16-bit mask registers per thread, which are part of the vector register file. The mask registers act as a filter per element for the 16 elements and thus allow you to control which of the 16 32-bit elements are active during a computation. For double precision the mask bits are the bottom eight bits.

Most of the VPU instructions are issued from the core through the U-pipe. Some of the instructions can be issued from the V-pipe and can be paired to be executed at the same time with instructions in the U-pipe VPU instructions.

TheV PUPipe line

Each VPU instruction passes through one or more of the following five pipelines to completion:

- *Double-precision*(DP) *pipeline*: Used to execute float64 arithmetic, conversion from float64 to float32, and DP-compare instructions.

- *Single-precision* (SP) *pipeline*: Executes most of the instructions including 64-bit integer loads. This includes float32/int32 arithmetic and logical operations, shuffle/broadcast, loads including loadunpack, type conversions from float32/int32 pipelines, extended math unit (EMU) transcendental instructions, int64 loads, int64/float64 logical, and other instructions.

- *Mask pipeline*: Executes mask instructions with one-cycle latencies.

- *Store pipeline*: Executesthe ve ctors toreope rations.

- *Scatter/gather pipeline*: Executes the vector register read/writes from sparse memory locations.

It should be noted that going between pipelines costs additional cycles in some cases. For example, since there are no bypasses between the SP and DP pipelines, intermixing SP and DP code will cause performance penalties, but executing SP instructions consecutively results in good performance, as there are many bypasses built in the pipeline.

The *vector execution pipeline*(or *vector pipeline*) is shown in Figure 3-1a. Once a vector instruction is decoded in stage D2 of the main pipeline, it enters the VPU execution pipeline. At E stage the VPU detects if there is any dependency stall. At the VC1/VC2 stage the VPU does the shuffle-and-load conversion as needed. At the V1-V4 stages it does the four-cycle multiply/add operations, followed by the WB stage, where it writes the vector/mask register contents back to the cache as instructed.

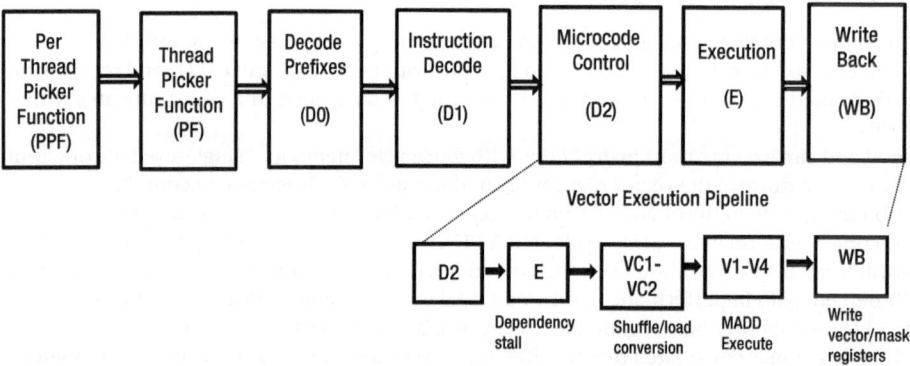

Figure 3-1a. *The vector pipeline stages relative to the core pipeline*

VPU Instruction Stalls

When there are two independent SP/SP instructions, as shown in Figure 3-1b, the pipeline can throughput one instruction per cycle, with each instruction execution incurring a latency of four or more cycles. The four-cycle minimum constitutes the best-case scenario, which involves a vector operation on registers without the need for any shuffle or writing back to memory, spent in the MADD computation unit shown as V1–V4 in Figure 3-1a.

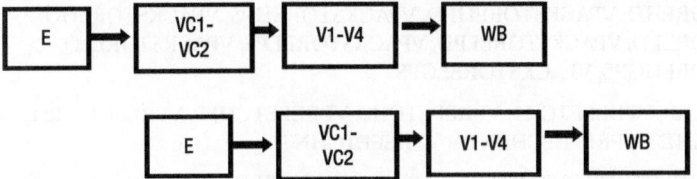

Figure 3-1b. *SP/SP-independent instruction pipeline throughput one per cycle*

If there are data dependencies—say for two consecutive SP instructions, as shown in Figure 3-1c—the second instruction will wait until data are produced at stage V4, where they will be passed over to the V1 stage of the second instruction using an internal bypass.

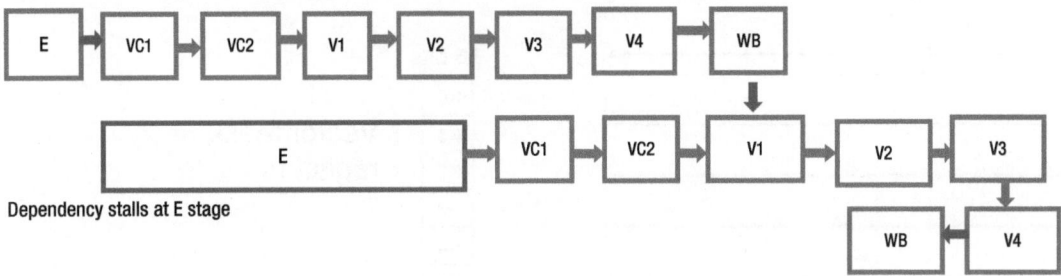

Dependency stalls at E stage

Figure 3-1c. *SP/SP-dependent instruction pipeline throughput one per cycle*

For an SP instruction followed by a dependent SP instruction, there is a forward path and, after the results of the first instruction are computed, the result is forwarded to the V1 stage of the second instruction, causing an additional three-cycle delay, as for the DP instructions.

For a SP instruction followed by another dependent SP instruction with register swizzle, the dependent data have to be sent to the VC1 stage, which does the swizzling, causing an additional five-cycle delay.

If the SP instruction is followed by an EMU instruction, because the EMU instruction has to look up the transcendental lookup table, which is done in VC1 stage, then the data have to be forwarded from V4 to VC1, as for the dependent swizzle case described, likewise resulting in an additional five-cycle dependency.

When an instruction in the DP pipeline is followed by a dependent instruction executing in an SP pipeline, the DP instruction has to complete the write before the dependent SP instruction can execute, because there are no bypasses between different pipelines. In this case the second instruction is stalled until the first instruction completes its write back, incurring a seven-cycle delay.

Pairing Rule

Although all vector instructions can execute on the U-pipe, some vector instructions can execute on the V-pipe as well. Table 3-1 describes the latter instructions. The details of these and other vector instructions are described in Appendix A. Proper scheduling of these pairable instructions with instructions executing on U-pipe will provide performance boost.

Table 3-1. *Instruction Pairing Rules Between U- and V-Pipelines*

Type	InstructionMn emonics
Vector mask instructions	JKNZ, JKZ, KAND, KANDN, KANDNR, KCONCATH, KCONCATL, KEXTRACT, KMERGE2L1H, KMERGE2L1L, KMOV, KNOT, KOR, KORTEST, KXNOR, KXOR
Vector store instructions	VMOVAPD, VMOVAPS, VMOVDQA32, VMOVDQA64, VMOVGPS, VMOVPGPS
Vector packstore instructions	VPACKSTOREHD, VPACKSTOREHPD, VPACKSTOREHPS, VPACKSTOREHQ, VPACKSTORELD, VPACKSTORELPD, VPACKSTORELPS, VPACKSTORELQ, VPACKSTOREHGPS, VPACKSTORELGPS
Vector prefetch instructions	VPREFETCH0, VPREFETCH1, VPREFETCH2, VPREFETCHE0, VPREFETCHE1, VPREFETCHE2, VPREFETCHENTA, VPREFETCHNTA
Scalar instructions	CLEVICT0, CLEVICT1, BITINTERLEAVE11, BITINTERLEAVE21, TZCNT, TZCNTI, LZCNT, LZCNTI, POPCNT, QUADMASK

VectorR egisters

The VPU state per thread is maintained in 32 512-bit general vector registers (zmm0-zmm31), eight 16-bit mask registers (K0-K7), and the status register (MXCSR), as shown in Figure 3-2.

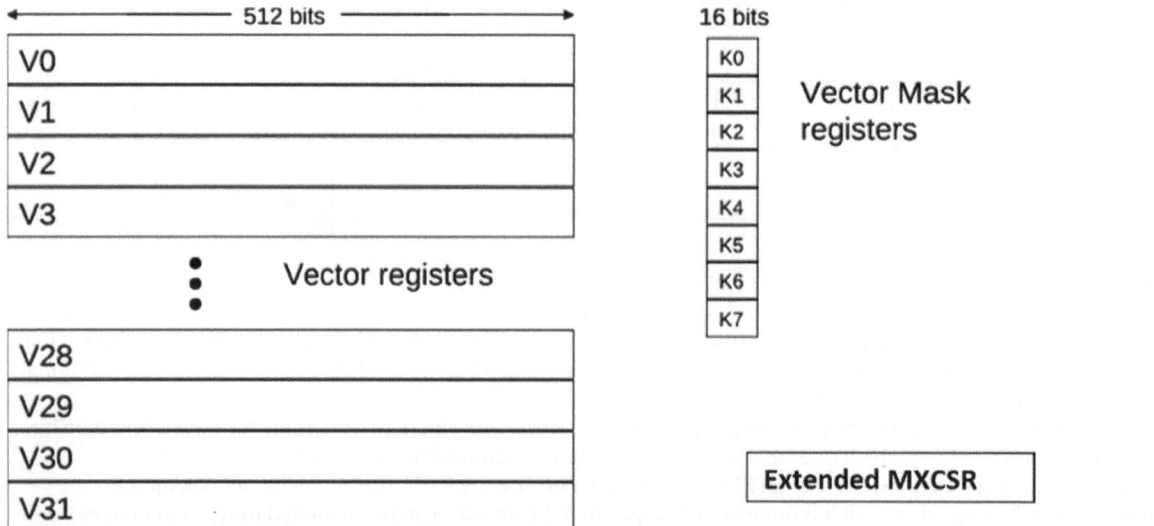

Figure 3-2. *Per-thread vector state registers*

Vector registers operate on 16 32-bit elements or eight 64-bit elements at a time. The MXCSR maintains the status of each vector operation, which can be checked later for exceptions during floating-point execution.

The VPU reads and writes the data cache at a cache-line granularity of 512 bits through a dedicated 512-bit bus. Reads from the cache go through the load conversion, swizzling before getting to the ALU. Writes go through store conversion and alignment before going to the write-commit buffer in the data cache.

VectorM ask Registers

Vector mask registers control the update of vector registers inside the calculations. In a nonmasked operation, such as a vector multiply, the destination register is completely overwritten by the results of the operation. Using write mask, however, one can make the update of the destination register element conditional on the bit content of a vector mask register, as shown in Figure 3-3.

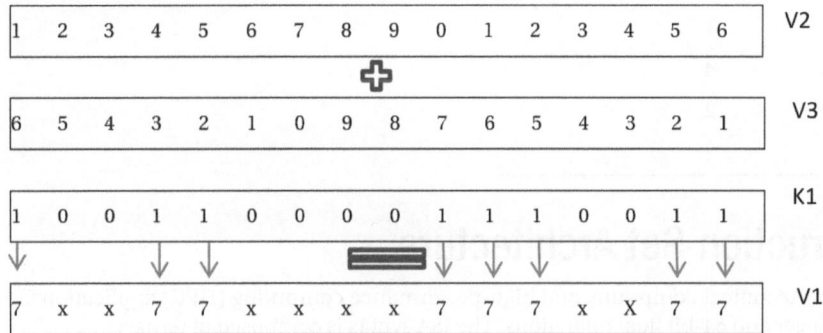

Figure 3-3. *A write mask register updates only the elements of destination register v1 based on mask k1*

Figure 3-3 shows the effect of the write mask register on SP vector operations. Here the two vectors v2 and v3a re added and, depending on the mask register bit values, only the V1 register element, which corresponds to 1 bit in the k1 register, gets updated. The other values corresponding to bit values 0 remain unchanged, unlike implementations where these elements can get cleared. For some operations, such as the vector blend operation (VBLEND*), the mask can be used to select the element from one of the operands to be output.

There is a small set of Boolean operations that can be performed on the mask registers—such as Xor, OR, and AND—but not arithmetic operations such as + or ×.

A write mask modifier can be used with all the vector instructions. If it is not specified, a default value of 0xFFFF is implied. There is a special mask register designated k0, which represents the default value of 0xFFFF and is not allowed to be specified as a write mask, because it is implied when no mask register is used. Although this mask register cannot be used for a write mask, it can be used for other mask register purposes, such as holding carry bits from integer arithmetic vector operations, comparison results, and so forth. One way to remember this restriction is to recall that any mask registers specified inside a braces {} mask specifier cannot be k0, but they can be used in other locations.

ExtendedM athU nit

The VPU implements the SP transcendental functions needed by various technical computing applications in various computing domains. These instructions are computed using quadratic minimax polynomial approximation and use a lookup table to provide a fast approximation to the transcendental functions. The EMU is a fully pipelined unit and can execute hardware transcendental instructions within one or two cycles. The hardware implements the following elementary transcendental functions: reciprocals, reciprocal square roots, base 2 exponential, and base 2 logarithms. There are three derived exponential functions dependent on these elementary functions: division using the reciprocal and multiplier; square root using the reciprocal square root and multiplier; and power using log 2, mult, and exp2. Table 3-2 shows the latency and throughput of vector transcendental instructions in Xeon Phi.

Table 3-2. *Latency and Throughput of Transcendental Functions*

instructions	Latency(cycles)	Throughput(cycles)
Exp2	8	2
Log2	4	1
Recip	4	1
Rsqrt	4	1
Power	16	4
Sqrt	8	2
Div	8	2

Xeon Phi Vector Instruction Set Architecture

The Vector ISA is designed to address technical computing and high-performance computing (HPC) applications. It supports native 32-bit float and integer and 64-bit float operations. The ISA syntax is composed of ternary instructions with two sources and one destination. There are also FMA (fused multiply and add) instructions, where each of the three registers acts as a source and one of them is also a destination. Although the designers of Xeon Phi architecture had every intention to implement an ISA compatible with the Intel Xeon processor ISA, the longer vector length, various transcendental instructions, and other issues prevented implementation at this time.

Vector architecture supports a coherent memory model in which the Intel-64 instructions and the vector instructions operate on the same address space.

One of the interesting features of vector architecture is the support for scatter and gather instructions to read or write sparse data in memory into or out of the packed vector registers, thus simplifying code generation for the sparse data manipulations prevalent in technical computing applications.

The ISA supports the proposed standard IEEE 754-2008 floating-point instruction rounding mode requirements. It supports denorms in DP floating point operations, round TiesToEven, round to 0, and round to + or - infinity. Xeon Phi floating point hardware achieves 0.5 ULP (unit in last place) for SP/DP floating point FP add, subtract, and multiply to conform to the IEEE 754-2008 standard.

Data Types

The VPU instructions support the following native data types:

- Packed32-b itin tegers(ordw ord)
- Packed 32-bit single-precision FP values
- Packed 64-bit integers (or qword)
- Packed6 4-bitd ouble-precisionF Pv alues

The VPU instructions can be categorized into typeless 32-bit instructions (denoted with the postfix "d"), type less 64-bit instructions (denoted with the postfix "q"), signed and unsigned int32 instructions (denoted with the postfix "pi" and "pu," respectively), signed int64 instructions (denoted with the postfix "pq"), and fp32 and fp64 instructions (denoted with the postfix "ps" and "pd," respectively).

For arithmetic calculations, the VPU represents values internally using 32-bit or 64-bit two's complement plus a sign bit—duplicate of the most significant bit (MSB)—for signed integers, 32-bit or 64-bit plus a sign bit tied to zero for unsigned integers. This is to simplify the integer data path and to avoid implementing multiple paths for the integer arithmetic. The VPU represents floating-point values internally using signed magnitude with an exponent bias of 128 or 1024 to adhere to the IEEE basic SP or DP format.

The VPU supports the up-conversion/down-conversion of the data types listed in Table 3-3 to/from either 32-bit or 64-bit values to execute instructions in the SP ALU or the DP ALU. These are the data types that the VPU can convert to native representation for reading and writing from memory to work with 32- or 64-bit ALUs.

Table 3-3. *VPU-Supported Memory Load Type Conversions*

Memory Stored Data Type	Destination Register Data Type			
	float32	float64	int32/uint32	int64/uint64
float16	Yes	No	No	No
float32	Yes	Yes	Yes	No
sint8	Yes	No	Yes	No
uint8	Yes	No	Yes	No
int16	Yes	No	Yes	No
uint16	Yes	No	Yes	No
int32	Yes	Yes	Yes	No
uint32	Yes	Yes	Yes	No
float64	Yes	Yes	Yes	No
int64/uint64	No	No	No	Yes

VectorN omenclature

This section introduces nomenclature helpful for describing vector operations in detail.

Each vector register in Xeon Phi is 512 bits wide and can be considered as being divided into four lanes numbered 0–3 with each being 128 bits long, as shown in Figure 3-4.

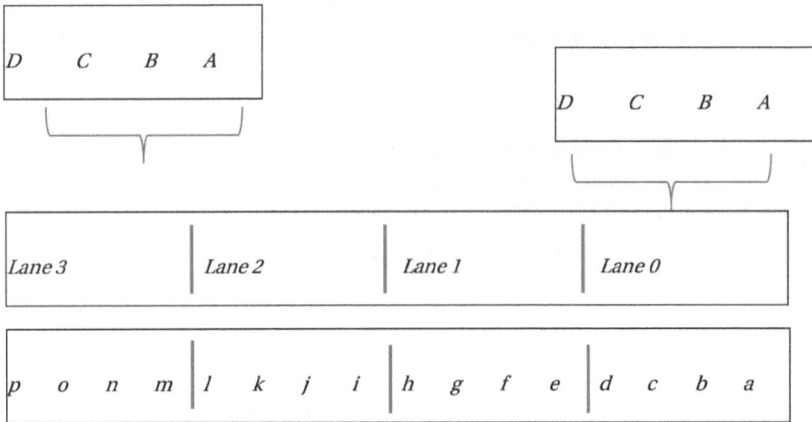

Figure 3-4. *Vector registers nomenclature*

There are four 32-bit elements in a 128-bit lane, identified by letters D through A regardless of which lane they belong to. All 16 elements in a vector are denoted by letters p through a, as shown in Figure 3-4.

The vectors are stored in the memory such that the lowest address is on the right-most side and the terms are read right to left. For example, when loading a 32-bit full vector from memory address 0xC000, the first element "a" will correspond to 32-bit memory content located at 0xC000, and the last element "p" comes from memory at location 0xC03C.

VectorI nstructionS yntax

Intel Xeon Phi uses three operand forms for its vector ISA. The basic form is as follows:

```
vop v0{mask}, v1, v2|mem {swizzle}
```

where vop indicates vector operator; v0,v1,v2 various vector registers defined in the ISA; mem is a memory pointer; {mask} indicates an optional masking operation; and {swizzle} indicates an optional data element permutation or broadcast operation. The mask and swizzle operations are covered in detail later in this chapter.

Depending on the type of operation, various numbers of vectors from one to three may be referenced as input operands. v0 in the above syntax is also the output operand of an instruction. The output may be masked with an optional mask, and the input operand may be modified by swizzleo perations.

Each Intel Xeon Phi instruction can operate on from one to three operands to support the ISA. Syntax for various operands izesa red escribedb elow:

1. One-input instructions, such as the vector converter instructions:

   ```
   v0 <= vop (v1|mem)
   ```

   where vop is the vector operator; v1 are vector registers; and mem represents a memory reference. The memory reference conforms to standard Intel-64 ISA and can be direct or indirect addressing—with offset, scale, and other modifiers to calculate the address.

   An example is vcvtpu2ps, which instructs a vector (vcvt part of the instruction mnemonics) of unsigned integers (pu) to convert to a (2) vector of floats (ps).

2. Two-input instructions, such as vector add operations:

   ```
   v0 <= vop (v1, v2|mem),
   ```

   where the operator vop operates on input v1 and v2 or mem and writes the output to v0. The swizzle/broadcast modifiers may be added to v2/mem, and the mask operator can be used to select the output of the vector operation to update the v0r egister.

   An example is vaddps, an instruction to add two vectors of floating point data.

3. Three-input instructions, such as fused multiply operations that work on three inputs:

   ```
   v0 <= vop (v0,v1,v2/mem),
   ```

   Where the operator operates on all three input vector register data v0, v1, and v2a nd writes the result of operation to one of the registers v0.

XeonP hiV ectorI SAb yC ategories

The Xeon Phi vector ISA can be broadly grouped into the following categories.:

Mask Operations

The Xeon Phi ISA supports optional mask registers that allow you to specify individual elements of a vector register to be worked on. The mask register is specified by curly braces {}. An example of their usage is:

```
vop v1[{k1}], v2, v3|mem
```

In this instruction, the bits in the 16-bit vector k1 determine which elements of the vector v1 will be written to by this operation. For 64-bit data types, the last eight bits of the mask register are used as mask bits. Here k1 is working as a write mask. If the mask bit corresponding to an element is zero, the corresponding element of v1 will remain unchanged; otherwise it will be overwritten by the corresponding element of the output of the computation. The square bracket indicates optional arguments.

There are 16 mask instructions: K*, JKXZ, JKNZ. The mask register k0 has all bits 1. This is a default mask register for all the instructions that do not have their mask specified. The behavior of mask operations was described in the section of this chapter, "Vector Registers."

Swizzle, Shuffle, Broadcast, and Convert Instructions

These instructions allow you to permute and replicate input data before being operated on by the instructions. The following subsections will look at these broad categories of instructions in detail.

Swizzle

Swizzle is an operation to perform data element rearrangement or permutations of the source operands before operating on the data element. A swizzle modifies the source operand by creating a copy of the input and generating a multiplexed data pattern using the temporary value and feeding it to the ALU as a source for the operation. The temporary value is discarded after the operation is done, thus keeping the original source operand intact.

In the instruction syntax, swizzles are optional arguments to instructions such as the mask operations described in the preceding section.

There are some restrictions on types of swizzles that may be used, depending on the microarchitectural support for the instruction. The instruction behavior is tabulated in Table 3-4.

Table 3-4. *Supported Swizzle Operations with Vector Instructions*

Function: 4 × 32 bits/4 × 64 Bits	Usage {`swizzle`}
No swizzle	No swizzle modifier (default) or {dcba}
Swapi nnerp airs	{cdab}
Swap with two away	{badc}
Crossp roducts wizzle	{dacb}
Broadcast 'a' element across 4-element packets	{aaaa}
Broadcast 'b' element across 4-element packets	{bbbb}
Broadcast 'c' element across 4-element packets	{cccc}
Broadcast 'd' element across 4-element packets	{dddd}

The swizzle command can be represented as follows:

```
vectorop v0, v1, v2/mem{swizzle},
```

where v0, v1, and v2 represents vector registers.

The swizzle operations are element-wise and limited to eight types. These operations are limited to permuting within four-element sets of a 32-bit or 64-bit element.

For register source swizzle, the supported swizzle operations are described in Table 3-4, where {dcba}d enotes the 32-bit elements that form one 128-bit block in the source (with *a* being least significant and *d* being most significant). {aaaa} means that the least significant element of each lane of a source register with shuffle modifier is replicated to all four elements of the same lane. When the source is a register, this functionality is the same for both integer and floating-point instructions. The first few swap patterns in the table ({cdab}, {badc}, {dacb}) are used to shuffle elements within a lane for arithmetic manipulations such as cross-product, horizontal add, and so forth. The last four patterns' "repeat element" are useful in many operations, such as scalar-vector arithmetic.

Figure 3-5 illustrates the swizzle operation for the register/register vector operation vorpi v0,v1,v2{aaaa}. It shows the replication of the least significant element across all lanes due to the swizzle operation {aaaa}.Intel compiler intrinsics define __MM_SWIZZLE_ENUM to express these permutations.

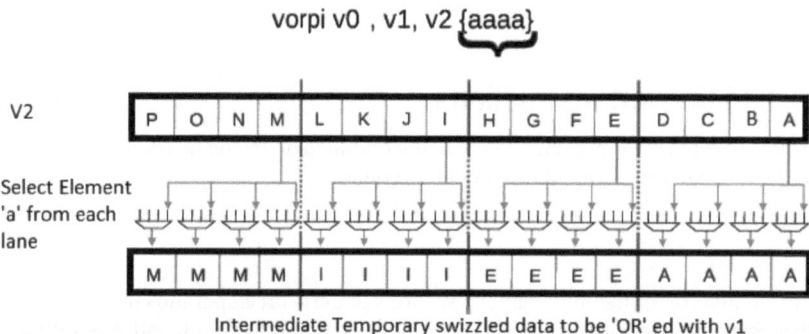

Figure 3-5. *Register/register swizzle operations*

Register Memory Swizzle

The register memory swizzle operations are available for all implicit loads. These operations perform data replication through broadcast operation or data conversion.

Data Broadcasts

If the input data is a memory pointer instead of a vector register, the swizzle operator works as a broadcast operator—that is, it can read specific elements from memory and replicate or broadcast them to the entire length of the vector register. This can be useful, for example, for vector expansion of a scalar.

The data broadcast operation allows you to perform data replication without having to load all of the 64-byte vector width from memory hierarchy, thus reducing memory traffic. In this operation, a subset of data is loaded and replicated the desired number of times to fill the 64-byte vector width. The three predefined swizzle modes for data broadcasts are: {1 to 16}, {4 to 16}, and {16 to 16}:

- In {1 to 16} broadcast swizzle pattern, one 32-bit element pointed to by the memory pointer is read from memory and replicated 15 times, which together with the single element read in from memory creates 16 element entries.

- For {4 to 16} broadcast, the first four elements pointed to by the memory pointer are read from memory and replicated three more times to create 16 element entries.

- {16 by 16} broadcasts are implied when no conversions are specified on memory reads and all 16 elements load from the memory into the registers. {16 by 16} is the default pattern in whichn or eplicationh appens.

Data Conversions

Data conversion allows the use of a swizzle field to convert various data formats in the memory to either 32-bit signed or unsigned integers or 32-bit floating point data types supported by native Xeon Phi operations on vector elements. The memory data types supported are 16-bit floats (float16), signed and unsigned eight-bit integers (sint8, uint8), and signed and unsigned 16-bit integers (sint16 and uint16). There is no load conversion support for 64-bit data types.

Intel Xeon Phi allows data transformations such as swizzle or data conversions on only one operand at most. For instructions that take more than one operand, the other operands are used unmodified. The ISA does not allow the swizzling and data conversion at the same time. However, the data conversion and broadcast can be combined when doing vector loads.

The vector registers are treated such that they contain either all 32-bit or all 64-bit data—not a mix of 32 and 64 bits. This means that data types other than 32- and 64-bit—such as float16—will have to be mapped to SP or DP floats before computations can be performed on them. Such mapping can generate different results than those obtained by working directly on float16 numbers, violating the commutative or associative rules of the underlying arithmetic. Allowed data conversions are listed in Table 3-3.

Shuffles

The shuffle instructions permute 32-bit blocks of vectors read from memory or vector registers using index bits in the immediate field. No swizzle, broadcast, or conversion is performed by this instruction. Unlike swizzle instruction, which is limited to eight predefined data patterns, as listed in Table 3-4, the shuffle operation can take arbitrary data patterns. For example, shuffle can generate the pattern dddc, whereas swizzle cannot.

There are two supported shuffle instructions:

```
vpshufd zmm1{k}, zmm2/mem, imm8
```

This instruction shuffles 32-bit blocks of the vector read from the memory or zmm2 using index bits in imm8. The results are written to zmm1 after applying appropriate masking using mask bits in k.

```
vpermf32x4 zmm1{k}, zmm2/mem, imm8
```

This instruction differs from the previous one in that it shuffles 128-bit lanes instead of 32-bit blocks within a lane—that is, it is an interlane shuffle as opposed to an intralane shuffle. These two shuffles can be combined consecutively to shuffle interlane and then within the lanes. One can use Intel compiler intrinsics enumeration _MM_SWIZZLE_ENUM to express these permutations.

Shift Operation

Intel Xeon Phi supports various shift operations on 32-bit integer vectors, as follow.

Logical Shifts

```
vpslld zmm1{k1}, Si32(zmm2/mem), imm8
```

This immediate shift version of the instruction uses the imm8 value to perform the shift. This instruction performs an element-by-element logical shift of the result of the swizzle, broadcast, or conversion of the input data zmm2/mem (indicated by the Si32 operation in the instruction mnemonic) by shift count given by the immediate value imm8a nd stores the result in zmm1 using write mask {k1}. If the shift count is more than 31, the result is set to all zeros. The write mask dictates which of the elements of the output registers will be written to. The elements in the destination register zmm1, for which the corresponding bits in {k1} are clear, retain their original values.

The conjugate operation, the right shift immediate operation, is indicated by vpsrld, where the r replacing lin vpslld indicates the right shift operation. The logical shift right shifts a 0-bit in the MSB for each shift count. Similar to the left shift, if the number of shifts is greater than 31, all bits are set to zero.

```
vpsllvd zmm1{k1}, zmm2, Si32(zmm3/mem)
```

This version of the instruction uses a vector Si32(zmm3/meme) to indicate the desired shift amount. This instruction performs an element-by-element logical shift of the 32-bit integer vector zmm2 by the int32 data computed by the swizzle, broadcast, or conversion of the zmm3/mem and stores the result in zmm1 using write mask {k1}. If the shift count is more than 31, the result is set to all zeros. The write mask dictates which of the elements of the output registers will be written to. The elements in the destination register zmm1, for which the corresponding bits in {k1}a re clear, retain their original values.

In the conjugate operation, the right shift vector operation is indicated by vpsrlvd, where the r replacing lin vpsllvd indicates the right shift operations. The logical shift right shifts a 0 bit in the MSB for each shift count. Similar to left shift, if the number of shifts is greater than 31, all bits are set to zero.

Arithmetic Shifts

Arithmetic shift Int32 vector right immediate:

```
vpsrad zmm1{k1}, Si32(zmm2/mem), imm8
```

This immediate arithmetic shift version of the instruction uses the imm8 value to perform the shift. This instruction performs an element-by-element arithmetic right shift of the result of the swizzle, broadcast, or conversion of the input data zmm2/mem (indicated by the Si32 operation in the instruction mnemonic) by the shift count given by the immediate value imm8 and stores the result in zmm1 using write mask {k1}. The arithmetic shift keeps the sign bit unchanged after each shift count and shifts the results into MSB bits. If the shift count is more than 31, the result is set to the original sign bit for all destination elements. The write mask dictates which of the elements of the output registers will be written to. The elements in the destination register zmm1, for which the corresponding bits in {k1} are clear, retain their original values.

Arithmetic shift Int32 vector right:

```
vpsravd zmm1{k1}, zmm2, Si32(zmm3/mem)
```

This version of the instruction uses a vector Si32(zmm3/mem) to indicate desired arithmetic right shift count. This instruction performs an element-by-element arithmetic right shift of the 32-bit integer vector zmm2 by the int32 data computed by the swizzle, broadcast, or conversion of the zmm3/mem and stores the results in zmm1 using write mask {k1}.

The arithmetic shift keeps the sign bit unchanged after each shift count and shifts the results into MSB bits. If the shift count is more than 31, the result is set to the original sign bit for all destination elements. The write mask dictates which of the elements of the output registers will be written to. The elements in the destination register zmm1, for which the corresponding bits in {k1} are clear, retain their original values.

Sample Code for Swizzle and Shuffle Instructions

Although I will be explaining how to program for a Xeon Phi coprocessor, here I am providing some code examples you can scan through to help you understand the concepts of swizzle and shuffle. You can try the code segment out when you are set up with Xeon Phi hardware and tools.

The code fragment in Listing 3-1 shows a simple C++ program using the C++ vector class Is32vec16p rovided with the Intel Xeon Phi compiler. In order to build and run this code, I went through the steps shown in the top of Listing 3-1. The middle section of Listing 3-1 shows the source code to test the shuffle instruction behavior using the C++ vector library and compiler intrinsics (these are functions you can call from C++ routines, which usually map into one assembly instruction).

The bottom section of Listing 3-1 shows the output from the run of the sample code. The swizzle form cdabs waps inner pairs of each lane; the intralane shuffle with the pattern aaaa on the same input data replicates element At o each element of each lane; and, finally, the interlane shuffle with the data pattern aabc reorganizes the lanes.

Listing 3-1. Simple C++ Program

Compiling and running sample shuftest.cpp **on Intel Xeon Phi**

```
//compiled the code
icpc -mmic shuftest.cpp -o shuftest
//copied output to Xeon Phi
scp shuftest mic0:/tmp
//Executed the binary
ssh mic0 "/tmp/shuftest"
```

Source Code for shuftest.cpp

```
//-------------------------
//-- Program shuftest.cpp
//-- Author: Reza Rahman
////-------------------------

#define MICVEC_DEFINE_OUTPUT_OPERATORS
#include <iostream>
#include <micvec.h>

int main()
{
    _MM_PERM_ENUM p32;

    __declspec(align(64)) Is32vec16  inputData(0,1,2,3,4,5,6,7,8,9,10,11,12,13,14,15);
    __declspec(align(64)) Is32vec16  outputData;

    std::cout << "input = "  << inputData;
```

```
    // swizzle input data and print
    // std::cout << "\nswizzle data for pattern 'cdab' \n" << inputData.cdab();

    // swizzle input data and print
    std::cout << "\n Intra lane shuffle data for pattern 'aaaa' \n";

    p32 = _MM_PERM_AAAA;

    //shuffle intra lane data
    outputData = Is32vec16(_mm512_shuffle_epi32(__m512i(inputData), p32));
    std::cout << outputData << "\n";

    std::cout << " Inter lane shuffle data for pattern 'aabc' \n";

    p32 = _MM_PERM_AABC;
    //shuffle inter lane data
    outputData = Is32vec16(_mm512_permute4f128_epi32(__m512i(inputData), p32));
    std::cout << outputData << "\n";
}
```

Output from shuftest.cpp **run on Intel Xeon Phi**

```
input = {15, 14, 13, 12, 11, 10, 9, 8, 7, 6, 5, 4, 3, 2, 1, 0}

swizzle data for pattern 'cdab'
{14, 15, 12, 13, 10, 11, 8, 9, 6, 7, 4, 5, 2, 3, 0, 1}

Intra lane shuffle data for pattern 'aaaa'
{15, 15, 15, 15, 11, 11, 11, 11, 7, 7, 7, 7, 3, 3, 3, 3}

Inter lane shuffle data for pattern 'aabc'
{7, 6, 5, 4, 11, 10, 9, 8, 15, 14, 13, 12, 15, 14, 13, 12}
```

Arithmetic and Logic Operations

There are 55 arithmetic instructions coded as V*PS for SP arithmetic, V*PD for DP arithmetic, VP*D for int32, and VP*Q for int64. These instructions include nine MAX/MIN instructions: V*MAX*, V*MIN*. There are four hardware-implemented (EMU) transcendental instructions (VEXP223PS, VLOG2PS, VRCP23PS, and VRSQRT23PS). The hardware supports SP and DP floating point denorms, and there is no performance penalty working on the denorms. So it does not assert DAZ (denormals are zero) and FTZ (flush to zero support). For logical operations, the ISA contains seven compare instructions—V*CMP*—which compare vector elements and set the vector masks. There are also 15 Boolean instructions to implement logical operations.

Fused Multiply-Add

Intel Xeon Phi supports IEEE 754-2008–compliant fused multiply-add/subtract (FMA/FMS) instructions, which are accurate to 0.5 ULP. The computation performed by a ternary FMA operation can be semantically represented by:

```
v1 = v1 vop1 v2 vop2 v3,
```

where vop1 can be set to multiply operation (×) and vop2 set to addition operation (+).

Other forms of these operations are possible by using implicit memory load or by using modifiers to broadcast, swizzles, and other conversions to source v3. In order to simplify the coding effort for the programmers, the ISA contains a series of FMA/FMS operations that can be numbered with three digits to signify the association of the source vectors with specific operations without remembering the rules that allow for specific sources to be tied to specific modifiers. For example, a basic SP vector FMA can have three mnemonics associated with it that are interpreted based on the three digits embedded in mnemonics, as follows:

```
vfmadd132ps  v1,v2,v3 => v1 = v1xv3 + v2
vfmadd213ps  v1,v2,v3 => v1 = v2xv1 + v3
vfmadd231ps  v1,v2,v3 => v1 = v2xv3 + v1
```

Memory load modifiers such as broadcast conversion are applicable only to v3, but by using the various mnemonics programmers it can apply the shuffle operators to the appropriate source vector of interest.

Another FMA mnemonic, vfmadd233ps, allows you to do a scale-and-bias transformation in one instruction, which could be useful in image-processing applications. This instruction uses four element sets—0-3, 4-7, 8-11, and 12-15—of source vector v2 and uses v3 elements as scale and bias to generate the results in vector v1; vfmadd233ps v1,v2,v3 generates code equivalent to the following:

```
v1[3..0]      = v2[3..0] x v3[1] + v3[0]
v1[7..4]      = v2[7..4] x v3[5] + v3[4]
v1[11..8]     = v2[11..8] x v3[9] + v3[8]
v1[15..12]    = v2[15..12] x v3[13] + v3[12]
```

Xeon Phi also introduces a vector version of carry-propagate instructions. These instructions can be combined to support wider integer arithmetic than the hardware default. In order to support this operation on vector elements, a carry-out flag can be generated for each individual vector element and a carry-in flag needs to be added to each element for the propagate operations. The VPU uses vector mask registers for both the carry-out bit vectors and carry-inb itv ectors.

Data Access Operations (Load, Store, Prefetch, and Gather/Scatter)

The data access instructions control data load, store, and prefetch from memory subsystem in the Intel Xeon Phi coprocessor.

Masked load store operations can be used to select the elements to be read or stored to or from a vector register by using mask bits, as described earlier in the "Mask Operations" section. I also discussed broadcast load instructions as part of the swizzle operations in the "Swizzle" section. There 22 load or store instructions—V*LOADUNPACK*, V*PACKSTORE* operations—and 19 scatter or gather instructions implement the semantics for the various scatter or gather operations that are required by the many technical computing applications supported by this ISA. The mnemonics for these instructions are V*GATHER*, V*SCATTER*. In addition, the ISA supports eight consecutive memory prefetch instructions V*PREFETCH* and six scattered memory gather or scatter prefetch instructions to help prefetch data reach various cache levels and to reduce data access latency when needed.

All vector instructions that access memory can take an optional cache line eviction hint (EH). The hint can be added to prefetch as well as memory load instructions.

Memory Alignment

All memory-based operations must be on properly aligned addresses. Each source-of-memory operand must have an address that is aligned to the number of bytes accessed by the operand. Otherwise, a #GP (General Protection) fault will occur. The alignment requirement is dictated by the number of data elements and the type of the data element. For example, if a vector operation needs to access 16 elements of four-byte (32-bit) SP floats, the referenced data elements must be 16x4=64 [number of elements times the size of (float)] byte aligned. The Intel Xeon Phi memory alignment rules for vector operations are shown in Table 3-5.

Table 3-5. *Memory Alignment Rules for Vector Instructions*

Memory Storage Form	Number of Load/Store Elements	Needed Memory Alignment (bytes)
4 bytes (float, int32, uint32)	1 (1 to 16 broadcast)	4
	4 (4 to 16)	16
	16 (16 to 16)	64
2 bytes (float16, sint16, uint16)	1 (1 to 16 broadcast)	2
	4 (4 to 16)	8
	16 (16 to 16)	32
1 byte (sint8, uint8)	1 (1 to 16 broadcast)	1
	4 (4 to 16)	4
	16 (16 to 16)	16

Pack/Unpack

The normal vector instructions read 64 bytes of data and overwrite the destination based on the mask register. The unpack instructions keep the serial ordering of the source and write them sparsely to the destination. You can use pack and unpack instructions to handle the case where the memory data have to be compressed or expanded as they are written to memory or read from memory into a register. The mask register dictates how the memory has to be expanded to fill the 64-byte form of the compressed memory data. Examples include the vloadunpackh*/vloadunpackl* instruction pairs. These instructions allow you to relax the memory alignment requirements by requiring alignment to the memory storage form only. As long as the address to load from is aligned to a boundary for memory storage form, then executing a pair of vloadunpackl* and vloadunpackh* will load all 16 elements with default mask.

Non-temporal data

Cache helps improve application performance by making use of the locality of data being accessed by a program. However, for certain applications, such as streaming data apps, this model is broken and cache is polluted by taking up space for non-reusable data. To allow programmers or compiler developers to support such semantics of non-temporal memory, all memory operands in this ISA have an optional attribute called the eviction hint to indicate that the data are non-temporal. That is, EH indicates that the data may not be reused in time. This is a hint and the coprocessor can ignore it. The hint forces the latest data loaded by this instruction to become "least recently used" (LRU) rather than "most recently used" (MRU) in the LRU/MRU cache policy enforced by the cache subsystem.

Streaming Stores

In general, in order to write to a cache line, the Xeon Phi coprocessor needs to read in a cache line before writing to it. This is known as read for ownership (RFO). One problem with this implementation is that the written data are not reused; you unnecessarily take up the memory BW for reading nontemporal data. Intel Xeon Phi supports instructions that do not read in data if the data are a streaming store. These instructions, VMOVNRAP*, VMOVNRNGOAP*, allow you to indicate that the data need to be written without reading the data first. In Xeon Phi the VMOVNRAPS/VMOVNRAPD instructions are able to optimize the memory BW in case of a cache miss by not going through the unnecessary read step.

The VMOVNRNGOAP* instructions are useful when the programmer tolerates weak write-ordering of the application data—that is, the stores performed by these instructions are not globally ordered. A memory-fencing operation should be used in conjunction with this operation if multiple threads are reading and writing to the same location.[1]

Scatter/Gather

The Intel Xeon Phi ISA implements scatter and gather instructions to enable vectorization of algorithms working with a sparse data layout. Vector scatters are store operations in which the data elements of a vector do not reside in consecutive locations. Rather, some may reside sparsely on the memory virtual address space. You can still use write mask to select the data elements to be written to, and every one of these elements that are not write masked must obey the memory alignment rules given in Table 3-5. Gather instructions have a syntax of vgatherd* to gather SP, DP, int32, or int64 elements in a vector register using signed dword indices for source elements. These instructions can gather up to 16 32-bit elements in up to 16 different cache lines. The number of elements gathered will depend on the number of bits set in the mask register provided as source to the instruction.

Prefetch Instructions

The Intel Xeon Phi hardware implements a hardware prefetcher..In addition, the ISA supports a software prefetch to L1 and L2 data caches. The vprefetch* instructions are implemented for performing these operations. Intel Xeon Phi also implements gather prefetch instructions vgatherpf*. These instructions are critical where the hardware prefetch is not able to bring in necessary data to the cache lines, causing cache-line misses and hence increased instruction retirement stalls. Prefetch instruction can be used to fetch data to L1 or L2 cache lines. Since this hardware implements an inclusive cache mechanism, L1 data prefetched are also present in L2 cache—but not vice versa.

For prefetch instructions, if the line selected is already present in the cache hierarchy at a level closer to the processor, no data movement occurs. Prefetch instructions can specify invalid addresses without causing a GP fault because of their speculative nature.

Gather or scatter prefetches can be used to reduce the data-access latency of sparse vector elements. The gather/scatter prefetches set the access bits in the related TLB page entry. Scatter prefetches do not set dirty bits.

Summary

This chapter looked at an important component of Xeon Phi architecture: the vector unit. Used properly, the vector unit allows the coprocessor to achieve teraflops double-precision performance. In order to achieve maximum application performance, you must understand how the vector units are organized and restructure their source as necessary to allow the compiler to generate efficient code and achieve high performance on the coprocessor. This chapter also examined vector pipelines and what might cause them to stall and hurt performance.

---

[1]Memory Fencing Instructions: Since Intel Xeon Phi cores are inorder machines, where instructions are executed in the order they appear in the program, there are no memory fence instructions in these cores—unlike Intel Xeon cores' mfence instructions. However, memory access ordering will be needed between threads for consistency. So, in order to provide memory-access ordering on Xeon Phi, you need to impose explicit ordering by using instructions, such as lock or xchg instructions, to create similar semantics.

CHAPTER 4

■ ■ ■

Xeon Phi Core Microarchitecture

A processor core is the heart that determines the characteristics of a computer architecture. It is where the arithmetic and logic functions are mostly concentrated. The *instruction set architecture* (ISA) is implemented in this portion of the circuitry. Yet, in a modern-day architecture such as Intel Xeon Phi, less than 20 percent of the chip area is dedicated to the core. A survey of the development of the Intel Xeon Phi architecture will elucidate why its coprocessor core is designed the way it is.

The Intel Pentium Pro-based processors, designed around a long execution pipeline and a high degree of out-of-order instruction execution, reached a power barrier to increasing processor performance by increasing frequency. The demand for computing was still in its infancy, and the computing industry started the move toward parallel and multicore programming to feed the demand. The technical computing industry needed more compute power than provided by existing multicore architecture to continue modeling real-world problems in a wide range of fields from oil and gas exploration to biomedical engineering. As an example, in the oil and gas exploration field, high-performance computing is a competitive advantage for those who can make use of these computing resources to drill efficiently for oil recovery. Reducing the number of holes drilled in the search for oil reservoirs helps the environment as well as the bottom line. However, the simulation capabilities needed for such applications require processor performance and efficiency levels to push the power envelope of current serial or multicore-based architectures. Meeting the technical computing demands of the near future will require the implementation of disruptive technologies that will make each core substantially faster.

As a result, the computing industry started looking for alternate approaches—including attached-coprocessor solutions from Clearspeed, various *field-programmable gate array* (FPGA) solutions, and graphics chips such as from AMD and NVIDIA—to improve the performance of the scientific applications. Developing and maintaining such software seemed, however, prohibitively costly for practical industrial development environments. What was needed was a universal coprocessor programming language and processor architecture to leverage the development and tuning expertise of today's software engineers to achieve the power and performance goals of future computational needs. The architecture team within Intel found that the cores based on Intel Pentium designs could be extremely power-efficient on current semiconductor process architecture thanks to short pipelines and low-frequency operations. These cores could also retain many of the existing programming models that most of the developers in the world were already using. For the technical computing industry, the value of the years of investment that have been put into software development must be preserved. The compatibility and portability of existing applications are critical criteria in selecting among different hardware platforms for technical computing applications.

Intel Xeon Phi Cores

The decision to use Intel Pentium cores started the effort to develop Intel's first publicly available *many-integrated-core* (MIC) architecture. In this architecture, a single in-order core is replicated up to 61 times in Intel Xeon Phi design and placed in a high-performance bidirectional ring network with fully coherent L2 caches. Each of the cores supports four hyperthreads to keep the core's computing process busy by pulling in data to hide latency. The cores are also designed to run at *turbo modes*—that is, if the power envelop allows, the core frequency can be increased to increase performance.

These cores have dual-issue pipelines with Intel 64 instruction support and 16 floating-point (32-bit) wide SIMD units with FMA support that can work on 16 single-precision or 8 double-precision data with a single instruction. The instructions can be pipelined at a throughput rate of one vector instructions per cycle. The core contains a 32-kB 8-way set-associative L1 data and instruction cache. There are 512 kB per core L2 cache shared among four threads, and there is a hardware prefetcher to prefetch cache data. The L2 caches between the cores are fully coherent.

Thec orei sa *2-wide processor*—meaning it can execute two instructions per cycle, one on the U-pipe and the other on the V-pipe. It also contains an x87 unit to perform floating-point instructions when needed.

The Intel Xeon Phi core has implemented a 512-bit Vector ISA that can execute 16 single-precision floating-point or 32-bit integer and 8 double-precision floating-point or 64-bit integer vector instructions. Vector units consist of 32x 512-bit vector registers and 8 mask registers to allow predicated execution on the vector elements. Support for Scatter/Gather vector memory instructions makes assembly code generation easier for assembly coders or compiler engineers. Floating-point operations are IEEE 745 2008-compliant. Intel Xeon Phi architecture supports single-precision transcendental instructions for exp, log, recip, and sqrt functions in hardware.

The vector unit communicates with the core and executes vector instructions allocated in the U or V pipeline. The V-pipe executes a subset of the instructions and is governed by instruction-pairing rules, which are important to account for in getting optimum processor performance.

■ **Calculating the Theoretical Performance of Intel Xeon Phi Cores**   For an instantiation of the Intel Xeon Phi coprocessor with 60 usable cores, running at 1.1 GHz, you can compute its theoretical performance for single-precision operations as follows:

- GFLOP/sec = 16 (SP SIMD Lane) × 2 (FMA) × 1.1 (GHz) × 60 (# cores) = 2112 for single-precision arithmetic

- GFLOP/sec = 8 (DP SIMD Lane) × 2 (FMA) × 1.1 (GHz) × 60 (# cores) = 1056 for double-precision arithmetic

---

■ **Note**   Since the Intel Xeon Phi processor runs an OS inside, which may take up a processor core to service hardware or software requests such as interrupts, a 61-core processor may end up with 60 cores available for pure compute tasks.

Core Pipeline Stages

The core pipeline is divided into seven stages for integer instructions, plus six extra stages for the vector pipeline (Figure 4-1). Each stage including E and prior stages is speculative, since events such as a branch mispredict, data cache miss, or *translation look-aside buffer* (TLB) miss can invalidate all the work done up to this stage. Once it enters the WB stage, it is done and updates the machine's states.

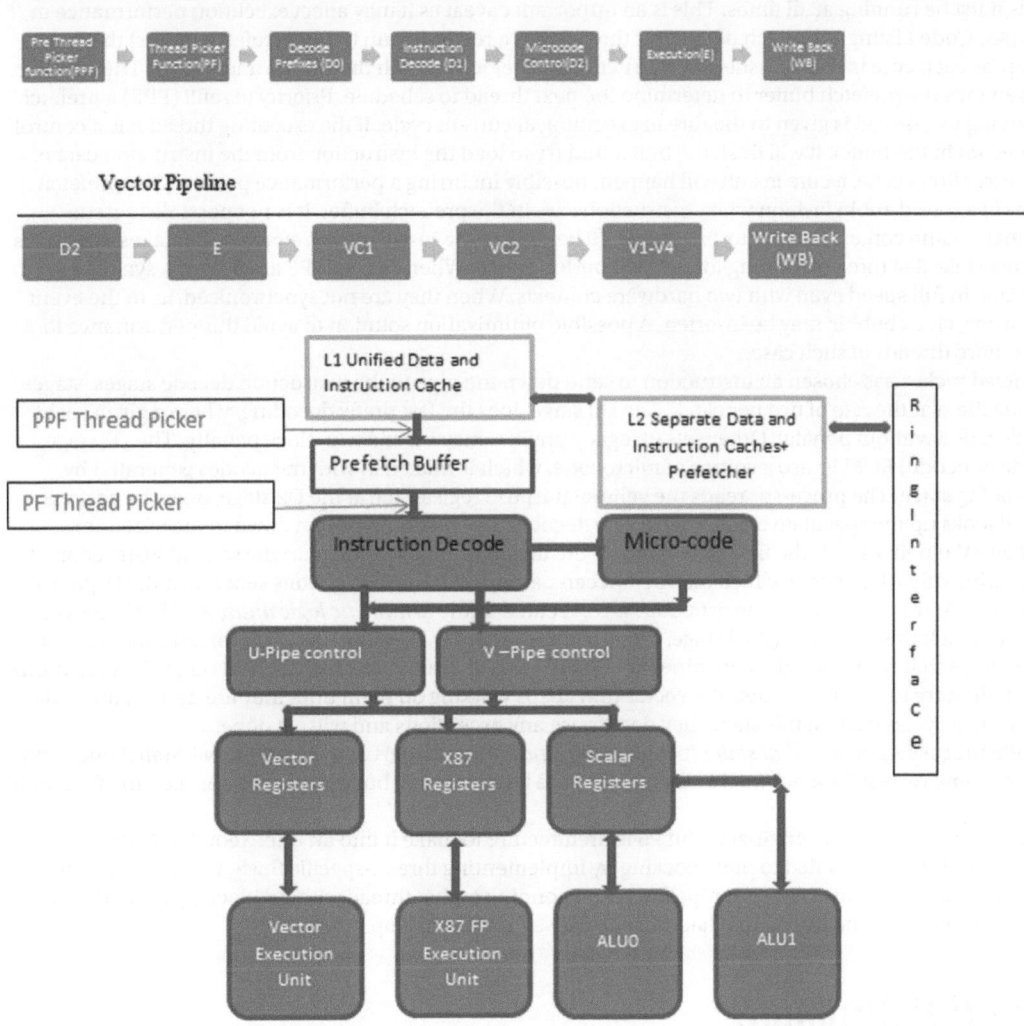

Figure 4-1. *Coprocessor core integer and vector pipeline and simplified instruction/data flow model*

Each core is *4-way multithreaded*, meaning that each core can concurrently execute instructions from four threads/processes. This helps reduce the effect of vector pipeline latency and memory access latencies, thus keeping the execution units busy.

The traditional *instruction fetch* (IF) stage is broken down into two *thread picker* stages for selecting the thread to execute: *pre-thread picker function* (PPF) and thread *picker function* (PF). The PPF stage prefetches instructions for a thread context into the prefetch buffers. There are four buffers per thread in the prefetch buffer space, and these can contain 32 bytes each per buffer. There are two streams per thread. When one of the streams is stalled, owing for example to a branch mispredict, a second stream is switched in while the branched target stream is being prefetched.

The PF stage selects the thread to execute by sending the instruction pairs to decode stages. The hardware cannot issue instructions back-to-back from the same thread in the core. To reach full execution unit utilization, at least two threads must be running at all times. This is an important caveat as it may affect execution performance in some scenarios (see Code Listing 4-1). Each of the four threads has a ready-to-run buffer (prefetch buffer) that is two instructions deep, as each core is able to issue two instructions per clock on both the U-pipe and V-pipe. The picker function (PF) examines the prefetch buffer to determine the next thread to schedule. Priority to refill (PPF) a prefetch buffer corresponding to a thread is given to the thread executing at current cycle. If the executing thread has a control transfer to a target not in the buffer, it will flush the buffer and try to load the instruction from the instruction cache. If it misses the instruction cache, a core install will happen, possibly incurring a performance penalty. The prefetch function behaves in a round-robin fashion when instructions are in the prefetch buffer. It is not possible to issue instructions from the same context in back-to-back cycles. The refill of the instruction prefetch buffer takes 4–5 cycles, which means it may take 3–4 threads running for optimal performance. When PPF and PF are properly synchronized, the core can execute in full speed even with two hardware contexts. When they are not synchronized, as in the event of a cache miss, a one-clock bubble may be inserted. A possible optimization solution to avoid this performance loss is to run three or more threads in such cases.

Once the thread picker has chosen an instruction to send down the pipe to the instruction decode stages, stages D0 and D1 decode them at the rate of two per clock. The D0 stage does the fast prefix decoding, where a given set of prefixes can be decoded without penalty. Other sets of legacy prefixes may incur a two-clock penalty. The D1 stage microcode(μcode or ucode) ROM is also a source of microcode, which is muxed in with the ucodes generated by the previous decoding stage. The processor reads the general purpose register file at the D2 stage, does the address computation, and looks up the speculative data cache. The decoded instructions are sent down to the execution unit using the U and V pipelines. U is the first path taken by the first instruction in the pair; the second instruction, if pairable under pairing rules that dictate which instruction can pair up with the instructions sent down the U-pipe, is sent down the V-pipe. At this stage, integer instructions are executed in the *arithmetic logic units*(ALU)s. Onces calar integer instructions reach the *writeback* (WB) stage, they are done. There is a separate pipeline for x87 floating-point and vector instructions that starts after the core pipeline. When vector instructions reach the WB stage, the core thinks they are done, but they are not done, because the vector unit keeps working on them until they are done at the end of the vector pipeline five cycles later. At this stage they don't raise any exceptions and will get done.

Intel Xeon Phi processors have *global stall pipeline architecture*—that is, part of the pipeline will stall if one of the stages is stalled for some reason. Modern Intel Xeon architecture has queues to buffer the stalls between the front and backe nd.

Many changes were made to the original 32-bit P54c architecture to make it into an Intel Xeon Phi 64-bit processor. The data cache was modified to non-blocking by implementing thread-specific flush. When a thread has a cache miss, it is now possible to flush only the pipeline corresponding to that thread without blocking other threads. When the data are available for the thread that had a cache misses, it will wake up.

Cache and TLB Structure

The details of the L1 instruction and data cache structure are shown in Table 4-1. The data cache allows simultaneous read and write, allowing cache line replacement to happen in a single cycle. The L1 cache consists of 8 ways set-associative 32-kB L1 instruction and 32-kB L1 data cache. The L1 cache access time is approximately 3 cycles, as measured in the "Understanding Intel Xeon Phi Cache Performance" section of this chapter. L2 cache is 8-way set-associative and 512 kB in size. The cache is *unified*—that is, it caches both data and instructions. The L2 cache latency could be as small as 14-15 cycles.

Table 4-1. *Intel Xeon Phi L1 I/D Cache Configuration*

Size	32k B
Associativity	8-way
Lines ize	64b ytes
Banks ize	8b ytes
Outstandingm isses	8
Data return	Out of order

L1 data TLB supports three page sizes: 4 kB, 64 kB, and 2 MB (Table 4-2). It also has a L2 TLB that acts as a true second-level TLB for 2-MB pages or acts as a cache for *page directory entries* (PDEs) for 4-kB and 64-kB pages. If one misses L1 and also misses L2 TLB, one has to walk four levels of page table, which is pretty expensive. For 4-kB/64-kB pages, if one misses the L1 TLB but hits the L2 TLB, it will provide the PDE (Figure 4-2) directly and be done with the paget ranslation.

Table 4-2. *Intel Xeon Phi TLB Configuration*

	PageSiz e	Entries	Associativity
L1D ataT LB	4K B	64	4-way
	64 KB	32	4-way
	2 MB	8	4-way
L1 InstructionT LB	4K B	64	4-way
L2 TLB	4 KB, 64 KB, 2 MB	64	4-way

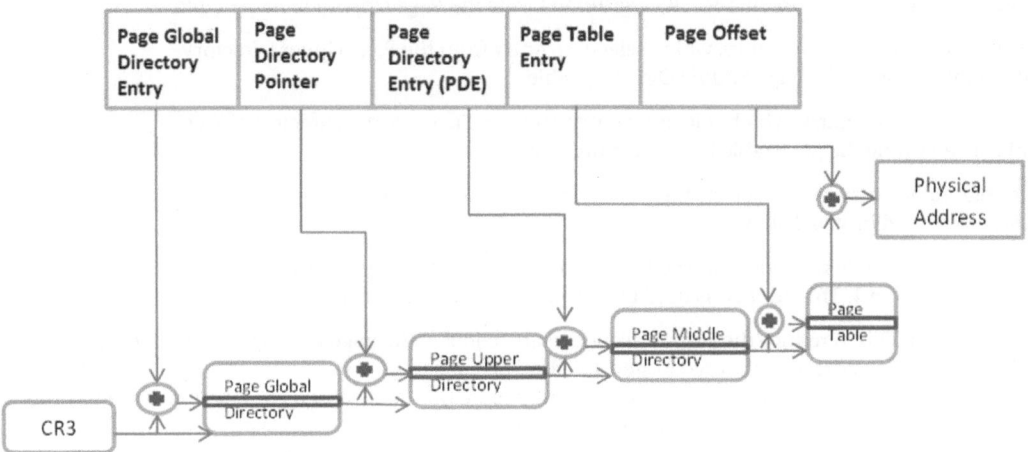

Figure 4-2. *Linear-to-physical address translation in Intel Xeon Phi coprocessor*

The page-translation mechanism allows the applications to use much larger address spaces than physically available in the processor. The size of a physical address is an implementation specific to the hardware. Intel Xeon Phi supports a 40-bit physical address in a 64-bit mode—that is, the coprocessor will generate a 40-bit physical address signal on the memory address bus of the coprocessor. Although Intel Xeon Phi supports various virtual address modes, such as 32-bit and physical address extension (36-bit) modes, I will focus here mainly on the 64-bit mode, as that is what is implemented through the micro OS running on the coprocessor. In the 64-bit mode, there is architectural support for applications to use a 64-bit linear address. The *paging* mechanism implemented in the operating system allows a linear address used by an application to map to a physical address, which can be less than 64 bits. A 64-bit linear address is used to address code, data, and stack. The micro OS running on the coprocessor uses 4-level hierarchical paging. Linear addresses generated by an application are grouped in fixed-length intervals known as *pages*. The micro OS running on Intel Xeon Phi supports 4kB and 2MB page sizes; 64KB implemented in the hardware is not yet supported by micro OS at time of writing. The application or OS may chose to move between various page sizes to reduce the TLB misses. The current micro OS implements *transparent huge page* (THP) to automatically promote or demote page sizes during an application run. You can use the madvise system API to control THPb ehavior.

The operating system creates data structures known as *page table data structures*, which the hardware uses to translate linear addresses into physical addresses. These page table data structures reside in the memory and are created and managed by the operating system or, in the case of Intel Xeon Phi, micro OS. There are four levels of page tabled atas tructures:

1. PageG lobalD irectory

2. PageU pper Directory

3. PageM iddleD irectory

4. PageT able

A special processor register, *CR3*, points to the base of the data structure Page Global Directory. Each data structure contains a set of entries that point to the next lower-level table structure. The lowest-level entries in the hierarchy point to the translated page, which, when combined with the offset from the linear address, provides the physical address that can be used to access the memory location. The translation process is shown in Figure 4-2.

The linear address can be logically divided into the following steps:

1. The Page Global Directory Offset, which combines with the base address of the Page Global Directory table found in the CR3 register to locate the Page Upper Directory table.

2. The Page Directory Pointer entry, which selects an entry from the Page Upper Directory Offset table to locate the Page Middle Directory table.

3. The Page Directory Entry, which selects an entry from the Page Middle Directory Offset table to determine the page table location in memory.

4. The Page Table Entry, which selects the physical page address by indexing into the Page Table discovered in step 3 above.

5. Page Offset, which then provides the actual physical address from the page address discovered in step 4. This address is used by the hardware to fetch the data.

The sole work of the TLB is to reduce the page-walk necessary to locate the page corresponding to steps 1 through 4 and save the page address discovered in step 4 in the TLB cache.

Applications running in the operating system have a separate set of this table structure and are switched in and out by changing the CR3 register value corresponding to the application.

L2 Cache Structure

The L2 cache is the secondary cache for the core. The L2 cache is inclusive of the L1 cache. It is all right to have a cache line in L2 only, but L1 cache lines must have a copy in L2. The L2 cache associated with each core is 512 kB in size. The cache is divided into 1024 sets and 8 ways per set with 64 bytes/1 cache line per way. The cache is divided into two logical banks. The L2 cache can deliver 64 bytes of read data to corresponding cores every two cycles and 64 bytes of write data every cycle.

Multithreading

The Intel Xeon Phi coprocessor uses time-multiplexed multithreading. The PPF thread picker prefetches instructions for a thread context into the prefetch buffers, and the PF selects what entries to read from the prefetch buffer and send them to the decoder. It uses a smart round-robin mechanism to pick only threads that have work to do and avoids threads that are inactive due to various conditions such as cache miss. For optimization, you can control thread scheduling by putting delay loops in the thread that the thread picker will not schedule in the actual hardware.

To support multithreading, all architectural states are replicated four times. Microarchitectural states of prefetch buffers, instruction pointers, segment descriptors, and exception logic are replicated four times as well. The design uses ID bits to distinguish between threads for shared structures such as *instruction TLB* (ITLB), *data TLB* (DTLB), and *branch target buffer* (BTB). All memory stalls are converted into thread-specific flushes.

PerformanceC onsiderations

Run two or more threads to keep the core completely busy. Integer operations and mask instructions are single-cycle. Most vector instructions have four-cycle latency and single-cycle throughput, so having four threads will not reveal the vector unit latency if all threads are executing vector instructions. Use four threads to hide vector unit latencies.

Address Generation Interlock

Address generation interlock (AGI) latencies are three clock cycles. When one writes to a *general-purpose register* (GPR) that is used as a base or index register, these instructions have to be spaced properly, as the address generation is done in a separate stage in the pipeline. For example, consider the following instruction sequence:

```
add rbx,4
mov rax,[rbx]
```

Here the calculation of the actual linear address from [rbx] is done in a separate stage before the memory fetch happens at line 2 above. In this case, hardware will insert two clock-delays between these two instructions. If running more than one thread, one may not see it as instructions from other threads can run during the dead clock-cycles for another thread.

There is also dependent load/store latency. The cores do not forward the store buffer contents, even if the data is available in the buffer to fulfill the request by the load instructions. So a load followed by a store to the same location will need the store buffer to write to the cache and then read back from the cache. In this case, the latency is four clock-cycles.

If there is a bank conflict—that is, if the U- and V-pipes try to access a memory location that resides on the same L2 cache bank—the core will introduce two clock-cycle delays for the V-pipe. When the cache line has to be replaced, it involves two clock-cycle delays. So if the code has a lot of vector instructions that miss cache, the core will have to put in a two-cycle delay for each miss to do the replacement.

Prefix Decode

There are two classes of prefixes. The fast prefixes are decoded in 0 cycles with dedicated hardware blocks and include the following prefixes: 62 for vector instructions, c4/c5 for mask instructions, *register extension* (REX) for integer instructions for 64-bit code, and 0f. All other prefixes are decoded in two-cycle latencies and include the following prefixes: 66 for selecting 16-bit operand size, 67 for address size, a lock prefix, a segment prefix, and an REP prefix for stringi nstructions.

Pairing Rules

There are specific instructions that are pairable and thus can execute in both the U- and V-pipelines. These instructions include independent single-cycle instructions. Some dependency exceptions occur where two dependent instructions can execute in pair—such as cmp/jcc, push/push, pop/pop—by incorporating the instructions' semantic knowledge into the hardware.

For pairing to occur, instructions cannot have both displacement and immediate values, and the instructions cannot be longer than 8 bytes. 62, c4, and c5 prefixed instructions with 32-bit displacement do not pair. Microcode instructions do not pair.

Scalar *integer multiples* (imul) are long latency instructions (10 cycles) in Xeon Phi as they are executed in x87 floating-point units. One needs to shift the integer operands to FP units to do the multiply and shift the results back to thei ntegerp ipeline.

Probingt heC ore

This section probes the behavior of the Xeon Phi core by executing various code fragments on it. This will provide you with practical experience on what the core is capable of achieving given the core architecture described so far in this chapter.

Measuring Peak Gflops

This section examines through experiments the core microarchitecture and pipelines described in the preceding sections. Code Listing 4-1 exemplifies how to measure the core computing power of a 61-core Intel Xeon Phi, of which 60 cores are available for computation while one of the cores services the operating system. Code Listing 4-1 is written in simple native code which can run on the card using the techniques discussed in Chapter 2.

The code needs to be designed such that the computation is core-bound and not limited by the memory or cache bandwidth. To do so, the data need to fit in the processor vector registers, limited to 32 for each thread in Intel Xeon Phi cores. The code uses OpenMP parallelism to run on 240 threads on the 60 core processors (with 4 threads/core). (See Appendix A for a background on OpenMP.) To build OpenMP code, I included the <omp.h> header file, which allows me to query various OpenMP parameters.

Writing the code in OpenMP will allow you to run the code from one core to multiple cores using an environment switch and gain an experimental understanding of the compute power of the processor.

Lines 42 and 43 in Code Listing 4-1 declare two constants. The first constant, 16, indicates the number of double precisions to be used for the computation. In this architecture, the vector units can work on 8 (DP) numbers per cycle. As discussed in the "Core Pipeline Stages" section of this chapter, each of the four threads per core has a ready-to-run buffer (prefetch buffer) two instructions deep, such that each core is able to issue two instructions per clock. Having 16 DP elements allows me to put a pair of independent instructions in the fill buffer. I have also made the number of iterations ITER multiple of 240, the number of maximum threads I shall be running to balance the workload.

The function-elapsed time uses the Linux gettimeofday function to get the time elapsed for computation. Line 52 declares the three arrays that I shall be working on each in each thread. I have aligned the arrays to 64-byte cacheline boundaries so that they can be loaded efficiently by the compiler. I let the compiler know however that the data are aligned by "pragma vector aligned" at line number 64 and 72 of Code Listing 4-1. If you look carefully, all threads will be writing back to array a[] in line 65 and 73. This will cause a race condition and will not be useful in real application code. However, for the sake of illustrative purposes, this effect may be ignored at this time.

In lines 62 through 66 I warm up the cache and initialize openmp threads so that these overheads are not counted during the code timing loops that happen between lines 70 through 74. For easy reference, if you look at the code fragment below, line 70 is a repetition of the omp parallel first encountered at line 62. As such, all OpenMP overhead related to thread creation is captured at line 62 and the threads are reused at line 70. The OpenMP "pragma omp parallel for" will divide up the loop iterations statically in this default case among the available threads set by the environment variable. The pragma vector aligned at line 72 tells the compiler that the arrays a, b, and c are all aligned to the 64-byte boundary for Intel Xeon Phi and do not need to do any special load manipulations needed for unaligned data.

At lines 78 and 79, the Gflops operations are computed. As the operations in line 73 are a fused multiply–add operation, it is in effect computing two DP FLOP operations. Since there are SIZE number of double-precision elements each operated over ITER number of times by one or multiple threads, depending on the OpenMP environment variable OMP_NUM_THREADS setting, the amount of computation is equal to 2*SIZE*ITER/1e+9 in Giga floating point operations or GFLOP. Dividing this number by duration measured by the timer routines at line 68 and 76 will allow us to compute the GFLOP/seconds which are an indication of the core performance. In addition, the Intel compiler allows us to control the code generation such that we can turn vectorization on or off.

Note that I have used special array notation supported by Intel Compiler known as *Cilk Plus notation*. Ci lk Plus array notation asks the compiler to work on SIZE elements of double-precision data and asserts that there is are no array data aliasing. This helps indicate to the compiler that the elements of the arrays (a, b, c in this case) are independent, thus allowing the compiler to vectorize the code, which otherwise could be ambiguous to the compiler as to its vectorizability.

Code Listing 4-1. Source Code to Measure Peak Gigaflops on Xeon Phi

```
38 #include <stdio.h>
39 #include <stdlib.h>
40 #include <omp.h>
41
42 unsigned int const SIZE=16;
43 unsigned int const ITER=48000000;
44
45 extern double elapsedTime (void);
46
47 int main()
48 {
49     double startTime, duration;
50     int i;
51
52     __declspec(aligned(64)) double a[SIZE],b[SIZE],c[SIZE];
53
54
55     //intialize
56     for (i=0; i<SIZE;i++)
57     {
58         c[i]=b[i]=a[i]=(double)rand();
59     }
60
61 //warm up cache
62     #pragma omp parallel for
63     for(i=0; i<ITER;i++) {
64     #pragma vector aligned (a,b,c)
```

```
65    a[0:SIZE]=b[0:SIZE]*c[0:SIZE]+a[0:SIZE];
66    }
67
68    startTime = elapsedTime();
69
70    #pragma omp parallel for
71    for(i=0; i<ITER;i++) {
72    #pragma vector aligned (a,b,c)
73    a[0:SIZE]=b[0:SIZE]*c[0:SIZE]+a[0:SIZE];
74    }
75
76    duration = elapsedTime() - startTime;
77
78    double Gflop = 2*SIZE*ITER/1e+9;
79    double Gflops = Gflop/duration;
80
81    printf("Running %d openmp threads\n", omp_get_max_threads());
82    printf("DP GFlops = %f\n", Gflops);
83
84  return 0;
85
86 }
```

Now that you are familiar with what the code is doing, you can proceed to measure the core performance of this architecture. You need to build the code with vectorization turned off, using the -no-vec command sent to the Intel compiler. To build with the Intel compiler with vectorization turned off, use the following command line:

```
Command_prompt > icpc -O3 -mmic -opt-threads-per-core=2 -no-vec -openmp -vec-report3 dpflops.cpp
gettime.cpp -o dpflops.out
```

where:

1. icpc is the Intel C++ Compiler invocation command.

2. The source file, dpflops.cpp, contains the code described in the Code Listing 4-1, and gettime.cpp contains calls to the gettimeofday function to get elapsed time in seconds, as shown in the following code segment:

   ```
   #include <sys/time.h>
   extern double elapsedTime (void)
   {
     struct timeval t;
     gettimeofday(&t, 0);
     return ((double)t.tv_sec + ((double)t.tv_usec / 1000000.0));
   }
   ```

3. The –mmic switch dictates to the compiler to generate cross-compiled code for Intel Xeon Phi coprocessor.

4. -opt-threads-per-core=2 switch allows the compiler code generator to schedule code generation assuming 2 threads are running in each core.

5. –no-vec switch asks the compiler not to vectorize the code, even if it can be vectorized.

6. `-openmp` switch allows the compiler to understand the OpenMP pragmas during the compile time and link in appropriate OpenMP libraries.

7. `-vec-report3` tells the compiler to print out detailed information about the vectorization being performed on the code as it is being compiled.

In order to see the effect of vectorization, first compile the code with the –no-vec switch and run it on a single core by setting OMP_NUM_THREADS=1.

Once the code is compiled, copy the file produces, dpflops.out, to the mic card by using the scp command as follows:

```
command_prompt-host >scp ./dpflops.out mic0:/tmp
dpflops.out                 100%  19KB 18.6KB/s  00:00
command_prompt-host >
```

This will upload the ./dpflops.out to the Intel Xeon Phi card and place it on the /tmp directory on the RAM disk of the card. The operating system on the Intel Xeon Phi usually allocates some portion of the GDDR memory to be used as a RAM disk and hosts the file system on the card.

You will also need to upload the dependent openmp library, libiomp5.so, to the card by the following command:

```
command_prompt-host >scp /opt/intel/composerxe/lib/mic/libiomp5.so mic0:/tmp
```

The libiomp5.so is the dynamic library necessary for running OpenMP programs compiled with Intel compilers. The Intel Xeon Phi version of the library is available at the location /opt/intel/composerxe/lib/mic/, provided you installed the compiler at the default install path on the system where you are building the application.

Once the card is uploaded with the file, you can log on to the card using the command:

```
command_prompt-host >ssh mic0
```

To run the code, you now need to set up the environment, as shown in the Figure 4-3 screen capture. The first thing you need to do is set the `LD_LIBRARY_PATH` to /tmp to be able to find the runtime openmp library loaded to the /tmp directory on the Xeon Phi card. Set the number of threads to 1 by setting the environment variable OMP_NUM_THREADS=1. Also set KMP_AFFINITY=compact, so that OpenMP threads for thread id 0-3 are tied to core 1 and so on.

Figure 4-3 shows that the single-threaded non-vectorized run only provided ~0.66 GFLOPs. Yet the expected DP flops for a single-core run are 2.2 Gflops [2(FMA) x1(DP non-vectorized elements) x1.1 GHz =]. As described in the "Core Pipeline Stages" section, however, the hardware cannot issue instructions back-to-back from the same thread in the core. To reach full-execution unit utilization, at least two threads must be running at all times. So running on 2 threads (OMP_NUM_THREADS=2) reaches 1.45 Gflops per core. As the core still uses vector units to perform scalar arithmetic, the code for scalar arithmetic is very inefficient. For each FMA on a DP element, the vector unit has to broadcast the element to all the lanes. Operate on the vector register with a mask and then store the single element back to memory. Note that increasing threads per core does not improve performance, as the instruction can be issued every cycle for this case. Now if you extend to 240 threads utilizing all 60 cores, you can achieve 86 Gflops, as shown in Figure 4-3. Let's see whether we can get close to the 1 teraflop designed for Intel Xeon Phi by turning on vectorization.

```
File Edit View Search Terminal Help
command_prompt-mic0 >export LD_LIBRARY_PATH=/tmp
command_prompt-mic0 >export KMP_AFFINITY=compact
command_prompt-mic0 >export OMP_NUM_THREADS=1
command_prompt-mic0 >./dpflops.out
Running 1 openmp threads
DP GFlops = 0.728247
command_prompt-mic0 >export OMP_NUM_THREADS=2
command_prompt-mic0 >./dpflops.out
Running 2 openmp threads
DP GFlops = 1.455630
command_prompt-mic0 >export OMP_NUM_THREADS=3
command_prompt-mic0 >./dpflops.out
Running 3 openmp threads
DP GFlops = 1.456115
command_prompt-mic0 >export OMP_NUM_THREADS=4
command_prompt-mic0 >./dpflops.out
Running 4 openmp threads
DP GFlops = 1.456233
command_prompt-mic0 >export OMP_NUM_THREADS=240
command_prompt-mic0 >./dpflops.out
Running 240 openmp threads
DP GFlops = 86.224700
command_prompt-mic0 >
```

Figure 4-3. *Executing non-vectorized code on Intel Xeon Phi*

Turn on the vectorization by removing the –no-vec switch. and recompile the code with the following command line:

```
icpc -O3 -opt-threads-per-core=2 -mmic -openmp -vec-report3 dpflops.cpp gettime.cpp -o dpflops.out
```

This prints out the following compiler report:

```
dpflops.cpp(58): (col. 29) remark: loop was not vectorized: statement cannot be vectorized.
dpflops.cpp(65): (col. 16) remark: LOOP WAS VECTORIZED.
dpflops.cpp(63): (col. 9) remark: loop was not vectorized: not inner loop.
dpflops.cpp(73): (col. 16) remark: LOOP WAS VECTORIZED.
dpflops.cpp(71): (col. 4) remark: loop was not vectorized: not inner loop.
```

This report shows that Lines 65 and 73 of Code Listing 4-1 have been vectorized by the compiler. Let's upload the binaries to Intel Xeon Phi by scp command as before and run it under various conditions. With an FMA and double-precision arithmetic which can work on 8 DP elements at a time, you should see around 2 x (for Fused Multiply and Add (FMA)) x 8 (DP elements) x 1.1 GHz = 17.6 Gflops per core.

Figure 4-4 shows the results of experimentation with the vectorized double-precision code. With 1 thread, you are able to reach 8.7 Gflops, not 17.6 as expected. As described in the "Core Pipeline Stages" section, this is due to the issue bandwidth of the core pipeline not being fully utilized by dispatching instructions only every other cycle. In order to achieve this, you need to use at least two threads. By setting OMP_NUM_THREADS=2 with KMP_AFFINITY=compact, you made sure the code was running on the same core, but two threads were executing and scheduling instructions every other cycle. This kept the execution unit fully utilized and it was able to achieve near-peak performance of 17.5 Gflops per core on the double-precision fused multiply–add arithmetic. Observe in Figure 4-4 that increasing the number of threads to 3 and 4 did not improve performance since we already saturated the double-precision execution unit on the core. Utilizing all 60 cores, with 2 threads each you could achieve 1022 Gflops, which is near the theoretical peak of 1055 Gflops on this coprocessor. You can also see that I have set KMP_AFFINITY=balanced to make sure that the threads are affinitized to different cores to distribute computations evenly when the number of threads is less than the maximum number of threads needed to saturate the cores, in this case 240 threads. Since I am running 120 threads with 2 threads per core on 60 cores, having affinity set to balanced, there will be two threads per core distributed across cores.

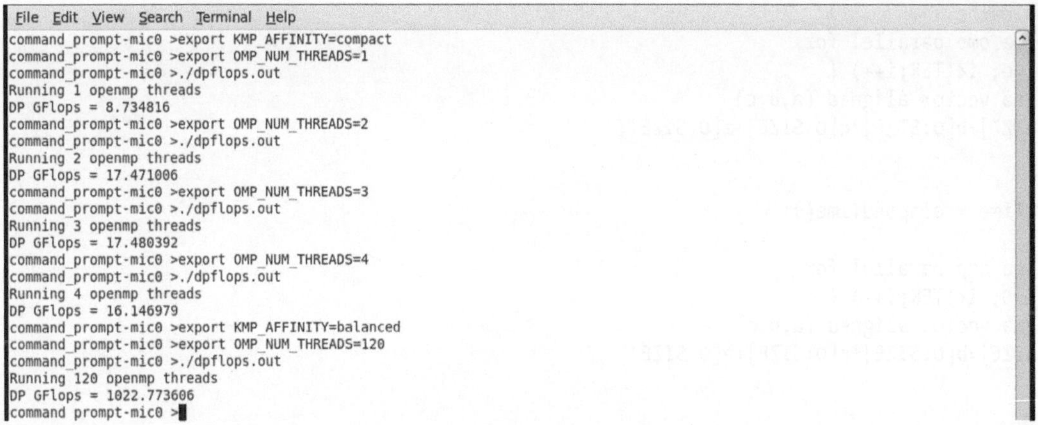

```
File  Edit  View  Search  Terminal  Help
command_prompt-mic0 >export KMP_AFFINITY=compact
command_prompt-mic0 >export OMP_NUM_THREADS=1
command_prompt-mic0 >./dpflops.out
Running 1 openmp threads
DP GFlops = 8.734816
command_prompt-mic0 >export OMP_NUM_THREADS=2
command_prompt-mic0 >./dpflops.out
Running 2 openmp threads
DP GFlops = 17.471006
command_prompt-mic0 >export OMP_NUM_THREADS=3
command_prompt-mic0 >./dpflops.out
Running 3 openmp threads
DP GFlops = 17.480392
command_prompt-mic0 >export OMP_NUM_THREADS=4
command_prompt-mic0 >./dpflops.out
Running 4 openmp threads
DP GFlops = 16.146979
command_prompt-mic0 >export KMP_AFFINITY=balanced
command_prompt-mic0 >export OMP_NUM_THREADS=120
command_prompt-mic0 >./dpflops.out
Running 120 openmp threads
DP GFlops = 1022.773606
command_prompt-mic0 >
```

Figure 4-4. *Execution of vectorized double-precision code on Intel Xeon Phi*

Let's turn our attention to single-precision arithmetic. You would expect the performance to be 2x the double precision. The changes to the code segment in Code Listing 4-1 will be to change double to float. We need to keep the float calculation the same, as the number of operations is the same. Since the vector unit can work on 16 elements at a time with the float, in order to be able to fill up the dispatch queue for each thread, we would need twice as many elements as double, and so I have adjusted the size to 32 elements instead of 16 elements as shown in Code Listing 4-2.

Code Listing 4-2. Single-Precision Peak Gigaflops Measurement

```
38 #include <stdio.h>
39 #include <stdlib.h>
40 #include <omp.h>
41
42 unsigned int const SIZE=32;
43 unsigned int const ITER=48000000;
44
45 extern double elapsedTime (void);
46
47 int main()
48 {
49     double startTime, duration;
50     int i;
51
52     __declspec(aligned(64)) float a[SIZE],b[SIZE],c[SIZE];
53
54
55     //intialize
56     for (i=0; i<SIZE;i++)
57     {
58         c[i]=b[i]=a[i]=(double)rand();
59     }
60
```

```
61 //warm up cache
62     #pragma omp parallel for
63     for(i=0; i<ITER;i++) {
64     #pragma vector aligned (a,b,c)
65     a[0:SIZE]=b[0:SIZE]*c[0:SIZE]+a[0:SIZE];
66     }
67
68     startTime = elapsedTime();
69
70     #pragma omp parallel for
71     for(i=0; i<ITER;i++) {
72     #pragma vector aligned (a,b,c)
73     a[0:SIZE]=b[0:SIZE]*c[0:SIZE]+a[0:SIZE];
74     }
75
76     duration = elapsedTime() - startTime;
77
78     double Gflop = 2*SIZE*ITER/1e+9;
79     double Gflops = Gflop/duration;
80
81     printf("Running %d openmp threads\n", omp_get_max_threads());
82     printf("SP GFlops = %f\n", Gflops);
83
84   return 0;
85
86 }
```

For single-precision arithmetic, I did the same experimentation as before and the output is captured in Figure 4-5. You can see that the single-precision behavior is the same for single-core execution where it can execute optimally with 2 threads per core to utilize the execution bandwidth properly, which it cannot do with a single thread. However, adding more threads to the core on this core-bound code does not help. Binding the threads to a core was enforced by the KMP_AFFINITY switch. After changing the affinity to balanced, we allowed the threads to spread out to various cores first to make use of independent execution units. Making the number of threads 120 (2 x number of cores for this case), we were able to get the performance to 1979 Gflops.

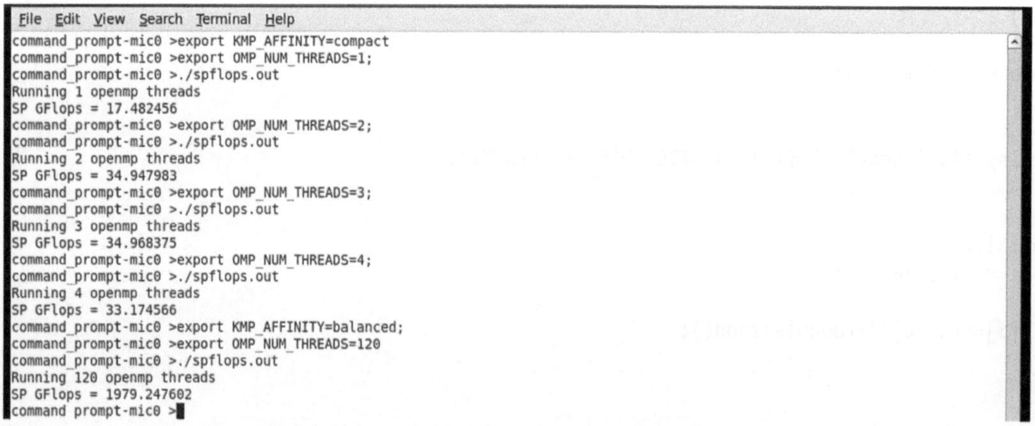

```
File  Edit  View  Search  Terminal  Help
command_prompt-mic0 >export KMP_AFFINITY=compact
command_prompt-mic0 >export OMP_NUM_THREADS=1;
command_prompt-mic0 >./spflops.out
Running 1 openmp threads
SP GFlops = 17.482456
command_prompt-mic0 >export OMP_NUM_THREADS=2;
command_prompt-mic0 >./spflops.out
Running 2 openmp threads
SP GFlops = 34.947983
command_prompt-mic0 >export OMP_NUM_THREADS=3;
command_prompt-mic0 >./spflops.out
Running 3 openmp threads
SP GFlops = 34.968375
command_prompt-mic0 >export OMP_NUM_THREADS=4;
command_prompt-mic0 >./spflops.out
Running 4 openmp threads
SP GFlops = 33.174566
command_prompt-mic0 >export KMP_AFFINITY=balanced;
command_prompt-mic0 >export OMP_NUM_THREADS=120
command_prompt-mic0 >./spflops.out
Running 120 openmp threads
SP GFlops = 1979.247602
command prompt-mic0 >
```

Figure 4-5. *Execution of vectorized single-precision vector code on Intel Xeon Phi*

Understanding Intel Xeon Phi Cache Performance

In order to understand the cache latencies, I shall be using the publicly available memory latency benchmark component of lmbench benchmark available at `http://www.bitmover.com/lmbench/`. I d ownloadedl mbench3t od o the experiment.

The lmbench was developed by its authors to make the benchmark portable and written in C. That was the reason I picked the benchmark to explore the memory hierarchy of Intel Xeon Phi architecture. One of the benchmark components that I was interested in was lat_mem_rd, which finds out memory-read latencies at various memory hierarchies.

In order to build this software, I downloaded the lmbench3 source from the benchmark download page. I set CC to point to icc or icpc, the Intel compiler to build the suite. I modified the scripts/compiler file as follows to point to icc:

```
/bin/sh

if [ "X$CC" != "X" ] && echo "$CC" | grep -q '`'
then
  CC=
fi

if [ X$CC = X ]
then   CC=cc
    for p in `echo $PATH | sed 's/:/ /g'`
    do   if [ -f $p/gcc ]
        then   CC="icc -mmic"
        fi
    done
fi
echo $CC
```

Once the Make file and compiler were set properly, I did a `command_prompt> make -f Makefile.mic` to build the benchmark binaries, which in my case ended up in the folder `bin/x86_64-linux-gnu`. The next step was to copy the benchmark binary I was interested in, lat_mem_rd, to the /tmp directory on the coprocessor micro OS using the scp command.

Once the benchmark binary was transferred to the card, I ran the latency benchmark as `command_prompt-mic0 >./lat_mem_rd -P 1 -N 10 32 64`.

The benchmark ran with 32 MB of memory that filled the L1 cache, in single-threaded mode with 64-byte stride, so I am reading data from different cache lines in subsequent calls. The output is captured in the screenshot in Figure 4-6. You can see that for sizes up to 32 kB, which is the L1-D cache size for each core, the cache latency is about 2.8 ns, which is approximately 3 cycles on this coprocessor. Moving beyond L1-D cache sizes, you can see that the latency goes up to 13.27 ns (~14.5 cycles).

```
 File  Edit  View  Search  Terminal  Help
command_prompt-mic0 >./lat_mem_rd -P 1  -N 10 32 64
"stride=64
0.00049 2.800
0.00098 2.800
0.00195 2.800
0.00293 2.800
0.00391 2.800
0.00586 2.800
0.00781 2.805
0.00977 2.805
0.01172 2.805
0.01367 2.785
0.01562 2.785
0.01758 2.785
0.01953 2.775
0.02148 2.776
0.02344 2.776
0.02539 2.771
0.02734 2.773
0.02930 2.778
0.03125 2.778
0.03516 13.266
0.03906 15.874
0.04297 18.477
0.04688 18.481
0.05078 18.486
0.05469 18.503
0.05859 21.091
0.06250 21.088
0.07031 21.091
0.07812 21.096
0.08594 21.089
0.09375 21.091
0.10156 21.092
```

Figure 4-6. *lmbenchmark lat_mem_rd running on Intel Xeon Phi*

Summary

This chapter surveyed the Xeon Phi core architecture. You examined the core pipeline and the instruction flow through the pipeline. You learned how to compute the theoretical peak Gigaflops of the machine for single-precision and double-precision floating-point arithmetic, and how to measure the practical gigaflops achievable on the hardware by writing simple code. You looked at the cache and translation lookaside buffer (TLB) structures, which are critical to achieving high performance on the Xeon Phi coprocessor.

The next chapter will cover the cache architecture in detail. You will learn the cache protocol that you will need to maintain cache coherency and the tools you will need to measure the cache latency at each cache level.

CHAPTER 5

■ ■ ■

Xeon Phi Cache and Memory Subsystem

The preceding chapter showed how the Intel Xeon Phi coprocessor uses a two-dimensional tiled architecture approach to designing manycore coprocessors. In this architecture, the cores are replicated on die and connected through on-die wire interconnects. The network connecting the various functional units is a critical piece that may become a bottleneck as more cores and devices are added to the network in a chip multiprocessor (CMP) design such as Intel Xeon Phi uses. The interconnect design choices are primarily determined by the number of cores, expected interconnect performance, chip area limitation, power limit, process technology, and manufacturing efficiencies. The manycore interconnect technology—although it has benefited from existing research on other interconnect topologies in multiprocessor systems and the close interaction among cores, cache subsystem, memory, and external bus—makes interconnect design for coprocessors especially challenging.[1]

The Interconnect Topologies for Manycore Processors

Various topologies can be used to connect the cores in a multicore chip. The most common interconnect topologies in current use are described in the following sections.

Bidirectional Ring Topology

The simplest interconnect topology is *bidirectional ring topology*, where the cores connect with one another through one or multiple hops in both directions (Figure 5-1). The low complexity of the implementation is attractive for a low number of cores. The average number of hops is N/4, where N is the number of cores.

---

[1]Rakesh Kumar, Victor Zyuban, and Dean M. Tullsen. "Interconnections in Multi-core Architectures: Understanding Mechanisms, Overheads and Scaling." *Proc. Intl. Symp. on Computer Architecture* (ISCA), 2005, pp. 408–419; and D. N. Jayasimha, Bilal Zafar, and Yatin Hoskote. "On-Chip Interconnection Networks: Why They Are Different and How to Compare Them." Technical Report, Intel Corp., 2006.

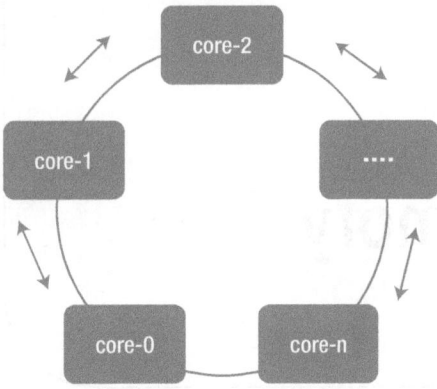

Figure 5-1. *Bidirectional ring topology*

This ring design's simplicity is offset by latency, bottleneck, and fault-tolerance issues:

- As the number of cores N increases, the number of hops and hence the latency increases.

- A single bidirectional path to move data from one core to another can easily become a bottleneck as the data transfer load increases.

- Any link failure will cause the chip to become nonfunctional.

Two-Dimensional Mesh Topology

Two-dimensional (2D) *mesh topology* (Figure 5-2) is a popular solution for interconnecting cores in a multicore design thanks to being more scalable than a ring network and a more simplified layout in 2D tiled architecture. The routing protocol plays a significant role in the performance of such a network.

Core 0

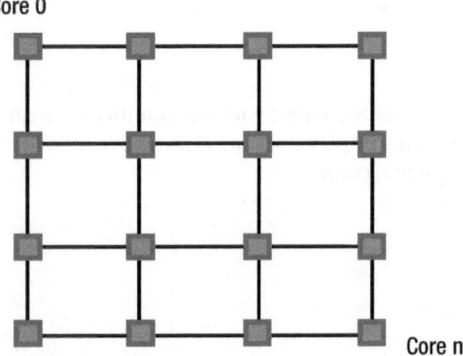

Core n

Figure 5-2. *2D mesh network*

2D mesh topology has the following drawbacks:

- The power efficiency of a 2D mesh network is relatively low compared to that of a ring network.

- The 2D mesh topology is nonuniform, because the cores at the edges and corners have fewer communication channels and hence less bandwidth available to them.

Two-DimensionalT orusT opology

Two-dimensional torus topology improves on 2D mesh by adding wrap-around wires to the mesh network, as shown in Figure 5-3. This topology removes the nonuniformity of the edge nodes in a 2D mesh, reduces the maximum and average hop counts, and doubles the bisection bandwidth. The downside is the extra wiring that spans the length of the die. Folded torus topology can be used, however, to reduce the wire length to two tiles.

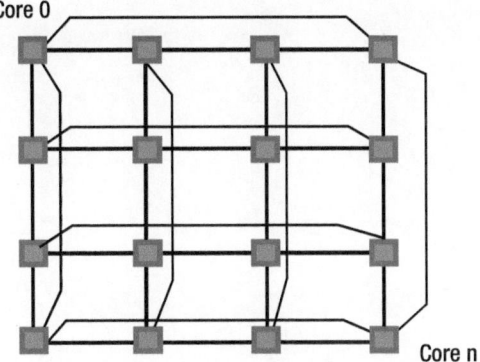

Figure 5-3. *2D torus topology*

OtherT opologies

Other networks—sucha s *3D mesh*, *3D torus*, *fat tree*, and *hierarchical ring networks*—havethe irr espective technological merits, but their wiring density and power requirements are impractical for on-chip interconnects at the current level of technology.

The Ring Interconnect Architecture in Intel Xeon Phi

The Xeon Phi coprocessor implemented bidirectional high performance on the chip ring carrying data and instructions to various agents, such as core, GDDR controllers, and *tag directory*(TD).[2] These agents are connected to the ring through ringstops, as shown in Figure 5-1. Ringstops handle all traffic coming on and off the ring for the attacheda gents.

---

[2]*Tags* are numbers used to uniquely identify the cache lines. The *tag directory* is a structure in the cache design that holds information about the cache lines residing in the processor cache.

In the Xeon Phi architecture, there are three pairs of independent rings traveling in two opposite directions (bidirectional), as shown in Figure 5-4. The three pairs carry data, addresses, and acknowledgments. The data ring is 64 bytes wide to feed the high data bandwidth required by a large number of cores. Messages placed on the ring are deterministically delivered to the destination or may remain (bounce) on the ring until they are captured by the destination. The address ring carries address and read/write commands and the acknowledgment ring carries flow control and coherence messages.

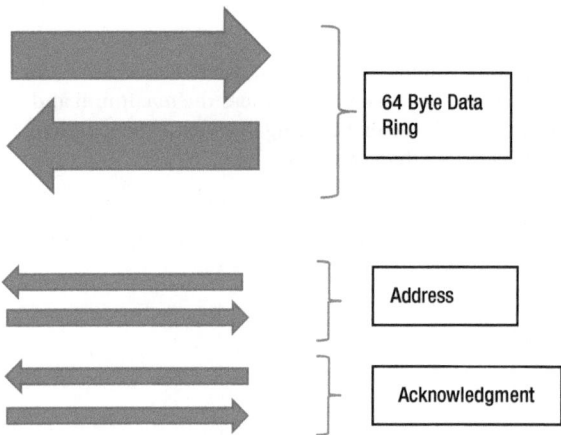

Figure 5-4. *Intel Xeon Phi bidirectional bus*

L2 Cache

The L2 cache is the secondary cache for the core. The L2 cache is inclusive of L1 cache. It is okay to have a cache line in L2 only, but L1 cache lines must have a copy in L2. TD, used for cache coherency, only tracks L2 entries. L2 has ECC, which implements single error correction and double error detections. With 32 GB (35 bits) of address range, each L2 cache associated with a core has 512 kB size divided into 1024 sets and 8-way associativity per set with 64 bytes/1 cache line per way. The cache is divided into two logical banks. There are 32 read buffers of one cache line each. There is a 16-entry write-out/snoop-out buffer of one cache line each, so that a minimum of four of these buffers is guaranteed to be available to snoop for outgoing data.

L2 latency is 11 cycles. If there is an L1 miss but an L2 hit, the latency is 17 cycles if the requesting thread is waiting for the data and 21 cycles if the thread is put to sleep. L2 cache uses pseudo-LRU implementation as a replacement algorithm.

TagD irectory

The Xeon Phi coprocessor implements a physically distributed TD for data coherency among the cores on the ring. It filters and forwards requests to appropriate receiving agents on the ring. It is also responsible for sending the snoop requests to various cores on behalf of the requesting core and returns global L2 line state to the requesting core. It also initiates the communication with the main memory via on-die memory controllers.

The TD is physically attached to each core and gets an equal portion of the whole address space to provide balanced load on the address ring. The TD that is referenced on a L2 miss is not necessarily collocated on the same core that generated the miss but is collocated based on the address. Every physical address is uniquely mapped through a reversible *one-to-one* mapping hash function. L2 caches are kept coherent through TDs and referenced on an L2 miss. A TD tag contains the address, state, and an ID for the owner of the cache line needed to perform the coherency functions.

DataT ransactions

On an L2 cache miss by an executing instruction, the core sends the address to TDs through the address ring. If the data are found in another core's L2, a forwarding request is sent to that core's L2 over the address link and the data are returned through the data ring. If the requested data are not found in any of the core's cache, a request is sent to the memory controller from the TD.

The memory controllers are distributed evenly on the ring and the address has *all-to-all* mapping between the TD and memory controllers. The addresses are evenly distributed among the memory controllers to reduce bottlenecks and to provide optimal bandwidth.

Once a memory controller retrieves the requested 64-byte size cache line, it is returned over the data ring to the requestingc ore.

The Cache Coherency Protocol

The Xeon Phi coprocessor uses a modified MESI protocol for cache coherency control between distributed cores using a TD-based *globally owned, locally shared* (GOLS) protocol. To start with, let's review what an unmodified MESI protocol looks like. The standard MESI state diagram and policies are shown in Table 5-1.

Table 5-1. *Standard MESI Protocol*

L2 Cache State	State Definition
M	*Modified*: Cache line is modified relative to memory. Only one core can have a given line in M state at a time.
E	*Exclusive*: Cache line is consistent with memory. Only one core can have a cache line in E state at a time.
S	*Shared*: Cache line is shared and consistent with other cores, but may not be consistent with memory. Multiple cores can have a given cache line in S state at a time.
I	*Invalid*: Cache line is not present in the cores L1 or L2.

Initially all cache lines are in the *invalid* (I) state. If the data are loaded for writing, the corresponding cache line changes to the *modified* (M) state. If the data are loaded for read and hits the cache in another core, it is marked *shared* (S) state; otherwise it is marked *exclusive* (E) state. If a modified cache line is read or written from the same core, it stays in the M state. If a second core reads this modified cache line, the data are sent to the second core and the GDDR memory update can be delayed due to the global coherency GOLS protocol with the help of TD. If a modified cache line has to be evicted due to a local capacity miss, or if a remote core tries to update the same cache line by a *read for ownership*(RFO),[3] the cache line is written back to GDDR memory and goes to the I state. If an eviction is caused by the remote core's write request, the corresponding cache line in the remote core gets to the E state first and then to the M state after the store retires. If a cache line in the E state is locally written to, it changes to the M state. If a cache line in the S state is requested by another core for write, the state changes to the I state and the cache line is sent directly to the requesting core. The state machine representing MESI policies implemented in a local L1/L2 cache is showni n Figure 5-5.

---

[3]The RFO is the process common to many cache-based processor architectures of reading a cache line from the memory into the cache before it can be written to.

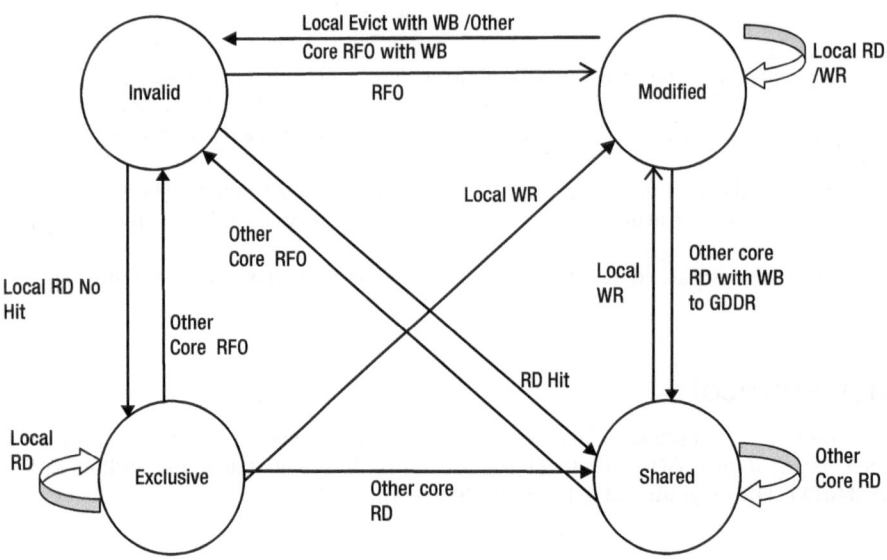

Figure 5-5. *Standard MESI cache coherency policies. RD = read; WR = write; WB = writeback to GDDR; RFO = read for ownership*

In order to remove the potential performance bottleneck resulting from its lack of the *owner* (O) state that is a component of the MOESI protocol, the Xeon Phi coprocessor has implemented TD to manage the global state so the modified cache lines can be shared between the cores without writing back to GDDR memory, thus reducing shared cache-line access between cores. The TD implements the GOLS protocol. By complementing the MESI protocol with the GOLS protocol, it is possible to emulate the O state. Table 5-2 and Figures 5-6a and 5-6b show the augmented MESIa ndG OLSp rotocols.

Table 5-2. *GOLS Protocol*

TDState	StateDe finition
GOLS	*Globally owned locally shared*: Cache line is present in one or more cores but inconsistent with memory (GDDR).
GS	*Globally shared*: Cache line is present in one or more cores and consistent with memory.
GE/GM	*Globally exclusive/modified*: Cache line is owned by one and only one core and may or may not be consistent with the memory. The TD does not know whether the core has modified the cache line or not.
GI	*Globally invalid*: Cache line is not present in any core.

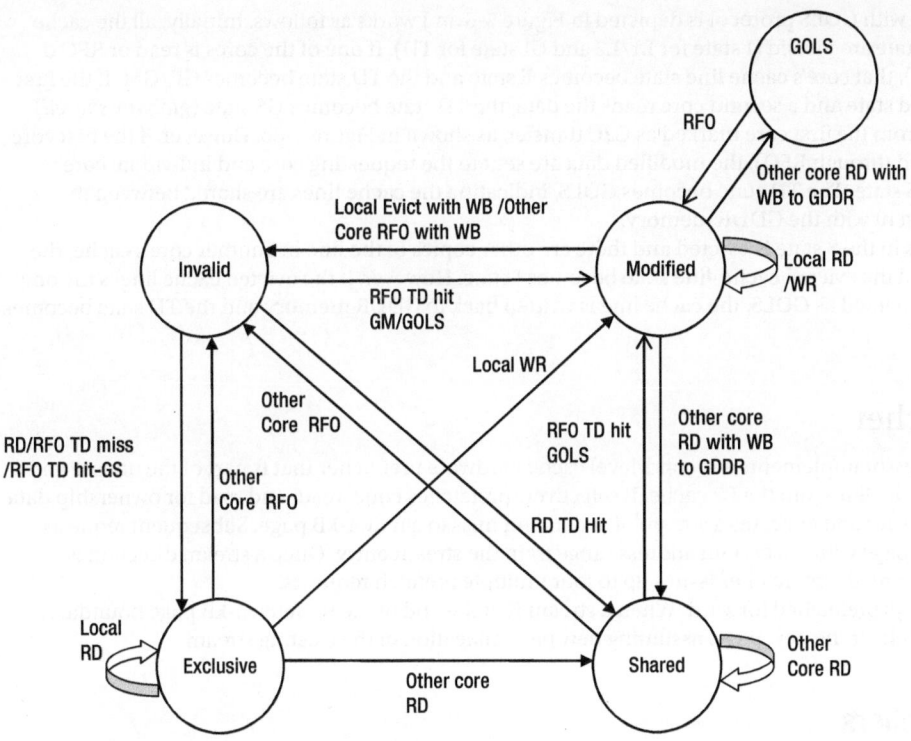

Figure 5-6a. *Intel Xeon Phi augmented MESI with GOLS protocol in the core. RD = read; WR = write; WB = writeback to GDDR; RFO = read for ownership; TD = tag directory*

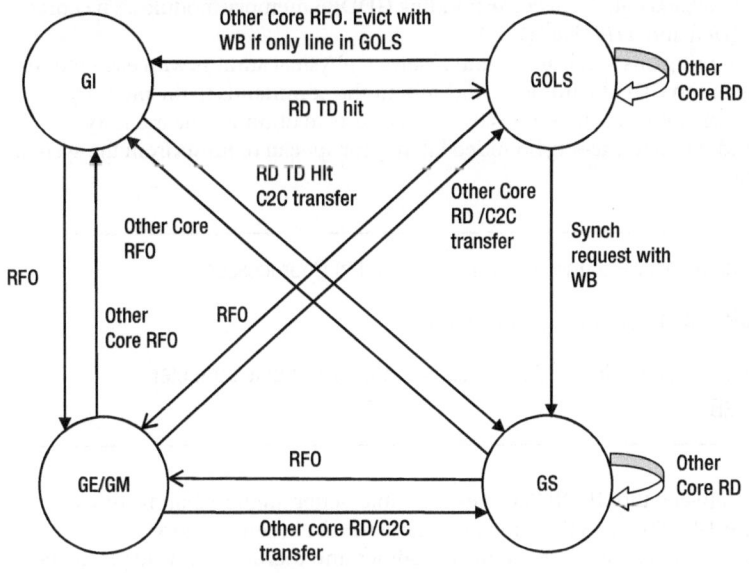

Figure 5-6b. *Intel Xeon Phi augmented MESI with GOLS protocol in the TD. RD = read; WR = write; WB = writeback to GDDR; RFO = read for ownership; TD = tag directory; C2C = cache to cache*

The augmented MESI with GOLS protocol is depicted in Figure 5-6 and works as follows. Initially, all the cache lines in the cores and TD state are invalid (I state for L1/L2 and GI state for TD). If one of the cores is read or RFO'd (to be written in the future), that core's cache line state becomes E state and the TD state becomes GE/GM. If the first core's data are in the shared state and a second core reads the data, the TD state becomes GS state (*globally shared*) and gets the data directly from the first core marked as C2C transfer, as shown in Figure 5-6b. However, if the first core modified the data (acquired through RFO), the modified data are sent to the requesting core and individual core's cache-line states become S state. The TD state becomes GOLS, indicating the cache lines are shared between the cores and may be inconsistent with the GDDR memory.

If the cache line that is in the S state is evicted and there are other copies of the line in another core's cache, the TD state remains GOLS and the evicted cache-line state becomes I state. However, if the evicted cache line is the only cache line and TD state is marked as GOLS, the cache line is written back to GDDR memory and the TD state becomes GIs tate.

HardwareP refetcher

The Intel Xeon Phi coprocessor implements a second-level cache hardware prefetcher that is part of the uncore and responsible for fetching cache lines into the L2 cache. It selectively prefetches code, read, and read for ownership data into L2. It has 16 stream entries and allocates a stream on a demand miss to a new 4-kB page. Subsequent requests that hit and miss the same page within a certain address range train the stream entry. Once a stream direction is detected, forward or backward, the prefetcher issues up to four multiple prefetch requests.

Code streams are always prefetched forward. When a stream is at the end of the prefetch 4-kB page boundary, it kick-starts an extra prefetch for the new page, assuming new page allocation of the existing stream.

The Memory Controllers

The Intel Xeon Phi coprocessor comes with eight memory controllers with two channels, each communicating with GDDR5 memory at 5.5 GT/s. The memory controllers are connected to a ring bus using ringstops on one end and GDDR5 on the other end. This provides approximately 352 GB/s of memory bandwidth. Memory access requests are directed to appropriate memory controllers to access data from corresponding GDDR5 memory modules. The cores support two types of memory: *un-cacheable* (UC) and *write-back*(WB).

The memory controllers interface with the ring bus at full speed and receive a physical address with each request. They translate the read/write requests from core to GDDR5 protocols and submit the commands to the memory devices. The memory controllers are also responsible for scheduling GDDR5 requests to optimize the memory bandwidth available from GDDR memory and for guaranteeing bounded latency for special requests from the system interface unit providing data over the PCI express bus.

■ **Note** Sample Calculation of the Theoretical Memory Bandwidth of an Intel Xeon Phi Coprocessor

Given eight memory controllers with two GDDR5 channels running at 5.5 GT/s

Aggregate Memory Bandwidth = 8 memory controllers × 2 channels × 5.5 GT/s × 4 bytes/transfer
= 352 GB/s

The memory addresses are interleaved between the GDDR5 devices to enable better memory bandwidth and ring bus utilization. The memory requests are 4-kB lines at a time and are interleaved between memory modules. This means consecutive memory locations are distributed among the memory modules and there is no way to place the memory close to a core for optimal memory bandwidth.

Memory Transactions Flow

A good understanding of how memory requests are handled by the memory controller may help in root-causing application performance issues running on the Xeon Phi coprocessor. This section will look at the details of how memory transactions are generated and handled by various servers and consumers of the data inside the Xeon Phi coprocessor.

Cacheable Memory Read Transaction

The memory address ranges can be divided into two broad categories: the cacheable and uncacheable memory ranges. Memory marked as *uncacheable* is not saved into cache for later access and directly delivered to the requester. For performance reasons, most memory transactions of interest to developers of applications running on Xeon Phi are cacheable. The memory transactions for address ranges that are cacheable in the core L1 and L2 caches are described below and shown in Figure 5-7.

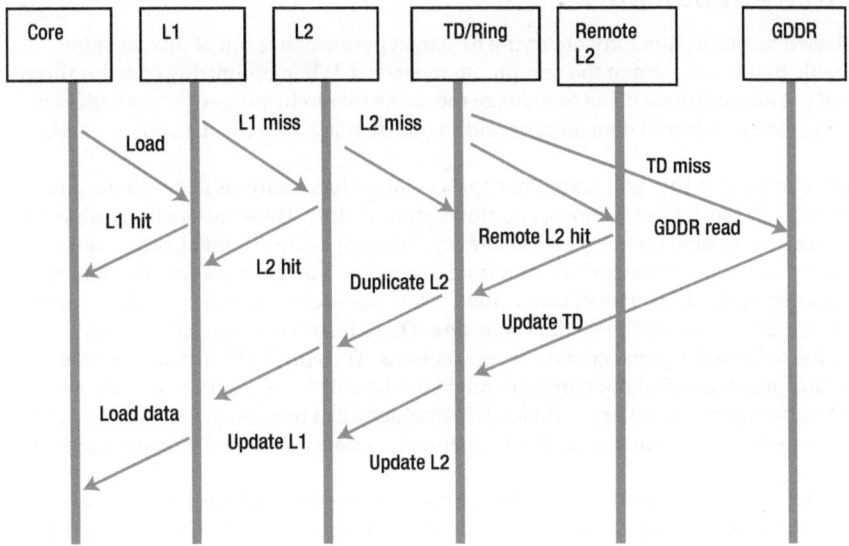

Figure 5-7. *Core/VPU load operation*

1. A read transaction request for data is generated from a core or vector unit.

2. If the data are found in L1 cache, the data are returned to the core, or else a local L2 lookup happens.

3. On a local L2 miss, a lookup to the TD happens. The TD contains all of the L2 occupancy information. The TD entry looked up might not be local to the core suffering the cache miss and sent through ring interconnect.

4. If the data are found in the L2 cache, the data are returned to the requesting core through an L1 update.

5. If not found in the L2 cache, the data have to be fetched from the GDDR memory to the L2 cache. The TD converts the address into a physical address and submits the physical addresses to the memory controller.

6. The memory controller converts the physical address to the appropriate memory access information channel/bank/row/column needed by the hardware.

7. There is a read queue for each memory channel and an entry is allocated when a read request is made to the memory controller. It uses a credit-based mechanism to prevent overflow of the read buffers.

8. The memory controller sends the read operation to GDDR memory, which returns the data to the read buffer.

9. The returned data update the TD, update the L2 cache with the appropriate cache, evict if needed, and return the data to the requesting core by appropriate cache level updates to L2a ndL 1.

Figure 5-7 shows the control and data flow for a memory read operation.

Managing Cache Hierarchy in Software

Because Intel Xeon Phi is a cache-based machine, any software trying to extract performance out of this machine must strive hard to make data available in the cache when the computation needs it. When optimizing code for this or any cache-based architecture, it is of the utmost importance to manage the cache hierarchy properly—through loop reorganization, data structure modifications, code and data affinity, and so on—to make sure the data are available in the cache as soon as needed.

To work with memory hierarchy complexity, the Intel Xeon Phi coprocessor includes various instructions and constructs such as prefetch, gather prefetch, clevict instructions, and nontemporal hints. These instructions allow one to pull in data to the appropriate cache level to hide memory access latency. The cache line eviction instructions— 'clevict'—are also useful when you want to remove unnecessary data from the cache to make space for new data or to keep useful data in the cache by managing the LRU state of cache lines. When the cache controller needs to select a cache line for eviction, the LRU state is used to select the victim cache line. These instructions are often useful when the hardware prefetcher fails due to irregularly spaced data access patterns. The vprefetch* instructions are implemented for performing cache line prefetches that the hardware might not be able to issue automatically. Xeon Phi also implements gather prefetch instructions—vgatherpf*. Prefetch instructions can be used to fetch data to L1 or L2 cache lines. Since this hardware implements an inclusive cache mechanism, L1 data prefetched is also present in L2 cache-but not vice versa.

For prefetch instructions, if the line selected is already present in the cache hierarchy at a level closer to the processor, no data movement occurs. Prefetch instructions can specify invalid addresses without causing a *general protection* (GP) fault because of their speculative nature.

The Intel compiler provides –opt-prefetch switch to tell the code generator to insert prefetch instructions in the code and the -opt-prefetch-distance switch to globally define the L1 and L2 prefetch distances. You can also tell the compiler not to generate prefetch instructions by setting the –no-opt-prefetch compiler switch or setting –opt-prefetch=0.

Let's look at how the compiler uses these flags to add instructions to your generated code. Code Listing 5-1 shows a small loop that runs on a single thread and performs memory access on an array of structures.

Code Listing 5-1. Compiler Prefetch Example

```
34 #include <stdio.h>
35 #include <stdlib.h>
36
37 #define SIZE    1000000
38 #define ITER         20
39
40
```

```
41 typedef struct pointVal {
42               double x, y, z;
43               double value;
44 }POINT;
45
46 __declspec(align(256)) static POINT  a[SIZE];
47
48 extern double elapsedTime (void);
49
50 int main()
51 {
52         double startTime, duration, tmp[SIZE];
53         int i, j;
54 //initialize
55         for( j=0; j<SIZE;j++){
56             a[j].x=0.1;
57         }
58
59      startTime = elapsedTime();
60
61      for(i=0; i<ITER;i++) {
62          for( j=0; j<SIZE;j++){
63            tmp[j]+=a[j].x;
64          }
65      }
66      duration = elapsedTime()-startTime;
67
68      double MB = SIZE*sizeof(double)/1e+6;
69      double MBps = ITER*MB/duration;
70      printf("DP ArraySize =  %lf MB, MB/s = %lf\n", MB, MBps);
71
72   return 0;
73 }
74
```

In order to turn off the prefetch instructions being generated by the compiler, I first compiled the code with the –no-opt-prefetch option and send the output gather.out code to the mic card using "scp gather.out mic0:/tmp" as follows:

```
Command_prompt-host >icpc  -mcmodel=medium -O3 -no-opt-prefetch -mmic   -vec-report3  gather.cpp
gettime.cpp -o gather.out
```

If I run the code on the mic card, I see that the code is able to achieve ~381 MB/s on the single-threaded run of this code.

```
command_prompt-mic0 >./gather.out
DP ArraySize =  8.000000 MB, MB/s = 381.794093
```

Now, I recompile the same code by removing the –no-opt-prefetch compiler option and upload the file to the mic card, as described above. The same run with the –no-opt-prefetch restriction removed will generate prefetch instructions and will cause substantial improvement in memory access performance, as shown below. The performance has gone up from 381 to 481 MB/s.

```
command_prompt-mic0 >./gather.out
DP ArraySize =  8.000000 MB, MB/s = 484.896942
command_prompt-mic0 >
```

You can generate the assembly file corresponding to Code Listing 5-1 by using –S switch as shown below. A fragment of the generated assembly code is shown in Code Listing 5-2. I also added the –unroll0 compiler switch to turn off code unrolling optimization so that the generated assembly is easier to read. Although I am not going to walk through the assembly listing here, I would like to point out some of the prefetch instructions highlighted in Lines 170 and 172 of the assembly in Code Listing 5-2, where it is prefetching the array a to Cache Level 1. You may also use the compiler option –opt-report-phase=hlo when building the code, so that the compiler will provide you diagnostics on where it generated the software prefetch instructions, if any:

```
Command_prompt-host >icc -mmic -vec-report3 -O3 -c -S -unroll0 –opt-report-phase=hlo gather.cpp
```

If you look at the kernel loop in Code Listing 5-1, you will notice that the code accesses nonconsecutive data elements: in this case, coordinate x in a[ ].

```
62              for( j=0; j<SIZE;j++){
63                 tmp[j]+=a[j].x;
64              }
```

This requires the compiler to use gather instructions as shown in Lines 180 and 183 of Code Listing 5-2. The Intel Xeon Phi ISA supports gather/scatter instructions to help sparsely placed data to move in/out of a vector register. These instructions simplify vector code generation for complex data structures and allow further hardware optimization of the instructions in future coprocessors. There are also prefetch instructions available corresponding to vector gather/scatter instructions. These are vgatherpf0dps for L1 and vgatherpf1dps for L2 prefetch.

Code Listing 5-2. Compiler Generated Prefetch Instruction

```
170          vprefetch0 a(%rip)                              #63.22 c17
171 ..LN46:
172          vprefetch0 256+a(%rip)                          #63.22 c21
173          .align    16,0x90
174 ..LN47:
....
177 ..LN48:
178          kmov      %k1, %k2                              #63.22 c1
179 ..LN49:
180          vprefetche1 512(%rsp,%rcx,8)                    #63.14 c1
181 ..L13:                                                   #63.22
182 ..LN50:
183          vgatherdpd a(%rdx,%zmm1), %zmm3{%k2}            #63.22
184 ..LN51:
185          jkzd      ..L12, %k2    # Prob 50%              #63.22
186 ..LN52:
187          vgatherdpd a(%rdx,%zmm1), %zmm3{%k2}            #63.22
188 ..LN53:
```

```
189        jknzd    ..L13, %k2    # Prob 50%              #63.22
190 ..L12:                                                #
191 ..LN54:
192        vaddpd    (%rsp,%rcx,8), %zmm3, %zmm4
194        vprefetch0 256(%rsp,%rcx,8)
196        vprefetch1 2048+a(%rdx)
197 ..LN57:
```

If vgatherpf0dps misses both L1 and L2, the resulting prefetch in L1 is nontemporal, but the prefetch into L2 is a normal prefetch.

The gather instruction 'vgatherd' is able to access up to 16 32-bit elements. The actual number of elements accessed is determined by the number of bits set in the vector mask provided as the source. In Intel Xeon Phi, vgatherd can load multiple elements with a single 64-byte memory access if all the elements fall in the same 64-byte cache line.

The gather instruction guarantees at least one element to be gathered for each call. In Lines 185 and 187 of Code Listing 5-2, the compiler uses a mask register, k2 to determine whether all the required elements are gathered or not.

Probing the Memory Subsystem

This section investigates the GDDR memory characteristics of the Xeon Phi coprocessor.

Measuring the Memory Bandwidth on Intel Xeon Phi

One key performance metric related to the cache subsystem is the GDDR memory bandwidth, seen by a computational code. To measure the GDDR memory bandwidth, we write and examine the small benchmark in CodeL isting5 -3.

Code Listing 5-3. Measuring GDDR Memory BW as Seen by Cores

```
34 #include <stdio.h>
35 #include <stdlib.h>
36 #include <omp.h>
37
38
39 #define SIZE     (180*1024*1000)
40 #define ITER         20
41
42 __declspec(align(256)) static double  a[SIZE],  b[SIZE],  c[SIZE];
43
44
45 extern double elapsedTime (void);
46
47 int main()
48 {
49        double startTime,  duration;
50        int i, j;
51
52        //initialize arrays
53        #pragma omp parallel for
```

```
54          for (i=0;  i<SIZE;i++)
55          {
56                  c[i]=0.0f;
57                  b[i]=a[i]=(double)1.0f;
58          }
59
60          //measure c = a*b+c performance
61          startTime = elapsedTime();
62          for(i=0; i<ITER;i++) {
63          #pragma omp parallel for
64              for( j=0; j<SIZE;j++){
65                  c[j]=a[j]*b[j]+c[j];
66              }
67          }
68          duration = elapsedTime() - startTime;
69
70          double GB = SIZE*sizeof(double)/1e+9;
71          double GBps = 4*ITER*GB/duration;
72          printf("Running %d openmp threads\n", omp_get_max_threads());
73          printf("DP ArraySize =  %lf MB, GB/s = %lf\n", GB*1000, GBps);
74
75      return 0;
76  }
```

The code consists of three double-precision arrays, a, b, and c. The size of arrays is set to (180*1024*1000). That number was chosen so that I can divide the work among 180 threads on the 60 available compute cores of the coprocessor. In order to create optimal code, I selected the number of elements to be 124 so that each vector access could be cacheline-aligned. The 1000 multiplier makes the size of the array large enough (each array ~ 1.4 GB) to go outside the cache. The ITER in Line 40 sets the number of times I need to run the bandwidth loop to account for run-to-run performance variations. The benchmark uses the timing routine described in Chapter 4 for core computational flops measurements.

The computation is a simple c = a*b+c operation, where each of the arrays is double-precision. At each iteration, we read in three DP numbers—a,b,c—and write out a single DP number 'c'. This is shown in Line 65 of Code Listing 5-3. Lines 53 to 58 initialize the array to some random numbers. I also make sure the arrays are aligned by declaring them as 256-byte align by __declrspec(align(256)) in Line 42.

In order to measure the BW, I run the inner compute loop ITER time and capture the start and end time during the whole run at Line 68. The amount of memory used by each array can be calculated with (GB = SIZE*sizeof(double)/1e+9;).

The total number of memory operations is 4 (3 reads and 1 write). Hence, the BW, as seen by this compute kernel, can be computed as:

```
4*GB*ITER/duration
```

where GB equals the gigabyte size of each of the arrays, ITER is the number of times the BW kernel iterates inside the timing count, and duration is obtained by collecting the total execution times from start to the end of the ITER loop.

This code is cross-compiled with the –mmic switch as follows:

```
icpc -mcmodel=medium -O3  -mmic  -openmp -vec-report3  bw.cpp gettime.cpp -o bw.out
```

Since the code uses three large arrays ~1.75GB each, we needed to use the switch -mcmodel=medium, which tells the compiler to expect the data size to be above 2GB and handle that accordingly, as it is for this case. This compile command will generate a bw.out binary that can run on the Intel Xeon Phi coprocessor.

Once the binary is generated, follow the commands in Chapter 4 to copy the binary over to the Intel Xeon Phi card native virtual drive using:

```
command-prompt-host>scp bw.out mic0:/tmp
```

Also, upload the necessary openmp file from the compiler to the card using the following command:

```
command-prompt-host>scp /opt/intel/composerxe/lib/mic/libiomp5.so mic0:/tmp
```

Once the binary and the corresponding files are on the card's virtual drive, you can execute the code by logging in to the card by ssh:

```
Command-prompt-host > ssh mic0
```

Inside the Intel Xeon Phi card, export LD_LIBRARY_PATH to point to the appropriate folder with openmp runtime library:

```
Command-prompt-mic0 > export $LD_LIBRARY_PATH=/tmp:$LD_LIBRARY_PATH;
```

Now set the number of openmp threads to 180 by "export OMP_NUM_THREADS=180" and execute the command ./bw.out as follows:

```
Command_prompt-mic0> export OMP_NUM_THREADS=180
Command_prompt-mic0>./bw.out
```

This should output the following on the terminal window:

```
Command_prompt-mic0> ./bw.out
Running 180 openmp threads
DP ArraySize = 1475.56 MB and GBs = 159.005
Command_promot-mic0 >
```

The output (Figure 5-8) shows that the code ran with 180 threads and was able to measure ~ 159 GB/s overall BW for memory access on this kernel.

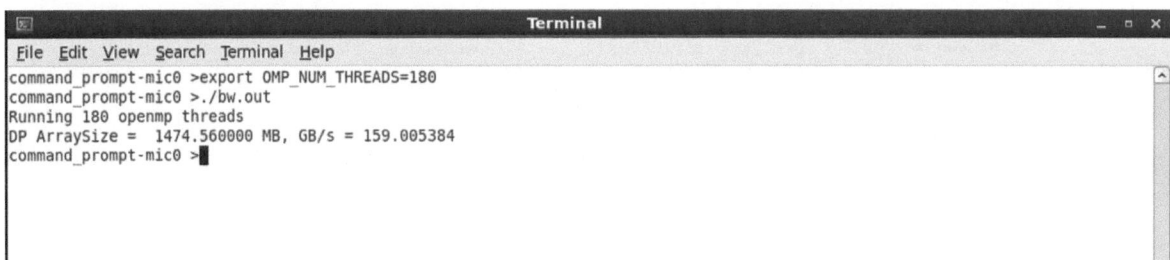

Figure 5-8. *Output of BW benchmark run*

Summary

This chapter covered the memory subsystem of the Xeon Phi coprocessor. You learned about the interconnect ring that connects various components of Xeon Phi, such as cores and memory controllers. You looked at various cache levels and how the cache coherency protocol MESI with GOLS extension is used to maintain data consistency among the caches associated with different cores. You saw how to measure the memory bandwidth on a Xeon Phi coprocessor.

The next chapter will explain the PCIe bus and power management support on the Xeon Phi coprocessor.

CHAPTER 6

■ ■ ■

Xeon Phi PCIe Bus Data Transfer and Power Management

This chapter looks at how the coprocessor is configured in a Xeon-based server platform and communicates with the host. It will also look at the power management capabilities built into the coprocessor to help reduce power consumption while idle. Figure 6-1 shows a system with multiple Intel Xeon Phi and two socket Intel Xeon processors. The coprocessor connects to the host using PCI Express 2.0 interface x16 lanes. Data transfer between the host memory and the GDDR memory can be through programmed I/O or through *direct memory access* (DMA) transfer. In order to optimize the data transfer bandwidth for large buffers, one needs to use the DMA transfer mechanism. This section will explain how to use high-level language features to allow DMA transfer. The hardware also allows peer-to-peer data transfers between two Intel Xeon Phi cards. Various data transfer scenarios are shown in Figure 6-1. The two Xeon Phi coprocessors A and B in the figure connect to the PCIe channels attached to the same socket and can do a local peer-to-peer data transfer. The data transfer between Xeon Phi coprocessors B and C will be a remote data transfer. These configurations play a key role in determining how the cards need to be set up for optimal performance.

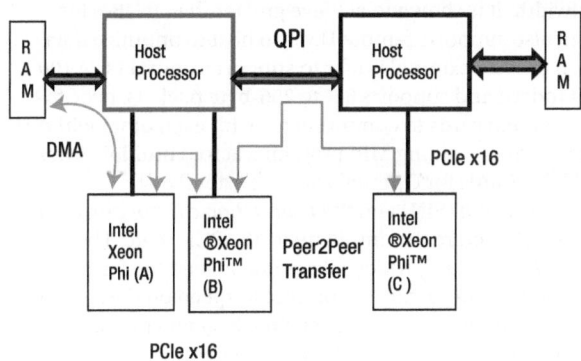

Figure 6-1. *Intel Xeon Phi-based system configuration*

Figure 6-2 shows the various important components of a card that allow it to operate as a coprocessor in conjunction with host processors and other PCIe devices and coprocessor in the system.

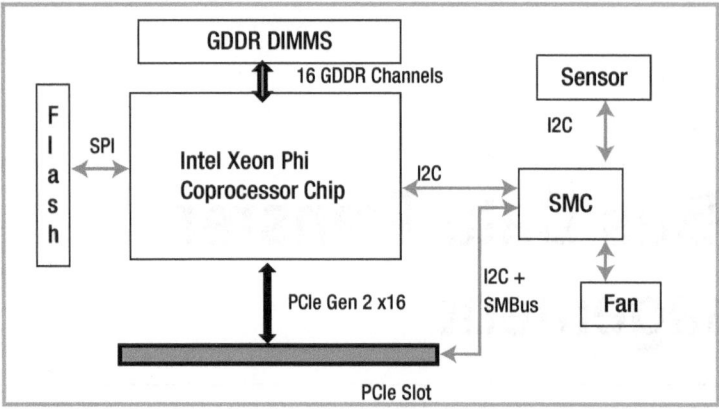

Figure 6-2. *Components of an Intel Xeon Phi card*

As seen in Figure 6-2, the card contains the Intel Xeon Phi coprocessor and is connected to the onboard DDR5 DIMMS with up to 16 channels distributed on both sides of the *printed circuit board* (PCB). Each memory channel supports two 16-bit-wide GDDR devices. The board also contains a *system management controller* (SMC in the diagram), thermal sensors, and a fan in actively cooled SKUs of the product. There are certain SKUs of Intel Xeon Phi which are passively cooled and do not require the cooling fan. The clock system uses a PCI Express 100 MHz reference clock and includes onboard 100 MHz ± 50 ppm reference. The card contains an onboard flash allowing it to load a coprocessor OS on boot. You can find full physical and electrical specifications in the Intel Xeon Phi coprocessor data sheet.[1]

The SMC shown in Figure 6-2 has three I2C interfaces. One of them connects directly to the coprocessor chip to collect coprocessor thermal and status data, the second one connects to on-card sensors, and the third one is the *system management bus* (SMBus) for system fan control for cards with passive heat sink. The SMBus is also used for integration with the node management controller using the *Intelligent Platform Management Bus*(I PMB)pr otocol.

The Intel Xeon Phi coprocessor uses a system interface functional unit to communicate with the host over a PCIe gen 2 interface and uses x16 lines for maximum transfer bandwidth. It is shown to achieve greater than 6 GB/s for both host-to-device and device-to-host data transfers. The unit also supports remote DMA to host to optimize data transfers. The PCIe clock mode supports both PCIe 1 and 2 and uses an external buffer to support external PCIe 100 MHz reference clocks. The PCIe conforms to the PCIe gen 2 standard and supports 64- to 256-byte packets, peer-to-peer read/writes. The peer-to-peer interface allows two Intel Xeon Phi cards to communicate with each other without host processor intervention. This capability is particularly useful when running MPI programs across multiple Intel Xeon Phi cards (see the section in this chapter, "Placement of PCIe Cards for Optimal Data Transfer BW").

The system interface consists of the coprocessor *system interface unit* (SIU) and the *transaction control unit* (TCU). The PCIe protocol engine is the part of the SIU of Intel Xeon Phi architecture that implements the PCIe logic. The system interface component also includes the *serial peripheral interface* (SPI), which allows one to load the flash and coprocessor OS. In addition, the SIU includes the I2C logic components necessary to control fan speed on the card and *advanced programmable interrupt controller* (APIC) logic to allow communication between the host and the card.

The TCU connects the system bus to the internal ring bus of the Intel Xeon Phi coprocessor core. The TCU implements the DMA engine and buffers to control the flow of data to and from the system bus to the ring interconnect encryption/decryption engine, memory mapped I/O (MMIO) registers, and flow-control logic and instructions.

---

[1]*Intel Xeon Phi Coprocessor Data Sheet*, Reference Number: 328209-001EN. www.intel.com/content/www/us/en/processors/xeon/xeon-phi-coprocessor-datasheet.html.

DMA Engine

The following data transfer scenarios are supported in a system with one or more Intel Xeon Phi cards:

1. Peer-to-peer communication between coprocessor GDDR5 apertures

2. Intel Xeon Phi coprocessor to host system memory (device-to-host)

3. Host system memory to Intel Xeon Phi coprocessor GDDR5 (aperture or DMA)

4. Intra-GDDR5 block transfers within Intel Xeon Phi coprocessors

DMA allows data transfer to happen between the host memory and the coprocessor memory without host CPU intervention. The DMA transfer is done by programming the DMA controller with the source and destination addresses in the *channel descriptor ring*. The descriptor contains the length of data in cache line sizes in addition to the source and destination addresses. One can use the DMA controller on the card or host to do the transfer either way.

A descriptor ring is a circular buffer with up to 128K entries and aligns to the cache line boundary. The software manages the ring by moving a head pointer to the circular buffer after it fills out a descriptor entry. The head pointer is copied to the DMA controller head pointer register for the appropriate DMA channel. The DMA channel contains a tail pointer which points to the same location as the head pointer upon initialization and is updated as descriptors are fetched by the DMA controller into a local descriptor queue inside the controller for each channel. The local descriptor queue has 64-bit entries and maps to a sliding window in the system descriptor ring. The tail pointer is periodically written to system memory to update the DMA transfer status. The head and tail pointers are 40-bit wide and the *most significant bit* (MSB) of the pointer indicates the location of the descriptor ring. If the high order bit is 1, the descriptor ring resides in the system memory; otherwise it resides in the Intel Xeon Phi coprocessor memory.[2]

The DMA descriptor rings can be programmed by the host driver or the coprocessor OS. Up to eight DMA channels, each corresponding to one circular DMA ring of descriptors, can be written by the driver or coprocessor OS and operate in parallel. The descriptor rings written by the host driver must be present in the host system memory, and those written by coprocessor OS must reside in the on-card GDDR5 memory.

The DMA can be host- or device-initiated and supports data transfer in both directions, from host to device and vice versa. The DMA transfer happens using the physical addresses and generates an interrupt after the transfer is done.

The DMA transfer happens at core clock rate, and the eight independent channels can move data in parallel from the host system memory to the Intel Xeon Phi GDDR5 and from the Intel Xeon Phi GDDR5 memory to the host system memory.

Intel Xeon Phi supports from 64 up to 256 bytes per DMA-based PCIe transaction. The transaction size is programmable by PCI commands.

The ring descriptors in a channel are operated on sequentially. The multiple DMA channels can, however, be opened to provide arbitration capabilities between the channels if needed.

Measuring the Data Transfer Bandwidth over the PCIe Bus

This section will walk you through actual data transfer using the offload programming language. In Code Listing 6-1, I show how you can use the offload programming language to set up a high-level data transfer between hosts to Intel Xeon Phi. Although there are lower level APIs exposed by Intel Xeon Phi programming environments available through Intel Xeon Phi system programming software, such as the *symmetric communication interface*(S CIF), Iw ill focus on high-level offload language extensions for C to do the data transfer. The Intel compiler uses appropriate lower-level system interfaces for such tasks as setting up the DMA channel for proper transfer and so forth. You will see, however, there are some requirements for optimizing data transfer performance.

---

[2]For details of the descriptor rings format, see *Intel Xeon Phi Coprocessor System Software Developers Guide.* IBL Doc. ID:488596.

Code Listing 6-1. Example of Host to Device Data Transfer Over the PCIe Bus

```
38 //Define number of floats for 64 MB data transfer
39 #define SIZE (64*1000*1000/sizeof(float))
40 #define ITER  10
41 // set cache line size alignment
42 #define ALIGN  (64)
43 __declspec(target(MIC)) static float *a;
44 extern double elapsedTime (void);
45 int main()
46 {
47     double startTime, duration;
48     int i, j;
49
50     //allocate a
51     a = (float*)_mm_malloc(SIZE*sizeof(float),ALIGN);
52
53     //initialize arrays
54     #pragma omp parallel for
55     for (i=0; i<SIZE;i++)
56     {
57         a[i]=(float)1.0f;
58     }
59     // Allocate memory on the card
60     #pragma offload_transfer target(mic) \
61      in(a:length(SIZE) free_if(0) alloc_if(1) align(ALIGN) )
62
63
65     startTime = elapsedTime();
66     for(i=0; i<ITER;i++) {
67     //transfer data over the PCI express bus
68      #pragma offload_transfer target(mic) \
69       in(a:length(SIZE) free_if(0) alloc_if(0) align(ALIGN) )
70
71     }
72     duration = elapsedTime() - startTime; ;
74     // free memory on the card
75     #pragma offload_transfer target(mic) \
76         in(a:length(SIZE) alloc_if(0) free_if(1) )
77
78
80 //free the host system memory
81     _mm_free(a);
83     double GB = SIZE*sizeof(float)/(1000.0*1000.0*1000.0);
84     double GBps = ITER*GB/duration;
85     printf("SP ArraySize = %0.4lf MB, ALIGN=%dB, PCIe Data transfer bandwidth Host->Device
GB/s = %0.2lf\n", GB*1000.0, ALIGN, GBps);
86
87  return 0;
88 }
```

Recall that the maximum data transfer performance can be achieved by using the DMA engine. Since DMA engines transfer data in 64 bytes (cache line size), you need to make sure the data length is a 64-byte multiple. At Line 39, I choose the data array size to transfer as 64MB. I chose a large size to amortize the DMA transfer overhead needed to set up the DMA engine with proper parameters. The second important datum of information needed to optimize the transfer is to make sure that the data to be transferred are cacheline-aligned to enable transfer of the data with the DMA engine. I used the 'C' macro '#define ALIGN' in Line 42 to make sure the allocated memory is 64-byte aligned. In Line 43, I define a pointer 'a' that will be visible to offloaded code executing on the card by declaring it with "__declspec(target(MIC))."

This pointer will be allocated on the host and transferred over to the coprocessor using offload pragmas. In order to do that, you need to allocate space for the buffer using _mm_malloc intrinsics supported by the Intel compiler in Line 51. The _mm_malloc intrinsic, in addition to behaving like a malloc function, also allows data alignment to be specified as part of the request. This line allocates 64MB of data area aligned to the cache line boundary (64 bytes).

The first data transfer happens in Line 60, as shown below:

```
60      #pragma offload target(mic) \
61       in(a:length(SIZE) alloc_if(1) free_if(0) align(ALIGN) )
62      {
63      }
```

The data transfer begins by a call "#pragma offload target(mic)" that tells the runtime library to start a process started on coprocessor. The 'in' parameter tells it to send the array pointed to by '*a' to the coprocessor, the alloc_if(1) clause in the offload statement allocates memory on the card for pointer 'a' and copies the data over to coprocessor. Since the size of the buffer and alignment is large enough, the underlying libraries will use the DMA engine to set up and transfer these data to the coprocessor. The free_if(0) clause tells the runtime not to free the buffer that was allocated on the card so it could be reused. The 'align(ALIGN)' clause in the same statement tells the buffer that is allocated on the card to be aligned to ALIGN bytes, in this case 64 bytes.

I have separated out the first offload pragma call as it involves start-up overhead that I do not want to count as part of the transfer time. The overhead involves sending the coprocessor part of the binary to the card and sending necessary runtime compiler library like openmp library to the card as well. You will also need to allocate space for array 'a' on the card to copy the data in, which happens during this first offload statement.

Lines 65 through 72 are the timing loop where the actual data transfer rate is measured. Here the data transfer is repeated ITER (10) times to average out the any run to run variation in transfer time. The 'pragma offload' statement is similar to what was discussed earlier to show the initialization of coprocessor code and data:

```
68      #pragma offload target(mic) \
69       in(a:length(SIZE) free_if(0) alloc_if(0) align(ALIGN) )
70       {}
```

The main thing to keep in mind is that in this statement we have both the 'free_if(0)' and 'alloc_if(0)' clause set to zero, thus telling the runtime not to allocate any more space for 'a' and also not to free the space created previously with pragma offload code. Note that if you made the previous statement to free the buffer allocated in the first call by calling with free_if(1), the buffer would have been freed after the 'pragma offload' statement.

In that case you would need to reallocate the buffer with the alloc_if(1) call instead of alloc_if(0) call. It is a common source of error in offload programming if the allocation and free clauses do not properly match up. If you have more 'alloc_if(1)' calls without matching free_if(1) calls, you will see memory leaks on the coprocessor card. Similarly, if you try to copy the input buffer with the alloc_if(0) call assuming the buffer is present, but where it was accidentally freed in the previous call, you will get a general protection fault.

In Line 75, I am done with the data transfer measurements and have freed the memory allocated on the card by using the free_if(1) call with a matching alloc_if(0) call so that I do not need to allocate the buffer on entering the offload region.

I also need to free the memory allocated on the host using _mm_malloc by matching _mm_free intrinsics. You need to make sure you use _mm_free instead of free calls since they use a different heap manager and a different space for buffer management. Figure 6-3a shows the output of "pciebw.out" application built by the following commandw ithI ntelc ompiler:

```
Command_prompt-host > icpc -O3  -openmp -vec-report3 pciebw.cpp gettime.cpp -o pciebw.out
```

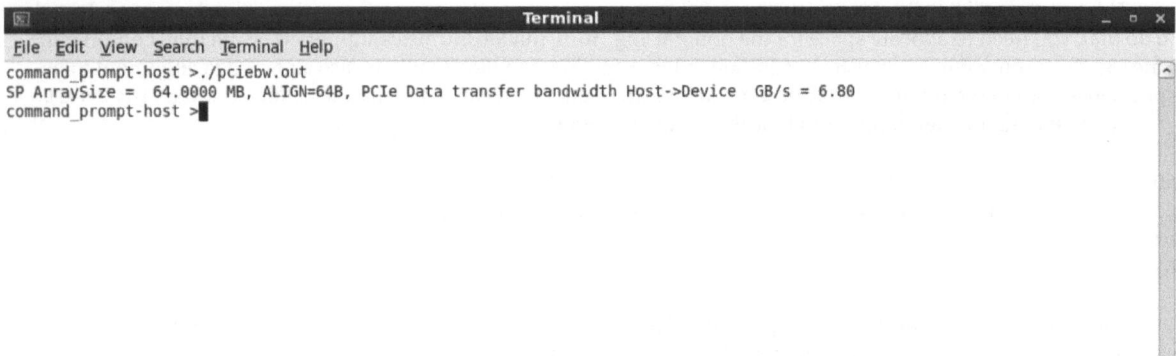

Figure 6-3a. *Output of pciebw test run*

The Intel compiler recognizes offload pragmas and generates the code necessary for data transfer to the coprocessor.

The output captured on Figure 6-3a shows that the data transfer of 64 MB buffer size with 64-byte aligned achieved an approximately 6.8 GB/s transfer rate over the PCIe bus in moving from the host to the coprocessor (device). You can also see the effect of various buffer sizes and alignment if you play around with the alignment and data buffer size. To see the effect of various buffer sizes, let's modify the code to run with 64 kB instead of 64 MB. This can be done by changing the buffer size in Line 39 to:

```
39 #define SIZE (64*1000/sizeof(float))
```

I recompiled and ran the same code with the modified buffer size and the output is shown in Figure 6-3b. As you can see, the BW drops to 3.88 GB/s compared to 6.8 GB/s for the 64 MB buffer size. This is due to DMA transfer overhead, because smaller data transfer sizes cut down on overall performance.

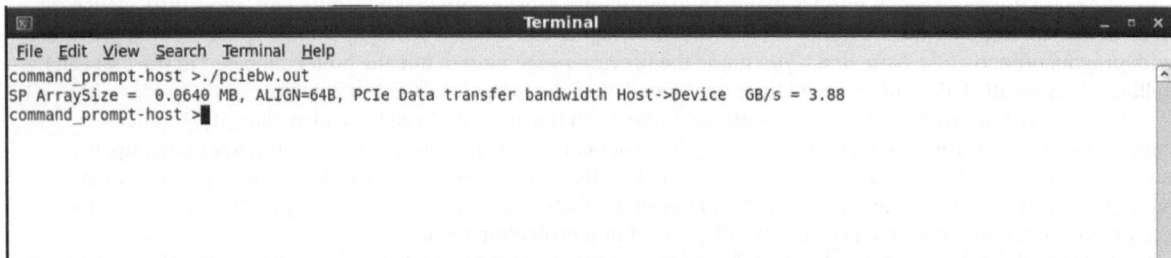

Figure 6-3b. *Output of the pciebw test with 64K data buffer*

Now, to see what the effect of alignment is, let's change the buffer alignment from 64 bytes to 6 bytes of unaligned data. As you can see from Figure 6-3c, the BW drops even further to 2.29 GB/s.

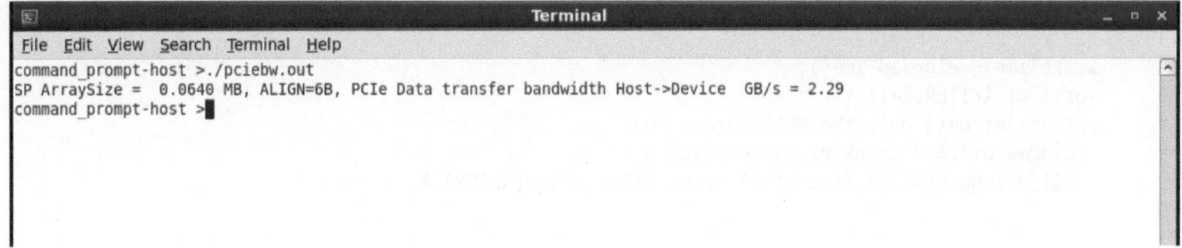

Figure 6-3c. *Output of the pciebw test with 64K data buffer with 6B alignment*

It has been found that for smaller data sizes (< 4 KB), the data transfer may be faster when it is done with MMIO through CPU write to card memory than through DMA transfer. The compiler may choose accordingly to use different data transfer methods depending on the data buffer size for optimal data transfer bandwidth. You could run the same example with OFFLOAD_REPORT=1. This will print out the CPU time taken to transfer the data and should correlate to the performance number for various alignment cases discussed in this section.

Reading Data from the Coprocessor

The previous section examined the bandwidth to transfer data from the host to the coprocessor. The data read back from the coprocessor to the host can be tested with very similar code. The main difference is that reading the data from the coprocessor involves using the 'out' clause instead of the 'in' clause in Line 69 of Code Listing 6-1. The code adjusted for device-to-host data transfer is shown in Listing 6-2.

Code Listing 6-2. Example of Device-to-Host Data Transfer Over the PCIe Bus

```
38 //Define number of floats for 64 MB data transfer
39 #define SIZE (64*1000*1000/sizeof(float))
40 #define ITER   10
41 // set cache line size alignment
42 #define ALIGN  (64)
43 __declspec(target(MIC)) static float *a;
44 extern double elapsedTime (void);
45 int main()
46 {
47     double startTime, duration;
48     int i, j;
49
50     //allocate a
51     a = (float*)_mm_malloc(SIZE*sizeof(float),ALIGN);
52
53     //initialize arrays
54     #pragma omp parallel for
55     for (i=0; i<SIZE;i++)
56     {
57         a[i]=(float)1.0f;
58     }
59     // Allocate memory on the card
60     #pragma offload_transfer target(mic) \
61       in(a:length(SIZE) free_if(0) alloc_if(1) align(ALIGN) )
```

```
62
63
65     startTime = elapsedTime();
66     for(i=0; i<ITER;i++) {
67     //transfer data over the PCI express bus
68      #pragma offload_transfer target(mic) \
69       out(a:length(SIZE) free_if(0) alloc_if(0) align(ALIGN) )
70
71     }
72     duration = elapsedTime() - startTime;
74     // free memory on the card
75     #pragma offload_transfer target(mic) \
76         in(a:length(SIZE) alloc_if(0) free_if(1) )
77
78
80 //free the host system memory
81     _mm_free(a);

88 }
```

The device-to-host code can be built using the same command line, and the output is shown in Figure 6-4. It can be seen from the output that the transfer bandwidth for read back is approximately 6.89 GB/s, which is slightly faster than the host-to-device transfer speed.

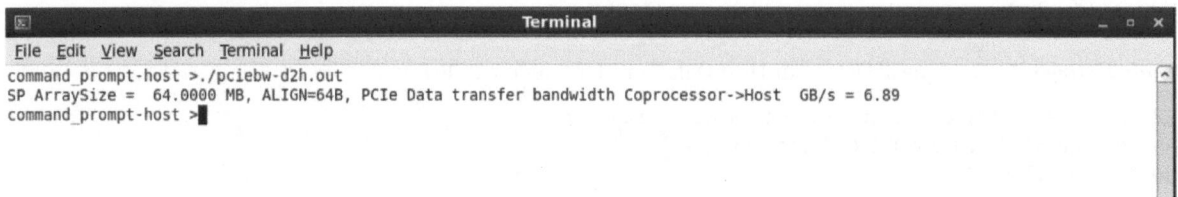

Figure 6-4. *Output of the PCIe BW-d2h test with 64MB data read with 64B alignment*

Low-Level Data Transfer APIs for Intel Xeon Phi

The Intel Xeon Phi MPSS software stack contains two lower-level APIs for more control over data allocation and transfer in case you need it. In general, developers are encouraged to use high-level programming constructs in Fortran and C/C++ to do the transfer. If the need arises, however, to have more control over data transfer, you can use either of two lower-level APIs: *Common Offload Infrastructure* (COI) and *Symmetric Communication Interface*(S CIF) (Figure 6-5). Although COI is an interesting interface, it is mainly used and exposed by the offload programming model and will not be discussed here. SCIF provides a low-latency communication channel between different SCIF clients, which can be any device including the host. SCIF provides the communication backbone between the host processor and the Xeon Phi coprocessors and between multiple Xeon Phi coprocessors. Other communication APIs such as COI, Virtual IP, and MPI can be built on top of the SCIF API.

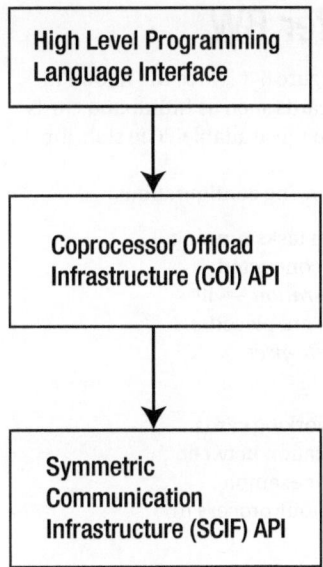

Figure 6-5. SCIF/COI API

The SCIF API exposes DMA capabilities for high-bandwidth data transfer. It also provides MMIO by mapping the host or coprocessor system memory address into the address space of the processes running on the host or coprocessor. SCIF uses the direct peer-to-peer memory access model for communicating with each of its nodes. So if two nodes are on two separate Xeon Phi coprocessors, the nodes can communicate with each other directly without going through the host memory.[3] SCIF does not provide any reliability features for the transmitted data but depends on the underlying PCIe reliability feature, thus making the software layer low-overhead.

As its name implies, SCIF is designed to provide you a symmetrical view, whether you are running on the host or on the coprocessor. With multiple Xeon Phi coprocessors in a system, SCIF treats each card and host as communication end points and supports an arbitrary number of nodes. The SCIF code is optimized for up to eight Xeon Phi devices. All of the coprocessor memory is visible to the host and other coprocessors; conversely, the host memory is visible to the coprocessors.

The SCIF implementations contain two components: one running in user mode (ring 3) and the other in kernel mode (ring 0). There are five categories of APIs provided by SCIF for lightweight communication purposes:

- *Connection API*: Establish connections among various SCIF nodes, following the socket programming paradigm.

- *Messaging API*: Support two-sided communications between SCIF nodes, intended for short-latency sensitive messages.

- *Registration API*: Allow mapping addresses for one node into the process space of the other node between which connections are established by the connection API.

- *RMA API*: Support communication using the address space mapped through registration APIs. This allows DMA and programmed I/O transfers to the mapped memory space and relevant synchronizationA PIs.

- *Utility API*: Provide the utility services necessary to perform above functionalities.

---

[3]*Intel Xeon Phi Coprocessor System Software Developers Guide.* SKU 328207-001EN. www.intel.com/content/dam/www/public/us/en/documents/product-briefs/xeon-phi-software-developers-guide.pdf.

Placement of PCIe Cards for Optimal Data Transfer BW

In a multisocket platform, there are multiple PCIe slots near the sockets, as shown in Figure 6-1. Since the Xeon Phi card is connected to the PCIe slots and can coexist with other Xeon Phi or networking cards such as Infiniband cards on the same node, you need to carefully consider placement of the coprocessor cards in the available PCIe slots for optimalp erformance.

For optimal communication bandwidth between the cards, you can create the following configurations:

1. For card-to-card data transfers, such as MPI ranks communicating between tasks running on two cards, it is better to have them connected to the PCIe lanes that are connected to the same socket. This configuration—known as *local peer-to-peer configuration*—will provide optimal bandwidth for data transfer between the cards. If the cards are placed on the PCIe bus corresponding to different sockets—known as *remote peer-to-peer configuration*—performancew ills uffer.

2. The card-to-card data transfer case is also true for Infiniband or other networking cards used in PCIe configurations. Always try to gravitate toward local communication between the cards or processor and the card for optimal data transfer bandwidth. For example, if you are setting up a cluster with Infiniband cards, it may be useful to pin your process to a socket which is local to the Infiniband card used for communication.

3. For configurations of one or more Intel Xeon Phi cards and Infiniband cards, putting them in *local P2P configuration* (i.e., connected to the same socket) will provide optimal performance.

Power Management and Reliability

According to top500.org, as of June 2013, the fastest supercomputer system was the Tianhe-2 with an Rpeak (theoretical peak performance of the system) of 54.9024 petaflops. According to computational power growth over time as recorded by top500.org,[4] if the trend continues, the top performing supercomputer will attain 1 exaflops around 2018, allowing us to perform technical computing to solve problems not yet attempted. Projecting the current rate of power consumption by the top 500 supercomputers, 100 MW—approximately the output of a small nuclear power station—will be required to power a 1 exaflops supercomputer, which is impractical. The Department of Energy projects that the power consumption needs to be cut to 20 MW or less to make an exaflops supercomputer practical.[5]

It was with this target in mind that Intel MIC architects designed the power management and reliability features in the Intel Xeon Phi implementation. The design philosophy has been that maximum power efficiency can be achieved when the software running on the machine is able to dictate to the hardware how to manage the power states the hardware supports. Accordingly, the Intel Xeon Phi is built so that the coprocessor OS/driver layer (the MPSS layer) manages the runtime power requirements of the hardware.

There are several power management states implemented by the Intel Xeon Phi coprocessor and controlled by system and application software: the Turbo mode, package P-states, core C-states, and memory M-states. In Turbo mode, the core can make use of power/thermal headroom to increase frequency and voltage depending on the number of active cores. There is a utility shipped with Intel Xeon Phi driver package that enables turbo on/off states of the coprocessor.

---

[4]Exponential growth of supercomputing power as recoded by top500.org. http://top500.org/statistics/perfdevel
[5]"The Opportunity and Challenges of Exascale Computing." Summary report of the Exascale Subcommittee of the Advanced Scientific Computing Advisory Committee (ASCAC), Fall 2010. http://science.energy.gov/~/media/ascr/ascac/pdf/reports/Exascale_subcommittee_report.pdf; and Thomas Sterling (with Peter Kogge). "An Overview of Exascale Architecture Challenges." SC08 Workshop on the Path to Exascale, 2008. www.lbl.gov/CS/html/SC08ExascalePowerWorkshop/Exarch.pdf.

P-states (shortf or *performance states*) are different frequency settings that the OS or applications can request when the cores are in executing state (also known as *C0 state* for cores). All cores run at the same P-state frequency, as there is only one clock source for the coprocessor. Since the frequency changes require voltage changes to the core, each P-state change changes the frequency and voltages in pairs. P1 is the highest P-state setting and it can have multiple sequentially lower frequency settings. As the device characteristics may vary from device to device, each device is carefully calibrated and programmed at the factory with the proper pair of voltage and frequency settings so that different devices may have different voltage settings for the same set of frequencies. All devices within an SKU will have the same P-state settings but may vary from SKU to SKU.

In C0 state, the core and memory (*M0 state*), the card runs at its maximum *thermal design power* (TDP) rating. In core C1 state, clocks are shut off to the core (including VPU). In order to enter this state, the threads have to be halted. The last thread's halt instruction performs the necessary housekeeping before shutting off the clock. A coprocessor can have some cores in C0 state and some in C1 state with memory in M0 state. In this case, clocks are gated on a core-by-core basis, allowing the cores in C1 state to lose clock source. For the actively cooled SKUs (where the coprocessor is cooled by a cooling fan on the card), it is possible to turn the fan speed down.

If all the cores enter C1 state, the coprocessor automatically enters the Auto-Package C3 (PC3) state. In this stage, the clock source to the memory can be gated off, thus reducing memory power. This is known as M1 state for the memory.

When all cores are in C1 halt state, the coprocessor package can reduce the core voltage and enters the Deep-PC3 state. The Package C3 state shuts off clocks once all the boxes are idle, enabling deeper package states. The fan runs at ~20 percent of peak for active SKUs in this phase. The VR (voltage regulator) on the cards also enters the low power stage in Deep-PC3 mode. The memory enters the M2 state, where it is put in self-refresh mode, further reducing memory power.

Core C6 state shuts the clock and power off for the core. If power down is desired, the coprocessor OS will write to a certain status register before issuing HALT to all the threads active on that core. Power is shut off after the specified delay and the core is electrically isolated. An interrupted active thread exiting core C6 state will use the content of an internal register to determine its branch address after completing CC6 reset. At this stage, the memory clock can be fully stopped to reduce memory power and memory subsystem enters M3 state.

Note that the time stamp counter lives in the uncore region and is always running except in the package C3/C6 state and it is restored to the core on C1 exit.

Power management in the MPSS is performed in the background. In periods of idle state, the coprocessor OS puts the cores in a lower power idle state to reduce the overall power consumption.

There are two major components to power management software running on Intel Xeon Phi. One is part of the coprocessor OS and the other is part of the host driver.

Power management capabilities in the coprocessor OS are performed in ring 0 except in PC6 states, where the power is shut down to the core and needs bootstrapping of the core. Here the OS boot loader helps in bringing the core up after the core shuts down. The OS kernel performs the following functions related to power management and exposes services to perform these functions:

- Selects and sets the coprocessor P-states, including Turbo mode. There is a utility (micsmc) shipped with the MPSS driver software package that lets users turn the Turbo mode on/off with the help of the coprocessor OS.

- Collects the device usage and power/thermal data for the coprocessor and exposes it through the MPSS utility to the coprocessor user.

- Sets the core power states as C-states.

- Saves and restores the CPU context on core C6 entry and exit. After C6 state exit, the boot loader performs reset initialization and passes control to the GDDR resident coprocessor OSk ernel.

Special instructions, such as HLT used by OS or MWAIT used by applications for idling routines, enable processors to take advantage of hardware C-states. The OS boot loader (see Chapter 7) helps to get the core back to the running state after a return to C6 power-saving state. It is put into service on PC6 state exit. The PC6 state lowers the core voltage VccP to zero. As a result, when the core voltage and clocks are restored, they start executing from the default instruction pointer address FFFF_FFF0h. However, rather than going through the normal boot sequence, as in the case of a cold restart, the PC6 state maintains the GDDR content by self-refresh and saves the hardware state before entering the C6 state. This minimizes the time required to bring the cores to full operational mode.

The host driver component of MPSS helps in power management by performing the following functions:

- Monitors and manages coprocessor idle states

- Replies to server management queries

- Provides a power management command status interface between the host and coprocessor software as may be required by cluster management tools

Power reduction is managed by the *power management* (PM) software using the states and services described above. Carefully selecting the P-states and idle states, the PM software can reduce power consumption without impacting application performance. It uses *demand-based switching* (DBS) to select the P-state. A decrease in CPU demand causes a reduction in the P-state (i.e., an increase in core frequency), and an increase in CPU demand causes an increase in the P-state (i.e., a reduction in core frequency). The P-state selection algorithm is thus tuned to detect changes in workload demands executing on the coprocessor with the help of some tunable system parameters. These system parameters can be set with the help of system policies selected by users. The P-state selection modules register with the coprocessor OS through a timer task and get invoked from time to time to evaluate the system P-states. The OS maintains a per-coprocessor running counter to compute the coprocessor core utilization. The evaluation tasks are invoked in the regular timer interval and executed in the background. These tasks use the per-core utilization data to compute maximum utilization values across all the cores to determine the target P-state and Turbo modes. (See the Intel Xeon Phi data sheet for the details of the power state management algorithm employed by MPSS.)

The P-state control module implements the P-states on the coprocessor. The P-state module of the system software exposes this functionality to the power management software. This module is part of the coprocessor's OS and allows the client software to set/get the P-state, register notifications, set core frequency, and voltage fuse values.

IdleS tareM anagement

Proper idle state selection allows the coprocessor to save even more power in addition to the P-state management described above. The policy uses the expected time that the cores are assumed to be idle together with the latency to get into and out of an idle state to select the specific idle state. The deeper sleep state requires longer latency to enter and exit the state.

The coprocessor supports package idle states such as Auto-C3, where all the cores and agents on the ring are clock-gated: the deeper-PC3 state, which reduces the voltage further, and the package C6 state, which shuts off the power to the package while keeping the GDDR memory content intact by autorefresh. The main differences between the package idle and core idle states are:

1. The package idle state requires all the cores to be idle.

2. The package idle state is controlled by the host driver except for Auto-C3 state.

3. Wake up from the package idle state requires external hardware events or coprocessor driver interrupts.

4. Package idle state causes the package *timestamp counter* (TSC) and local APIC timer to freeze, thus requiring an external timer, such as the *elapsed time counter* (ETC), outside the core to synchronize TSC when the package wakes up.

The coprocessor OS and host driver together play a central role in managing package idle states. The host processor may overwrite the coprocessor OS determination of PC3 selection, as the coprocessor may not have visibility in the uncore events. Also some package states, such as the Deep-PC3 and PC6 states, need host driver intervention to wake up the core.

Reliability Availability and Serviceability Features in the Intel Xeon Phi Coprocessor

Intel Xeon Phi is expected to be used in a cluster environment requiring reliability as a feature to support technical computing applications. It has built-in hardware support and tools to reduce the error rate and improve node availability and serviceability for fault tolerance. Intel Xeon Phi coprocessors implement extended machine check (MCA) features to help the software detect imminent failure and perform graceful service degradation when a component such as the core fails. An Intel Xeon Phi coprocessor reads bits from flash memory at boot time to disable the coprocessor component that MCA has reported as failing. (Please refer to the Intel Xeon Phi data sheet for details of MCA implementation in Xeon Phi.)

The memory controller of the coprocessor uses *cyclic redundancy control*(CR C)a nd *error correction code*(ECC) protection of the memory content. These enable machine MCA events. The controller can detect single- and double-bit errors and fix the single-bit errors. The coprocessor supports parity on the command and address interface as part of the error detection mechanism. ECC is also used to reduce error rates in cache lines and other memory arrays in the coprocessor.

Summary

This chapter discussed the characteristics of the communication and system management hardware of the Xeon Phi coprocessor. You looked at how data are transferred between the host and the coprocessor using DMA, and you saw the conditions that cause poor data transfer and how to avoid them. The chapter also covered reliability and power management features built into the Xeon Phi coprocessor.

The next chapter will introduce you to the system software layers that will help you manage and use the XeonP hic oprocessor.

PART 2

Software Foundation: Intel Xeon Phi System Software and Tools

CHAPTER 7

■ ■ ■

Xeon Phi System Software

Intel Xeon Phi needs support from system software components to operate properly and interoperate with other hardware components in a system. The system software component of the Intel Xeon Phi system, known as the Intel Many Integrated Core (MIC) Platform Software Stack (MPSS), provides this functionality. Unlike other device drivers implemented to support PCIe-based hardware, such as graphics cards, Intel Xeon Phi was designed to support the execution of technical computing applications in the familiar HPC environment through the MPI environment, as well as other offload programming usage models. Because the coprocessor core is based on the traditional Intel P5 processor core, it can execute a complete operating system like any other computer. The disk drive is simulated by a RAM drive and supports an Internet protocol (IP)-based virtual socket to provide networking communication with the host. This design choice allows the coprocessor to appear as a node to the rest of the system and allows a usage model common in the HPC programming environment. The operating system resides on the coprocessor and implements complementary functionalities provided by the driver layer on the host side to achieve its system management goals.

The system software layer is responsible for following functionalities:

- Boots the Intel Xeon Phi card to a usable state. Works with the host to enumerate and configure the card.

- Manages memory address space for configuration, I/O, and memory.

- Implements the device driver to run under the HOST OS to help system software functions such as interrupt handling, power state management, data transfer, communication, and supporting application layer requests through API support.

- The system software layer implements various protocols such as the socket protocol over TCP/IP to support the HPC programming model, which can treat Intel Xeon Phi as an independent cluster node from the system point of view. It provides low-level virtual ethernet and Symmetric Communication Interface (SCIF) APIs to help implement the standard communication protocols.

- The OS (also called coprocessor OS) running on the coprocessor manages the memory, I/O, and the processes of the application and/or application-offloaded functions running on the coprocessor by implementing all the necessary OS functionalities to support massively parallel tasks. The OS is based on an open-source Linux kernel to provide these functionalities. The OS implements the file system sysfs to expose communicate-system states and provide configurability of the OS runtime parameters, such as whether to use automated 2MB pages support in the OS for *transparent huge page* (THP).

- Allows users to develop their own applications and tools for value-added implementation, such as an MPI on top of the supplied system functionalities.

- Provides underlying support layers for user-level application execution such as Intel MPI, OpenCL, OpenMP 4.0, Cilk Plus, and the Intel proprietary shared memory and offload execution model. Some of these execution models were covered in Chapter 2 and others will be covered in Chapter 8 on tools.

System Software Component

The high-level software components for Intel Xeon Phi are depicted in Figure 7-1. The Xeon Phi system software has symmetric architecture. The software components on the card are complemented by an equivalent component on the host side to help abstract communication between the host and the coprocessor.

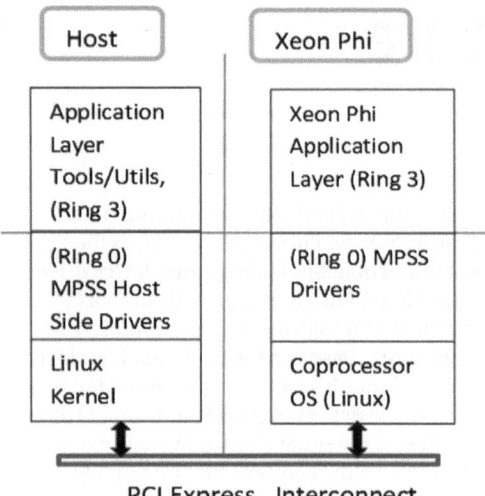

Figure 7-1. *Xeon Phi software layers*

The application layer is built on top of the system software running at Ring 0 (the most protected mode of operation of the processor, where the OS kernel and drivers usually run) on both the host and the coprocessor card. The application layer uses runtime libraries to provide the communication and control necessary to send the code and data to the coprocessor and get the results back. The application layer also contains utilities and libraries that can be used to query the system status and allow socket communications and other communication supports (such as InfiniBand protocols).

The coprocessor tools and utilities are part of the MPSS that allows the platform user to query the device status, as shown in Figure 7-2. Here the application is known as *MIC system management and configuration*(m icsmc)a nd is available with the MPSS. The application runs on the host at the Ring 3 user level and goes through the system drivers to communicate with the corresponding software piece on the coprocessor in order to retrieve such system information as core and memory utilization, core temperature, and power received from the system management component and controller (SMC) hardware on the coprocessor system, as discussed in Chapter 6.

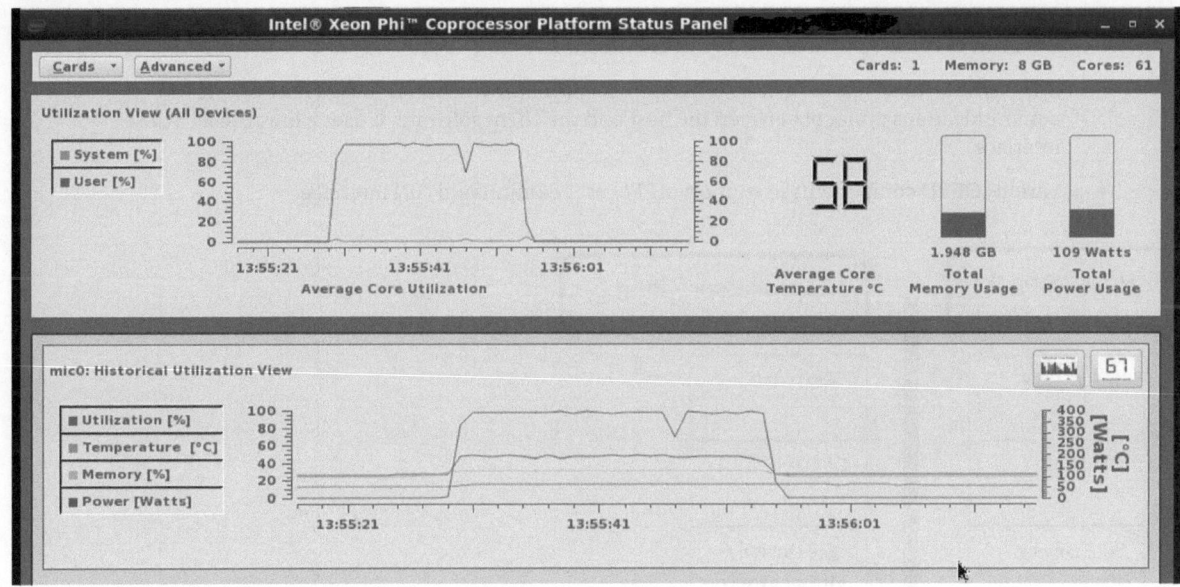

Figure 7-2. *Application layer system utility showing Xeon Phi coprocessor runtime status*

Applications running on the host side can also send computation and data over to the coprocessor via the PCIe bus using the system software layers on the host side. The data and code sent over to the coprocessor side are executed as a separate process (offload_main process) under the coprocessor OS. It is also possible to log in to the coprocessor OS with a remote shell such as the ssh command and run an application natively as one would run it on the host side. The MPSS subsystem also exposes common APIs to the applications running in the Ring 3 layer. These APIs include socket-level APIs over TCP/IP using a virtual ethernet interface and such MPI communication components as the Direct Access Programming Library (DAPL) provided to the fabric (communications hardware) independent API, Open Fabric Enterprise Distribution (OFED) verbs, and the Host Channel Adapter (HCA) library for InfiniBand technology. The coprocessor OS provides a command-line interpreter, such as the host Linux OS, to interact with the user connected directly to the coprocessor OS with tools such as secured shell functionality (ssh).

Ring 0 Driver Layer Components of the MPSS

The Ring 0 layers of the MPSS consist of the following basic components to support application and system functionalities(Figure 7-3):[1]

- *Host-side Linux kernel device driver for the Xeon Phi card*: The primary job of the host-side driver is to initialize the Xeon Phi coprocessor hardware. The driver is responsible for loading the OS in the coprocessor during the coprocessor boot process.

- *Symmetric Communication Interface*: The SCIF layer provides low latency communications between the host and the coprocessor. Other communication abstractions such as an IP-based network depend on the SCIF layer to perform their functions.

---

[1]*Intel Xeon Phi Coprocessor System Software Developers Guide*: http://www.intel.com/content/dam/www/public/us/en/documents/product-briefs/xeon-phi-software-developers-guide.pdf.

- *Xeon Phi coprocessor OS*: The coprocessor OS is based on the Linux kernel from kernel.org modified to fit the specifics of Xeon Phi architecture.

- *Symmetric virtual ethernet drivers*: This software layer provides an IP-based networking communications protocol between the host and the client software. It uses a lower-level SCIF interface.

- Various OFED components to support MPI over the InfiniBand (IB) interface.

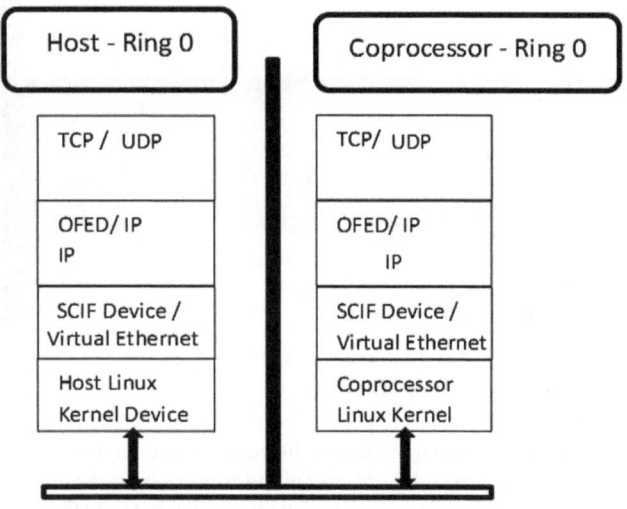

Figure 7-3. *Ring 0 components of the MPSS stack during runtime*

Applications and tools communicate with these components to perform their functionalities. The software layers are available when the system is booted and in the running state. It is possible to boot the coprocessor card through tools provided as part of the MPSS stack without booting the host system itself. The tool can be used to reboot the coprocessor at any time. In a cluster environment, for security purposes, the card may be rebooted to reset all the memory contents, including the RAM drive, to bring the coprocessor to clean reboot state.

SystemB ootP rocess

For the system administrator, it may be useful to understand the bootstrap process of the card to debug a system failure. *Bootstrap* is the process of initializing the card and loading the coprocessor OS. The coprocessor card contains firmware (ROM) that helps boot the card when first powered on reset by the host utilities. After the card reset, one of the cores of the coprocessor, known as a *boot strap processor* (BSP), starts execution. The first instruction executed is located in the default location in all x86-family processors: 0xfffffff0. The instruction pointer of the coprocessor points to this memory location after the power reset. This location points to the firmware section known as fboot0. This section of code is trusted code and cannot be reprogrammed, as it serves as the *root of trust*. This section of code authenticates the second stage of the boot process fboot1. If the authentication fails, the power is cut off from the core and ring by the boot strap code in fboot1 ROM area. At this stage, the host can reprogram the fboot1 to recover a bad or compromised fboot1 code block. If the power is cut from the core and ring, the coprocessor goes into zombie state. A jumper on the card then needs to be physically reset for the card to be recovered from this zombie state.

If the fboot1 passes the authentication check, the control is passed over to the fboot1 entry point and continues execution. Fboot1 code initializes the coprocessor cores, memory, and other coprocessor components. It copies code to the GDDR5 memory to improve performance. Then it moves on to boot the rest of the cores. Once all the cores are booted, the cores go into halt state. The coprocessor lets the host know when it is done with initialization. At this point, the host downloads the coprocessor OS image from the hard drive on the host side (Figure 7-4) to the predefined address location on the GDDR5 memory on the card. Once the download is complete, it signals the coprocessor through interrupt. The next step is to authenticate the coprocessor OS image. This is done by all the cores in parallel using an authentication code available in fboot0. If the authentication fails, the coprocessor OS is prevented from accessing sensitive registers and intellectual properties on the card. However, authentication will allow the coprocessor OS to boot by communicating necessary information—such as the number of CPUs, memory, and capabilities—to the OS loader code and handing control over to the OS for further execution. To be able to access the sensitive area in the coprocessor, one will need the maintenance OS released by Intel and signed with a special private key that matches the public key used by the authentication code in the fboot0 authentication code sequence.

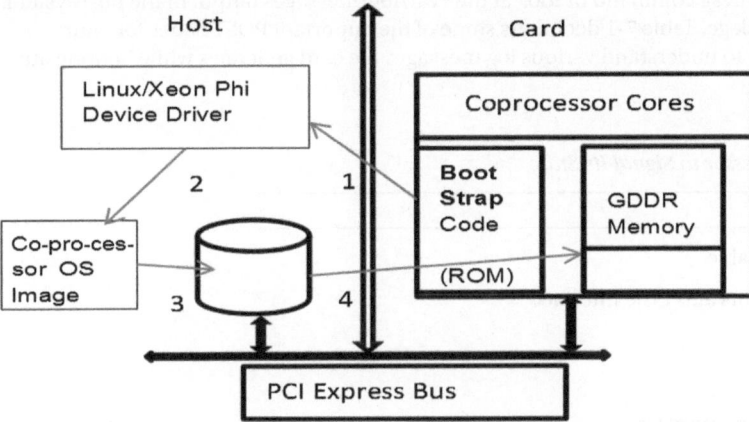

Figure 7-4. *Coprocessor OS load during boot strap process. 1. Coprocessor cores intialize and notify host. 2,3. Host driver reads the coprocessor image from the disk. 4. Host loads the coprocessor OS image to the GDDR memory. Coprocessor starts executing coprocessor OS, completing the boot process*

CoprocessorO S

The coprocessor OS provides the execution environment and runtime support to execute applications on the manycore Xeon Phi hardware. It supports other components of the MPSS stack such as SCIF communication and virtual ethernet. The coprocessor OS shipped as part of the MPSS is based on the standard Linux kernel source from kernel.org with minimal changes. Some of the main modifications needed are specific to the Xeon Phi hardware.

The coprocessor provides the necessary support for applications running on the coprocessor. This includes process, memory, and device and power management. One can also add loadable kernel modules to increase the functionality of the OS through kernel drivers. Intel tools such as profiling tools and debugging tools use the loadable kernel modules to interact with the hardware.

The OS provides the standard Linux base libraries such as libc, libm, librt. It also implements a minimal Shell environment using BusyBox.[2]

---

[2]Refert o http://www.busybox.net/about.htmlf orde tailsa boutB usyBoxf eatures.

Creating a Third-Party Coprocessor OS

The Xeon Phi coprocessor supports third-party OSs developed for the Xeon Phi processor. A third-party OS may be desirable for a customized operating system, such as one needing real-time response, light-weight processes, or other requirements not satisfied by the manufacturer's default OS. The boot strap code is written to conform to certain configurations required to boot the Linux OS as documented in the Linux kernel.

There are 16-bit, 32-bit, and 64-bit entry points for the Linux kernel. Xeon Phi supports the 32-bit entry points. The 32-bit entry point requires certain structures, such as the boot parameter and core and other hardware-related structures defined in the Linux documentation. The CPU mode also needs to be set in 32-bit protected mode as expected for a 32-bit entry point with paging disabled. A global descriptor table (GDT) with the proper boot code and data segment selectors must be provided, and other conditions must be fulfilled by the custom coprocessor OS as written in the boot.txt of the Linux kernel documentation.

During the boot process described earlier, the Xeon Phi processor logs the power on selftest (POST) messages to the host kernel log. These messages help in debugging the card in case the card fails to start. So if you are having issues starting the card, look at the Linux dmesg command or look at the /var/log/messages output in the host system. This inspection will require superuser privilege. Table 7-1 deciphers some of the important POST codes for your reference, which can be handy when trying to understand various log messages the card generates while booting and resettingt hec ard.

Table 7-1. *POST Code Provided by Coprocessor to Signal Its State*

POSTCo de	Interpretations
01	Load Interrupt Descriptor table
02	Initialize System Components and PCIe interface
03	SetG DDRm emory
04	Beginm emoryt est
05	Creates a table to describe memory layout
06	Initialize other parts of the coprocessor
09	Enablec aching
0b	Initialize application processor (cores other than boot strap processor core-0)
0c	Cachec ode
0d	Program multiprocessor configuration table (MP table)
0E	Copy application processor boot code to GDDR to speed up processing
0F	Wakeup application processors (AP)
10	Wait for APs to boot
11	Signal host to download coprocessor OS
12	Coprocessor in ready state to receive OS
13	Signal received from host after the coprocessor OS download completed
15	Reportp latformi nformation
17	Paget ables etup

(continued)

Table 7-1. (*continued*)

POSTCo de	Interpretations
30-3F	GDDR Memory Training phase
40	Beginc oprocessora uthentication
50-5F	Coprocessor OS load and setup
bP	Interrupt 3 (int3) break point
EE	Memoryte stf ailed
F0	GDDR parameter not found in flash
F2	GDDR failed memory training
F3	GDDR memory module query failed
F4	Memoryp reservationf ailed
FF	Bootstrapf inishede xecution
Ld	Locking down hardware access
nA	Coprocessor OS failed authentication

If you do a `sudo dmesg` after a card reboot on the host, you may find the logged message in Listing 7-1, which you can interpreted using Table 7-1. Here you see the card going through GDDR training (POST code 3C-3F) and finally getting to 'ready state' (code '12') to receive the coprocessor OS from the host. After the OS download, it starts the boot process and takes approximately 15 seconds to complete.

Listing 7-1. 'dmesg' output on host OS

```
mic0: Transition from state online to shutdown
host: scif node 1 exiting
mic0: Transition from state shutdown to resetting
mic0: Resetting (Post Code 3C)
mic0: Resetting (Post Code 3d)
mic0: Resetting (Post Code 3d)
mic0: Resetting (Post Code 3d)
mic0: Resetting (Post Code 3d)
mic0: Resetting (Post Code 3E)
mic0: Resetting (Post Code 3E)
mic0: Resetting (Post Code 3F)
mic0: Resetting (Post Code 09)
mic0: Resetting (Post Code 12)
mic0: Transition from state resetting to ready
mic0: Transition from state r eady to booting
MIC 0 Booting
Waiting for MIC 0 boot 5
Waiting for MIC 0 boot 10
MIC 0 Network link is up
```

mic0: Transition from State Booting to Online Host Driver

The MPSS ships with several host-side Linux device drivers to provide the necessary functionality. As we have seen, the host-side driver is responsible for starting the boot process of each of the cards attached to the system, loading the coprocessor OS, and setting the required boot parameters for the cards. Host drivers provide the basic communication layer through the SCIF driver layer and virtual ethernet driver layer, supporting the interfaces necessary for power management, device management, and configuration. User-level programs interact with these drivers to expose the user interface to these functionalities. For example, ssh functionality is built on top of the TCP/IP, which in turn depends on the virtual ethernet layer of host or coprocessor drivers.

The host driver load or unload functionality is provided through the standard Linux system `service start/stop` mechanism, which is provided by the commands `service mpss start/stop/restart` for booting and shutting down thec ard.

Linux Virtual File System (Sysfs and Procfs)

Two virtual file systems—Sysfs (/sys) and Procfs (/proc)—expose the coprocessor OS kernel and device status and control someo ft heb ehavior.

Sysfs (/sys) is a standard mechanism in Linux 2.6 for exporting information about the kernel objects to the user space. The user can query this file system content to view and manipulate these objects that map back to the kernel entities they represent. To see the usefulness of such a setup, suppose that you want to turn on huge page support in the coprocessor OS. In Chapter 4 you saw that the coprocessor supports 2MB-page sizes to reduce the TLB pressure. To reduce the TLB pressure as needed, the coprocessor can transparently promote memory pages to 2MB pages, controllable through the kernel parameter in the virtual file "enabled" located at /sys/kernel/mm/transparent_hugepage/.

If you cat the file, you see that the current configuration of the kernel is set to enable the transparent huge page supportb yd efault:

- `Cat /sys/kernel/mm/transparent_hugepage/enabled`, you can see the content

- `[always] madvise never`

In order to turn this default off, you can echo "never," as shown in Figure 7-5. Once you have echoed "never" to the enabled file, it is set in the kernel "enabled" property.

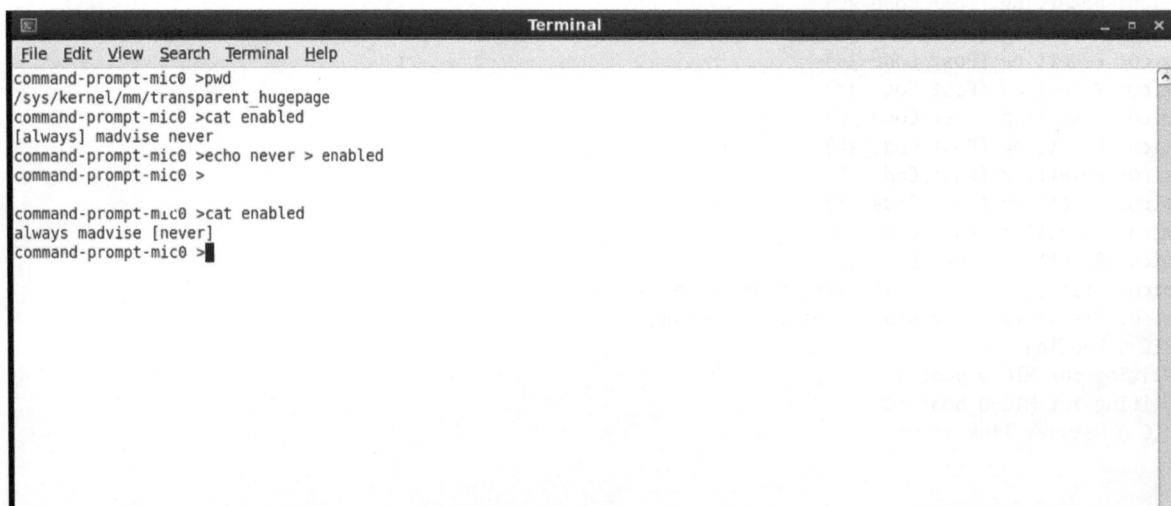

Figure 7-5. *Xeon Phi Coprocessor Sysfs virtual file system /sys*

The host also exposes some of the coprocessor information through its virtual file system. For example, on the Linux host with a Xeon Phi coprocessor, if you type the following cat command, it returns the memory size on the device in hex, which is 8GB in this case.

- `cat /sys/class/mic/mic0/memsize`

- `7c0000`

This useful interface may be used by system and card management software to query Xeon Phi configuration and status.

You can also use the /proc file system on the card to gather information related to the number of cores, memory usage, and so forth. You can type `cat /proc/cpuinfo` on the coprocessor command prompt to get information about the cores running on the coprocessor. Figure 7-6 captures the last fragment of the output of such a command on Xeon Phi. Because the hardware I was using had 61 cores with 4 threads per core, it had a total of 244 (processor id 243 since the first core is id = 0) logical processors.

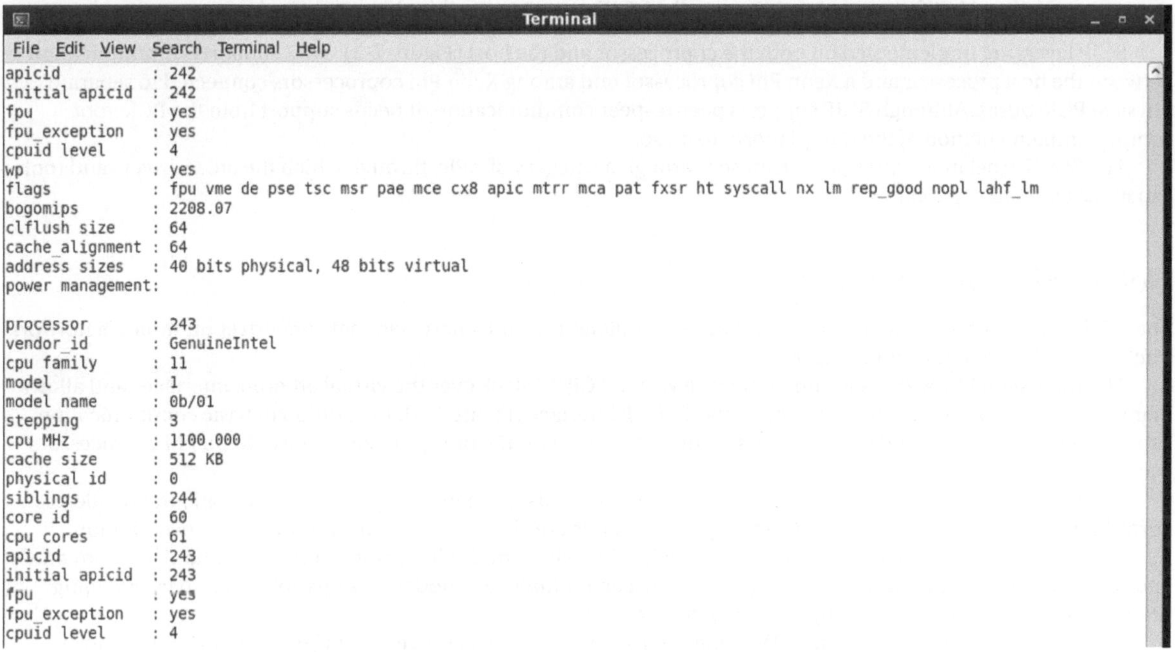

```
Terminal                                                    _ □ ×
File  Edit  View  Search  Terminal  Help
apicid           : 242
initial apicid   : 242
fpu              : yes
fpu_exception    : yes
cpuid level      : 4
wp               : yes
flags            : fpu vme de pse tsc msr pae mce cx8 apic mtrr mca pat fxsr ht syscall nx lm rep_good nopl lahf_lm
bogomips         : 2208.07
clflush size     : 64
cache_alignment  : 64
address sizes    : 40 bits physical, 48 bits virtual
power management:

processor        : 243
vendor_id        : GenuineIntel
cpu family       : 11
model            : 1
model name       : 0b/01
stepping         : 3
cpu MHz          : 1100.000
cache size       : 512 KB
physical id      : 0
siblings         : 244
core id          : 60
cpu cores        : 61
apicid           : 243
initial apicid   : 243
fpu              : yes
fpu_exception    : yes
cpuid level      : 4
```

Figure 7-6. */proc virtual file system listing CPU cores available on a Xeon Phi coprocessor*

Cluster management and monitoring software such as Ganglia[3] can use the information exposed by the Sysfs/Procfs virtual file system in the coprocessor OS and hosts to relay the data to its management interface to help manage the clusters containing Xeon Phi coprocessor cards. SCIF Layer

The SCIF layer sits above the coprocessor OS (Figure 7-3). It is a fast and lightweight communication layer that is responsible for abstracting PCIe data transfers between Xeon Phi devices and the host. It abstracts the end points (the host processor and the coprocessor) connected to the PCIe bus as "nodes" and thus can treat the nodes symmetrically. The symmetry means that the same interface is exposed to the host and the coprocessor. As a result, an application written against the SCIF interface can execute on both the host and the coprocessor.

---

[3]Ganglia is open-source cluster management software (`http://ganglia.sourceforge.net/`).

SCIFs supports:

- Reliability, accessibility, and serviceability (RAS). SCIF provides the communication channel for RAS feature implementation.

- Power management SCIF supports power management events to allow the coprocessor to enter and exit PC6 states.

- The Xeon Phi coprocessor supports direct-assignment virtualization. *Virtualization* is the process of running multiple virtual machines (VM) and corresponding guest OS or applications simultaneously on the same hardware. In direct assignment, a guest OS has a dedicated Xeon Phi coprocessor and corresponding SCIF network. The SCIF networks of multiple guest OSs do not interfere with one another.

- SCIF can support an arbitrary number of coprocessors by design. The current implementation of SCIF is optimized for up to eight coprocessors.

- VariousM PSSs ystemt oolss upportedb yS CIFa ret reatedi nt hisc hapter.

SCIF layers are implemented on both the coprocessor and the host (Figure 7-3). SCIF supports communication between the host processor and a Xeon Phi coprocessor and among Xeon Phi coprocessors connected to separate physical PCIe buses. Although SCIF supports peer-to-peer communication, it needs support from the PCIe root complex implementation of the host platform to do so.

The SCIF kernel mode interface is exposed through a category of APIs, through which the other drivers and tools can make use of its capabilities.[4]

Networking on Xeon Phi

The MPSS implements a virtual ethernet driver that emulates the Linux hardware network driver underneath network stacks on the host and the coprocessor.

The Intel Xeon Phi MPSS stack implements a virtual TCP/IP stack over the virtual ethernet interfaces and allows many tools and applications to run on top of the TCP/IP interface (Figure 7-3). In addition to basic communication support between the host and the coprocessor, there is support for the bridge to connect two Xeon Phi coprocessors over the TCP/IP network.

The support assigns unique IP addresses to each of the cards, configurable by means of a configuration file default.cfg supported by the MPSS. Currently, connections are class C subnets by Internet protocol definition.

If required, it is possible to create a network bridge that allows multiple coprocessors to communicate with one another on a node. If communication is expected between multiple host nodes, it is possible to do so by assigning unique addresses to the cards through the configuration process.

The virtual ethernet (VE) uses the DMA operations to transfer packets over the PCIe bus. It uses the following procedure for data packet transfer using TCP/IP:

1. The host VE device creates descriptor rings as needed by the DMA on the host memory.

2. During initialization, the host and coprocessor provide receive-buffer space using Linux socket buffer structure (skbuffs).

3. The card maps the host descriptor ring to its address space.

4. The card allocates and posts a number of receive buffers to the host-side VE driver.

---

[4]Refer to Intel Xeon Phi software guides for details of the interfaces, such as *Intel Xeon Phi Coprocessor System Software Developers Guide* (http://www.intel.com/content/dam/www/public/us/en/documents/product-briefs/xeon-phi-software-developers-guide.pdf).

5. During host transfer, the host VE driver DMAs the TCP/IP buffers to the receive buffers on thec oprocessor.

6. Theh osti nterruptst hec oprocessor.

7. The coprocessor VE sends the data up to the TCP/IP stack and allocates a new receive buffer for host use.

8. On the coprocessor send, the skbuffs is DMAed to the receive buffer posted by the host and interrupts the host.

9. The host interrupt routine of the VE device driver sends the skbuff to the TCP/IP stack.

10. Theh osta llocatesa n ewr eceiveb ufferf ort hec oprocessort ou se.

NetworkF ileS ystem

The coprocessor OS also supports the *Network File System* (NFS) to expose the host file system on the card. It is part of the MPSS. Because the NFS requires TCP/IP networking, it requires you to have the network set up so that the host can act as a file server for the NFS mount and allow access to the disks on the host.

The NFS file system is extremely handy when using the native mode of execution or the symmetric mode of application execution. These modes require the application binaries, the dependent libraries, and input dataset to be available on the coprocessor. As copying these files over would waste time, it is often possible to mount the host file system onto the coprocessor for the run. The program will then write output to its local NFS-mounted drive so that the output can be used on the host side as well without explicit copying. It is important to be aware, however, that the NFS file system is slow on Xeon Phi, and performance-sensitive files may be copied over to the coprocessor RAM drive explicitly.

The process of mounting the NFS file system is similar to the Linux NFS mount process using NFS server–client architecture. The following steps need to be executed by a superuser on both the host and the coprocessor:

1. **Export the file system you want to share with a Xeon Phi coprocessor through /etc/exports.** As a superuser you can add an entry to export fs. For example, to export the /opt/intel folder on the host where the default Intel Compiler library is available to a Xeon Phi coprocessor, you could add the following line to your /etc/exports file. /opt/intel mic0(rw,no_root_squash). Then execute exportfs -a to make sure the modification to exportfs is seen by the NFS daemons.

2. **Allow the file exported file system to be accessible to coprocessor.** To allow the coprocessor to access the file system, set /etc/hosts.allow. You can do this by adding the following line, if 172.31.1.1 is your coprocessor card IP address. Add the appropriate address if your card address differs.

   ```
   ALL:172.31.1.1
   ```

3. **Mount the exported file system on the coprocessor.** First create a folder /opt/intel on the coprocessor through the mkdir command. Then issue a mount command as follows:

   ```
   mount -t nfs -o rsize=8192,wsize=8192,intr,nolock host:/opt/intel /opt/intel
   ```

Open Fabrics Enterprise Distribution and Message Passing Interface Support

One of the key requirements for Intel Xeon Phi to be applicable to high-performance computing or technical computing applications is the support for MPI communication APIs and high-performance, low-latency communication fabrics. For this purpose, the MPSS stack has built-in support for OFED. The Intel MPI stack is built on top of the OFED module to implement the *remote direct memory access* (RDMA) transport available in the Xeon Phi coprocessor. The Intel MPI library on the coprocessor can use the SCIF or physical InfiniBand host channel adaptor (HCA) between various MPI ranks running on hosts and coprocessors. These allow a coprocessor to be treated like a node in a cluster of nodes.

There are two ways to communicate with an HCA device in a node:

1. *Coprocessor Communication Link* (CCL): This is a hardware proxy driver that allows internode communication by allowing a Xeon Phi coprocessor to communicate with an InfiniBand HCA device directly. This can provide good performance in a cluster environment. The CCL provides the benefits of RDMA architecture, which allows applications to write buffers directly to a network device without kernel intervention, resulting in lower latency and higher performance data transfer. The CCL allows RDMA hardware devices on the host to be shared between the host and the Xeon Phi coprocessor. RDMA operations are performed as "verbs," which are functions that are implemented by OFED package. The user-level verbs can be executed by the application running at the same time on the Xeon Phi and the host.

2. *OFED/SCIF*: The MPI can use the TCP/IP or OFED interface to communicate with other MPI processes. The OFED on top of the SCIF interface allows InfiniBand HCA (IBHCA) on the PCIe bus to directly access the physical memory on the Xeon Phi coprocessor. If the IBHCA device is not available, the OFED/SCIF driver emulates the IBHCA device to allow OFED-based applications such as Intel MPI to run on Intel Xeon Phi without a physical HCS device. OFED/SCIF is only used for intranode communication, whereas CCL can be usedf ori nternodec ommunication.

System Software Application Components

The MPSS provides various tools to help manage Xeon Phi–based compute nodes. These tools help in installing and managing the card, particularly in creating user accounts on the coprocessor OS and other utilities to query the cards' status. The sections that follow will look at some important components of the MPSS system software that can help you manage system functions.

micinfo

The micinfo utility, together with the micchek utility (discussed later in this section), can be used to see whether your Xeon Phi hardware is up and running and to collect information about the hardware and system software on your installation. By default, the system installed software puts it in the /opt/intel/mic/bin path. The command must be run in superuser mode to execute properly. The output of an instance of micinfo execution is displayed below. Here I invoked the micinfo command without any arguments, which tells it to print all the information about the device and the system software. You can also invoke it with specific arguments, such as –listdevice or –deviceinfo, to display only part of the following output. The output is categorized in the following sections:

- *System software information*: The host OS version and the Xeon Phi coprocessor MPSS version numbers are displayed. Also displayed for each Xeon Phi device on the platform are the logical device number and name, the firmware version (flash version), the coprocessor OS version, and other information such as the SMC boot loader version and device serial number.

- *Board information*: Information relevant to the board is displayed, including the coprocessor stepping, board SKU, ECC mode on the card, vendor, and system.

- *Core information*: This section is specific to the coprocessor core, including information on the voltage, frequency, and number of active cores.

- *Thermal section*: Information includes the SMC firmware version and the die temperature.

- *Memory section*: This GDDR-related information includes supplier, size, and data transfers peed.

Listing 7-2 provides a sample micinfo utility log.

Listing 7-2. Sample micinfo Utility Log

```
Created Wed May 15 09:26:02 2013

    System Info
            HOST OS                  : Linux
            OS Version               : 2.6.32-279.el6.x86_64
            Driver Version           : 5889-16
            MPSS Version             : 2.1.5889-16
            Host Physical Memory     : 65917 MB

Device No: 0, Device Name: mic0

    Version
            Flash Version            : 2.1.02.0383
            SMC Boot Loader Version  : 1.8.4326
            uOS Version              : 2.6.38.8-g9b2c036
            Device Serial Number     : [XXXXX]

    Board
            Vendor ID                : 8086
            Device ID                : 225c
            Subsystem ID             : 2500
            Coprocessor Stepping ID  : 3
            PCIe Width               : x16
            PCIe Speed               : 5 GT/s
            PCIe Max payload size    : 256 bytes
            PCIe Max read req size   : 4096 bytes
            Coprocessor Model        : 0x01
            Coprocessor Model Ext    : 0x00
            Coprocessor Type         : 0x00
            Coprocessor Family       : 0x0b
            Coprocessor Stepping     : B1
```

```
        Board SKU             : B1QS-7110P
        ECC Mode              : Enabled
        SMC HW Revision       : Product 300W Passive CS

  Cores
        Total No of Active Cores : 61
        Voltage               : 1013000 uV
        Frequency             : 1100000 KHz

  Thermal
        Fan Speed Control     : N/A
        SMC Firmware Version  : 1.13.4570
        FSC Strap             : 14 MHz
        Fan RPM               : N/A
        Fan PWM               : N/A
        Die Temp              : 55 C

  GDDR
        GDDR Vendor           : -----
        GDDR Version          : 0x1
        GDDR Density          : 2048 Mb
        GDDR Size             : 7936 MB
        GDDR Technology       : GDDR5
        GDDR Speed            : 5.500000 GT/s
        GDDR Frequency        : 2750000 KHz
        GDDR Voltage          : 1000000 uV
```

micflash

This utility is installed by default in the /opt/intel/mic/bin path and is used to update the coprocessor firmware, also known as flash memory. It can also be used to query and save the existing flash version before update. It is advisable to check compatibility of a given flash to the device in question by using –compatible switch before doing the flash update.

micsmc

The micsmc utility shows the coprocessor status. It can run in graphical or text mode interface. In graphical mode, it displays for all the Xeon Phi coprocessors installed in the system the details of such features as core utilization, memory usage, temperature, and power and error log. This utility can also be used for setting coprocessor features like ECC, turbo, and others. For example to turn off ECC you can run the sequence provided in Listing 7-3.

Listing 7-3. Sequence to Turn Off ECC

```
command_prompt_host > micctrl -r
command_prompt_host > micctrl -w
command_prompt_host > /opt/intel/mic/bin/micsmc  --ecc disable
command_prompt_host > service mpss restart
To check  ECC status:
command_prompt_host > /opt/intel/mic/bin/micsmc --ecc status
```

miccheck

The miccheck utility is used to check the current install status of a Xeon Phi installation in a node. It detects all devices and checks for proper installation, driver load status, status of the Xeon Phi network stack, and successful boot by POST code. An instance of miccheck output is displayed in Listing 7-4. It shows that the test failed because the flash version did not match the install log file (the manifest).

Listing 7-4. Sample miccehck Utility Output

```
miccheck 2.1.5889-16, created 17:08:24 Mar  8 2013
Copyright 2011-2013 Intel Corporation  All rights reserved

Test 1 Ensure installation matches manifest : OK
Test 2 Ensure host driver is loaded         : OK
Test 3 Ensure drivers matches manifest       : OK
Test 4 Detect all listed devices             : OK
MIC 0 Test 1 Find the device                      : OK
MIC 0 Test 2 Check the POST code via PCI          : OK
MIC 0 Test 3 Connect to the device                : OK
MIC 0 Test 4 Check for normal mode                : OK
MIC 0 Test 5 Check the POST code via SCIF         : OK
MIC 0 Test 6 Send data to the device              : OK
MIC 0 Test 7 Compare the PCI configuration        : OK
MIC 0 Test 8 Ensure Flash versions matches manifest : FAILED
MIC 0 Test 8> Flash version mismatch. Manifest: 2.1.01.0385, Running: 2.1.02.0383
Status: Test failed
```

micctrl

Micctrl is the Swiss army knife for the system administrator. This tool can be used to boot, control, and status check the coprocessor. After the system software is installed on a coprocessor host, micctrl --initdefaults is used to create the default set of the coprocessor OS boot configuration files. Any change in configuration can be reflected by using the micctrl --resetconfig command. The coprocessor can be booted, shut down, reset, and rebooted using micctrl commands with --boot,--shutdown, --reset, and --reboot commands, respectively. Since the coprocessor runs an OS with full user access, the micctrl utility also allows the system administrator to add, remove, or modify users or groups by managing the /etc/passwd file on the coprocessor.

micrasd

The micrasd process can be run on the host to handle log hardware errors and test hardware in the maintenance mode. It can also run as a host Linux system utility as service micras start/stopc ommands.

micnativeloadex

Micnativeloadex is a handy utility to run a cross-compiled binary targeted for the Xeon Phi coprocessor to be launched from the host. It also allows the same functionality from inside the coprocessor to reverse offload. When executed, it copies the binary and dependent libraries to the destination without needing to do it explicitly, as would bethe ca sew henus ingthe s cp/sshc ommand.

Summary

This chapter examined the system software layers needed to support the operations of the Intel Xeon Phi coprocessor. There are three major layers of the system software. Two of these layers run at Ring 0 protection level, which allows them to provide low-latency access to the Xeon Phi hardware. The bottommost layer is the Linux kernel or the Linux coprocessor OS, which interfaces with the hardware and provides basic OS supports, including memory and process management functionalities. The device-driver layer runs on top of the basic OS layer and provides interfaces for the applications and utilities running in Ring 3 layer to access and interact with the Xeon Phi hardware necessary to manage, query, and execute applications on the coprocessor.

The next chapter will look at the tools available for developing applications on Xeon Phi and provide some pointers on how to use these tools.

CHAPTER 8

∎ ∎ ∎

Xeon Phi Application Development Tools

In Chapter 2 we looked at how the Intel compiler may be used to build code for the Intel Xeon Phi coprocessor. This chapter will go more deeply and widely into the tools available for development on Intel Xeon Phi coprocessor. However, Intel tools have a lot of features that are outside of the scope of this book, which only focuses on the features relevant to Xeon Phi development. For a general introduction to the tools, please refer to the documentation installed with the tools themselves. The tools can be divided into four broad categories:

1. Development tools that let you build the code you write for Intel Xeon Phi and Intel Xeon processors and to debug issues with serial and parallel codes

2. Profiling and performance analysis tools that help you optimize the code you have written

3. Libraries that help you perform scientific computing efficiently on Xeon Phi

4. Cluster tools that allow you to run the applications on more than one node or within a node using message passing interface or other parallel methods

The following sections look at only a subset of the tools that are supported on Xeon Phi. Some of the tools such as Intel Inspector XE for checking multithreaded program correctness and performance analysis have not yet been ported to Xeon Phi as of time of writing.

The Application Development Tools

The application development tools allow the developer to compile and debug code for running programs on Intel Xeon Phi. Intel provides a compiler for the following languages that are relevant to Xeon Phi development. The version of the Intel compiler shipping as part of Intel Composer XE 2013 supports the following languages:

1. C/C++

    a. With offload extensions that includes upcoming OpenMP 4.0 specification.

    b. Intel proprietary offload extensions. Although there are a lot of commonalities between OpenMP 4.0 specification and the proprietary extensions, there are some useful features in these extensions that may not be included in the OpenMP 4.0 specifications or may be available later than the features already supported for the Intel compiler. These Intel compiler features are covered in this chapter.

    c. Thread Parallel programming support through Intel Cilk Plus, Intel Threading Building Blocks, OpenMP, and pthread.

2. Fortran

    d. OpenMP 4.0 and Intel proprietary Offload extensions as in C++

    e. Thread Parallel Programming support through OpenMP and Fortran 2008 Parallel Constructs(Coarraya ndD oC oncurrent)

Intel C/C++ Composer XE

The C/C++ development tool is packaged as Intel Composer XE. This package includes the compiler, debugger, and the libraries. Chapter 2 covered some introductory material on how to use these tools to build the offload and cross-compiled version of the source for Intel Xeon Phi coprocessors. This chapter details the compiler-supported syntax and its usage with respect to Intel Xeon Phi.

In addition to generating code for Intel MIC Architecture, the Intel C++ Compiler can also generate code for 32-bit Intel Architecture instruction set architecture (IA-32) and Intel 64-bit–based applications on Intel-based Linux systems. IA-32 architecture applications (32-bit) can run on all Intel-based Linux systems, including Intel 64-bit processors. Intel 64-bit architecture applications are supported on Intel 64-bit-architecture-based Linux systems but not 32-bit Intel processor architecture. The compiler can be used in command shell form or in an integrated development environment (IDE) environment such as Eclipse.

In order to support Xeon Phi programming, the Intel compiler supports the following components.

OpenMP 4.0 and Language Extensions

The Intel compiler has defined and implemented language extensions for C/C++ and Fortran to support offloading computation to Intel Xeon Phi coprocessors. With the release of OpenMP 4.0 to perform that same functionality, the Intel compiler has also implemented this standard to allow your code to take advantage of Xeon Phi coprocessors. Chapter 2 covered OpenMP 4.0 extensions by way of introducing offload programming for Xeon Phi.

This chapter specifically looks at the Intel proprietary extensions implemented in the Intel compiler for programming Xeon Phi. These extensions include keywords to support the computation offload and data transfer between Xeon Phi and the host, which support new compiler pragmas, keywords, macros, intrinsics, class libraries, and application programming interfaces. This chapter specifically covers the extensions for C/C++, but all of these have equivalent Fortran extensions as defined in the Intel Compiler users guide.

Pragmas
pragma offload

The pragma offload pragma allows you to copy in/out data and execute a block of code specified inside the pragma. The pragma greatly simplifies programming by requiring only changes to the code segment you would like to offload. There are some considerations and declarations that need to be made to make sure this block of code and all its functions in its call tree are made available to the coprocessor. This is accomplished by declaring them to be coprocessor executable through declarations. This is supported in both C++ and Fortran compilers and is the preferable offload model when the data are exchanged between a CPU and a coprocessor, but it is limited to arrays of bit-wise copyable elements or scalar data types.

Syntax

```
#pragma offload specifier[ specifier...]
{
  <expressions-statements>
}
```

Where `specifier` can be:

> `target` (target-name [:target-number]) where:

>> 'target name' must be `mic`,

> 'target-number' is a signed an integer value having the following interpretations:

>> -1: The runtime system selects the target. If no coprocessor is available, the program fails with an error message.

>> >=0: the code will be executed on the (coprocessor number = target-number %(modulo) total number of coprocessors). For example, if you have two coprocessors, a number '4' will signify mic0 (4 modulo 2) or the first coprocessor enumerated by the runtime system and so o n.

>> If the 'target-number' is not specified, the runtime system determines which coprocessor to use for offload and falls back to the host execution if no coprocessor is available.

> `if`-specifier: A Boolean expression. If `true`, the offload takes place according to the runtime decision on where to run the code depending on coprocessor availability. If `false`, it runs on the host processor.

> `signal` (tag): An optional integer expression that is used with asynchronous data transfers or compute operations. In this case, the offload computation and data transfer happen concurrently with host computation code after the pragma offload code block. Without this clause, the offload operation is done synchronously, that is, the host code running on the thread causing the offload must wait for the offload code to return. However, you can still have a separate thread running in parallel on the host while the offload thread waits for the coprocessor computation to complete. Note that the 'tag' integer expression could be a pointer value as well. Thus you can use the address of a variable as a signal for an asynchronous offload.

> `wait` (tag[, tag, ...]): An optional integer expression to wait on a previously initiated asynchronous offload call with signal specifier to complete. Note that both the signal and the wait clause must be associated with a target device and they must match. Otherwise, there may be a runtime abort.

> `mandatory`: An optional clause to specify that the execution on the coprocessor is required and cannot fall back to a host processor if the coprocessor is not available. If the correct target hardware is not available, the execution will fail with an error message.

> `offload-parameter` [, offload-parameter,..]: Describes the data transfer directions between host processor and the coprocessor for scalar and pointer data. For pointer data, one can specify the size of array to be bitwise copied to the target device. It is in one of these forms:

>> `in(variable [,variable] [modifier [,modifier]])`: Input to the target; the data are flowing only in one direction from host to the coprocessor.

>> `out(variable [,variable] [modifier [,modifier]])`: Output from the target; the data are flowing only in one direction from coprocessor to the host.

>> `inout(variable [,variable] [modifier [,modifier]])`: Both input and output to and from the target; this is the default if no in or out clause is specified.

>> `nocopy(variable [,variable] [modifier [,modifier]])`: This parameter allows the data previously copied from a previous offload call to the coprocessor to be reused without being sent back and forth between the host and the coprocessor.

The variables in the argument of the offload-parameters can be a C/C++ identifier, an array, or a segment of an array called an *array slice*, which is a contiguous memory area of an array and designated by a start index and the length of the segment. It is of the form:

```
variable [integer expression [: integer expression]]
```

[modifiers]: The modifiers as described in the definition of the offload-parameter can be one of the following:

length(integer expression): The length specifies the number of elements to be copied from the source object pointed to by the pointer variable or variable length array to or from the offload target variable. Note that because they are in disjoint memory regions, the pointer values are completely independent of each other between the host and the coprocessor.

alloc_if(Boolean condition)|free_if(Boolean condition): These constructs allow data persistency on the coprocessor.

alloc_if controls the allocation of a new block of memory on the target when the offload is executed on the target. If the Boolean condition evaluates to true, a new memory allocation is performed for each variable listed in the clause. If false, the existing allocated memory blocks on the target are reused.

free_if controls the deallocation of memory allocated for the pointer variables in an in clause. If the Boolean condition is true, the memory pointed to by each variable listed in the clause is deallocated. If false, no action is taken on the memory pointed to by the variables in the list (i.e., the memory allocated on the target remains intact and can be reused in a subsequent offload call). These two modifiers work in conjunction to provide persistent memory constructs for Xeon Phi processors. If the alloc_if or free_if is omitted, the default assumes alloc_if and free_if is invoked with the Boolean condition set to true. This way each invocation allocates and frees memory on entering and exiting the offloaded block of code.

align(expression): This modifier applies to the pointer variable and requests runtime to allocate memory on the coprocessor to be aligned to size as computed by the integer expression. The expression must evaluate to a number that is the power of two.

alloc(array_slice): Array_slice is a set of elements of the array that needs allocation. The array_slice must be contiguous and of the form (start_element_index:length). Only the portion of the array specified by the in or out expression is transferred, thus reducing the transfer bandwidth requirement. When the array slice has more than one dimension, the second and subsequent index expression must specify all elements of that dimension. For example, in #pragma offload in (data[10:100]:alloc(data[5:1000])), the modifier will allocate 1000 elements on the coprocessor in the index range 5-1004 and copy elements data[10] through data[109] to the target index location 10-109. The first usable array index on the target is 5, as specified by the data_slice expression.

into (var-exp): By default the variable names used in the offload parameter are the same for the CPU and coprocessor side. You can transfer data from one variable in the host processor to a different variable name in the target coprocessor. For example, using #pragma offload in(var1[10:100] : into(var2[100:100])) will copy data from the var1 array on the host side to the var2 array on the coprocessor side.

Offload Execution Process

The execution of an offload process by the compiler runtime is as follows:

1. If there is an 'if', evaluate the if expression. If it evaluates to `false`, execute the region on the host CPU and you are done; if not, continue with the following steps.

2. Acquire the coprocessor. If the target is not available to run the offload code, execute the region on the host CPU and you are done; if the target is acquired, continue.

3. Evaluate alloc_if, free_if, and length expressions used in 'in' and 'out' clauses.

4. Gather all input values and send them to the coprocessor.

5. On the target coprocessor, allocate memory for pointer based on out variables.

6. On the target coprocessor, copy input variable values into the corresponding target variables. This includes scalar variables, arrays, and pointer data.

7. Execute the offloaded region on the coprocessor.

8. On the coprocessor, compute all length expressions used in out clauses.

9. On the coprocessor, gather all variable values that are outputs of the offload.

10. Send output values back from the target to the host CPU.

11. On the host, copy the output values received into the corresponding host CPU variables.

pragma offload_attribute

The `offload_attribute` pragma is used to declare code or data sections that need to be available on the coprocessor. This goes hand in hand with the 'pragma offload' to be used for function and variable declarations. It specifies that all functions and variables declared following this pragma are made available on the coprocessor by generating and allocating appropriate functions codes and data on the coprocessor.

You can also use `declspec` to define the variables and functions that should be available on the Xeon Phi coprocessor, but that requires you to use that for each individual variable or function declaration. However, with the `pragma offload_attribute` pragma given below, you can declare a block of variables or functions to be available on the coprocessor environment.

Syntax

```
#pragma offload_attribute([push, ] target(target-name))
<declarations>|<definitions>
#pragma offload_attribute(pop|{target(none)})
```

Where:

'target name' must be `mic`

`push`: All function and variable declarations and definitions are targeted for Intel MIC architecture until the statement #pragma `offload_attribute(pop|{target(none)})`or end of compilation unit is reached.

`pop/target(none)`:T urnso ffp ragma.

The following example shows how to declare a block of functions and variables so that the compiler can have them available to codes executing on the coprocessor:

```
#pragma offload_attribute (push, target(mic))
<function/variable declarations>
#pragma offload_attribute (pop)
```

pragma offload_transfer and pragma offload_wait

The offload _transfer and offload_wait pragmas are used to perform a synchronous or asynchronous data transfer between the host and Xeon Phi coprocessor. Offload_wait is specifically used for asynchronous data transfer and waits for any previously initiated transfer to complete. This clause is designed to control data transfer between the host and the coprocessor; as such the clause does not have any execution code block as was provided with pragma offload.

Syntax

```
#pragma offload_transfer specifier[ specifier...]
#pragma offload_wait specifier[, specifier...]
```

Where the 'specifier' is the same as defined for 'pragma offload' above and reproduced for easier reference. *target* (target-name [:target-number]) where:

'target name' must be mic,

'target-number' is a signed integer value having the following interpretations:

-1: The runtime system selects the target. If no coprocessor is available, the program fails with an error message.

>=0: The code will be executed on the (coprocessor number = target-number %(modulo) total number of coprocessors). For example, if you have two coprocessors, the number '4' will signify mic0 (4 modulo 2) or the first coprocessor enumerated by the runtime system and so on.

If the 'target-number' is not specified, the runtime system determines which coprocessor to use for offload and falls back to the host execution if no coprocessor is available.

if-specifier: A Boolean expression. If true, the offload takes place according to the runtime decision on where to run the code depending on coprocessor availability. If false, it runs on the host processor.

signal (tag): An optional integer expression that is used with asynchronous data transfers or compute operations. In this case, the offload computation and data transfer happen concurrently with the host computation code after the pragma offload code block. Without this clause, the offload operation is done synchronously, that is the host code running on the thread causing offload must wait for the offload code to return. However, you can still have a separate thread running in parallel on the host while the offload thread waits for the coprocessor computation to complete. Note that the 'tag' integer expression could be a pointer value as well. Thus you can use the address of a variable as a signal for asynchronous offload.

wait (tag[, tag, ...]): An optional integer expression to wait for a previously initiated asynchronous offload call with a signal specifier to complete. Note that both the signal and the wait clause must be associated with a target device and they must match, otherwise, there may be a runtime abort.

mandatory: An optional clause to specify that the execution on the coprocessor is required and cannot fall back to the host processor if the coprocessor is not available. If the correct target hardware is not available, the execution will fail with an error message.

offload-parameter [, offload-parameter,..]: Describes the data transfer directions between the host processor and the coprocessor for scalar and pointer data. For pointer data, you can specify the size of the array to be bitwise copied to the target device. It is in one of these forms:

> in(variable [,variable] [modifier [,modifier]]): Input to the target. The data are flowing only in one direction from host to the coprocessor.

> out(variable [,variable] [modifier [,modifier]]): Output from the target. The data are flowing only in one direction from coprocessor to the host.

> inout(variable [,variable] [modifier [,modifier]]): Both input and output to and from the target. This is the default if no in or out clause is specified.

> nocopy(variable [,variable] [modifier [,modifier]]): This parameter allows the data previously copied from a previous offload call to the coprocessor to be reused without being sent back and forth between the host and the coprocessor.

The variables in the argument of the offload parameters can be a C/C++ identifier, an array, or a segment of an array called an *array slice*, which is a contiguous memory area of an array and designated by a start index and the length of the segment.

variable [integer expression [: integer expression]]

[modifiers] The modifiers as described in the definition of the offload parameter can be one of the following:

> length(integer expression): The length specifies the number of elements to be copied from the source object pointed to by the pointer variable or variable length array to or from the offload target variable. Note that because they are in disjoint memory regions, the pointer values are completely independent of one another between the host and the coprocessor.

> alloc_if(Boolean condition)|free_if(Boolean condition): These constructs allow data persistency on the coprocessor.

> alloc_if controls the allocation of a new block of memory on the target when the offload is executed on the target. If the Boolean condition evaluates to true, a new memory allocation is performed for each variable listed in the clause. If false, the existing allocated memory blocks on the target are reused.

> free_if controls the deallocation of memory allocated for the pointer variables in an in clause. If the Boolean condition is true, the memory pointed to by each variable listed in the clause is deallocated. If false, no action is taken on the memory pointed to by the variables in the list (i.e., the memory allocated on the target remains intact and can be reused in a subsequent offload call). These two modifiers work in conjunction to provide persistent memory constructs for Xeon Phi processors. If the alloc_if or free_if is omitted, the default assumes alloc_if and free_if is invoked with Boolean condition set to true.T his way each invocation allocates and frees memory on entering and exiting the offloaded block of code.

> align(expression): This modifier applies to pointer variables and requests runtime to allocate memory on the coprocessor to be aligned to the size computed by the integer expression. The expression must evaluate to a number that is the power of two.

> alloc(array_slice): array_slice is a set of elements of the array that needs allocation. The array_slice must be contiguous and of the form (start_element_index:length). Only the portion of the array specified by the in or out expression is transferred, thus reducing the transfer bandwidth requirement. When the array slice has more than one

dimension, the second and subsequent index expressions must specify all of the elements of that dimension. For example, the #pragma offload in (data[10:100]:alloc(data[5:1000])) modifier will allocate 1000 elements on the coprocessor in the index range 5-1004 and copy elements data[10] through data[109] to the target index location 10-109. The first usable array index on the target is 5, as specified by the data_slice expression.

into (var-exp): By default the variable names used in the offload parameter are the same for the CPU and coprocessor side. You can transfer data from one variable in the host processor to a different variable name in the target coprocessor. For example, using #pragma offload in(var1[10:100] : into(var2[100:100])) will copy data from the var1 array on the host side to the var2 array on the coprocessor side.

For pragma offload_wait, only the following specifiers are valid:

```
target ( target-name [ :target-number ])
if ( if-specifier )
wait ( tag[, tag ...] )
```

Asynchronous Data Transfer Over PCI Express

The attribute offload_transfer with the implementation of a signal provides a way to transfer data asynchronously. The tag in the signal specifier is associated with the data to be transferred. The complementary wait specifier usually follows the some host computation and causes code execution at that point to wait for the data transfer initiated with signal clause to complete.

The wait clause must be executed after the signal clause specific transfer is initiated and must be enforced if the wait call is executed in a different thread. Otherwise, a runtime program abort will happen.

The source code in Listing 8-1 shows how to perform an asynchronous data transfer by using the offload_transfer pragma. To test the asynchronous transfer, we allocate 64MB of memory (memory pointer a) on the host at line 51. We also preallocate data on the coprocessor at line 60-63 so that the transfer time does not include the data allocation time. Listing 8-2 shows the output of a run of this code on a host with the Xeon Phi processor.

Listing 8-1. An example of asynchronous data transfer using Intel compiler offload pragmas

```
34. #include <stdio.h>
35. #include <stdlib.h>
36. #include <omp.h>
37.
38. //Define number of floats for 64 MB data transfer
39. #define SIZE (64*1000*1000/sizeof(float))
40. #define ITER    1
41. // set cache line size alignment
42. #define ALIGN   (64)
43. __declspec(target(MIC)) static float  *a;
44. extern double elapsedTime (void);
45. int main()
46. {
47.         double startTime,  duration;
48.         int i, j;
49.
50.         //allocate a
51.         a = (float*)_mm_malloc(SIZE*sizeof(float),ALIGN);
52.
```

```
53.          //initialize arrays
54.          #pragma omp parallel for
55.          for (i=0; i<SIZE;i++)
56.          {
57.                  a[i]=(float)1.0f;
58.          }
59.          // Allocate memory on the card
60.          #pragma offload_transfer target(mic:0) \
61.            in(a:length(SIZE) free_if(0) alloc_if(1) align(ALIGN) )
62.
63.
64.          // test synchronous transfer time
65.          startTime = elapsedTime();
66.              //transfer data over the PCI express bus
67.            #pragma offload_transfer target(mic:0) \
68.              in(a:length(SIZE) free_if(0) alloc_if(0) align(ALIGN) )
69.
70.          duration = elapsedTime() - startTime;
71.          printf("Synchronous data transfer time %lf milliseconds \n",duration*1000);
72.          // test asynchronous transfer time
73.          startTime = elapsedTime();
74.              //transfer data over the PCI express bus
75.      #pragma offload_transfer target(mic:0) \
76.      in(a:length(SIZE) free_if(0) alloc_if(0) align(ALIGN) ) signal(a)
77.
78.          duration = elapsedTime() - startTime;
79.          printf("Asynchronous data transfer time after start of the transfer %lf milliseconds
            \n",duration*1000);
80.          // test asynchronous transfer time
81.          startTime = elapsedTime();
82.              #pragma offload_wait target(mic:0) wait(a)
83.
84.          duration += elapsedTime() - startTime;
85.          printf("Asynchronous data transfer time with wait clause %lf milliseconds
            \n",duration*1000);
86.          // free memory on the card
87.          #pragma offload_transfer target(mic:0) \
88.                  in(a:length(SIZE) alloc_if(0) free_if(1) )
89.
90.
91. //free the host system memory
92.          _mm_free(a);
93.          double GB = SIZE*sizeof(float)/(1000.0*1000.0*1000.0);
94.          double GBps = ITER*GB/duration;
95.          printf("SP ArraySize =  %0.4lf MB, ALIGN=%dB, PCIe Data transfer bandwidth Host->Device
            GB/s = %0.2lf\n", GB*1000.0, ALIGN,  GBps);
96.    return 0;
}
```

Listing 8-2. Output from the Code Running on a Host with Xeon Phi Coprocessor

- ./pciebw.out

```
Synchronous data transfer time 9.397984 milliseconds
Asynchronous data transfer time after start of the transfer 2.367973 milliseconds
Asynchronous data transfer time with wait clause 9.452820 milliseconds
SP ArraySize =  64.0000 MB, ALIGN=64B, PCIe Data transfer bandwidth      Host -> Device  GB/s = 6.77
```

At lines 67 through 69 of the source code, the code performs a synchronous transfer by invoking 'offload_transfer' without the signal command:

```
#pragma offload_transfer target(mic:0) \
   in(a:length(SIZE) free_if(0) alloc_if(0) align(ALIGN) )
```

The output shows that the synchronous transfer took approximately *9.39*m illiseconds.

Then the code performs an asynchronous transfer at lines 75 and 76 by invoking 'offload_transfer' with a signal(a) clause. This causes the code to start the transfer and return almost immediately. It takes approximately *2.36* milliseconds to do this, as shown in Listing 8-2. Finally, the code waits for the transfer to complete with pragma offload_wait with the wait(a) clause in line 82. We see from Listing 8-2 that the total time to start the asynch transfer plus wait time is *9.45* milliseconds, close to the synchronous transfer time. You can do some computing on a host on the same thread in between the start of the transfer and the offload_wait pragmas.

Keywords

There aret wok eywords: _Cilk_offload and _Cilk_shared. _Cilk_offload allows you to offload a function to a card. You can use _Cilk_offload with _Cilk_spawn to perform an asynchronous offload. What if you want to execute a loop on the Xeon Phi rather than a function? In order to run a loop rather than a function, you can use _Cilk_offload with the _Cilk_for construct. The _Cilk_shared clause is used to declare the functions or data to be shared between the host processor and the coprocessor. For example, before calling _Cilk_offload to offload a function, you need to declare them with a _Cilk_shared clause. The memory declared with _Cilk_shared is at the same virtual address on the host and coprocessor.

I will not be covering syntax of these keywords here, but you can find those details in the Intel C++ Compiler XE users and reference guides installed as part of the Intel Composer XE package.

Using Shared Virtual Memory

We have seen in pragma offload section above that the data need to be bitwise copyable in order to be shared between the host and the coprocessor. However, Intel Compiler C++ runtime library provides a shared virtual memory model where the data do not need to be bitwise copyable. For example, it can use pointers or composition of 'C' structures and pointers. Pointers to a shared variable have the same value, although they point to different virtual address spaces on the host processor and the coprocessor. This allows offload code to work on the linked data structures as the pointer values are preserved in their respective disjoint virtual address space. Here the runtime maintains the data consistencies between the copies residing on the host and the coprocessor(s).

You need to use the _Cilk_shared clause for declaring such data. There are also library functions, _Offload_shared_malloc(), _Offload_shared_aligned_malloc(), _Offload_shared_free(),a nd _Offload_shared_aligned_free() that allow you to allocate space for such shared objects. The data in the shared virtual address are synchronized between the host and the coprocessor at the following points during program executions:

1. When the offload function is invoked on the host and upon entering the offload function on the target coprocessor.

2. On return from the offload execution call to the host processor.

No other synchronization point exists, so simultaneous access to the shared memory location outside these sync points creates a race condition.

Valid Use of the Keywords

The following are some of the rules for using the _Cilk_shared and _Cilk_offloadk eywords:

- Apply them to C++ classes. In this case all the member functions of the class and the objects instantiated of that class are shared.

- Apply them to static fields of a class.

- Assign an address of a shared variable to a shared pointer.

- The functions called directly or indirectly by _Cilk_offload must be declared as _Cilk_sharedo rp ointer-to-shared.

- Pointer arguments passed to an offload function must be pointer-to-shared.

- Global variables and functions referenced within _Cilk_offload must be marked _Cilk_shared.

- _Cilk_shared cannot be used on a field in a structure, a static variable, or a local variable.

Macros

The functions or code fragment of the offload functions can be designated to be compiled for Xeon Phi or MIC coprocessor only. This is useful when you want to use some intrinsics or assembly instructions that are only valid for the Xeon Phi instruction set and will not compile for the host. This is done through the macro __MIC__r ecognized by the compiler and designated as the part of the code that should be built for Xeon Phi only. Do not use it inside a #pragma offload statement, but rather inside a function offloaded to the Xeon Phi card. The reason for not using it inside a #pragma offload is that the Intel compiler goes through two different phases while compiling the source code. In the first phase, it compiles for the host, and in the second phase, it compiles for Xeon Phi. In some cases where a variable is defined on the host side, it is only used inside an offload region bracketed by the __MIC__m acro and is not explicitly passed by the pragma offload clause. The variable will not be sent in when the code is compiled for the host. This is because the __MIC__ macro is undefined in this phase and removes the code that uses this variable. As a result, the host side code will not send in the variable. However, the code version created for Xeon Phi will need this variable, which is not available on the coprocessor and will cause the runtime abort as the variable is not sent in by the code running on the host.

Listing 8-3 shows the effect of using the __MIC__ macro inside an offload region directly. Listing 8-4 shows the host version of the code in Listing 8-3. Listing 8-5 shows the coprocessor version of the code in Listing 8-3. Listing 8-6 presents the output for the code in Listing 8-3.

Listing 8-3. Wrong Use of the __MIC__ Macro

```
int main()
{
   printf("y = %d\n", f());
}

int f()
{
  int x=1, y=3;
  #pragma offload target(mic)
  {
      #ifdef __MIC__
         y = x;
      #endif
         y++;
  }

return y;
}
```

Listing 8-4. Host Version of Listing 8-3

```
//host version of f()
int f()
{
  int x, y;
  #pragma offload target(mic)
  {
         y++; // only sends in Y variable, x is not sent in.
  }
}
```

Listing 8-5. Coprocessor Version of the Code in Listing 8-3

```
// coprocessor version of f()
int f()
{
  int x, y;
  #pragma offload target(mic)
  {
      y = x; // Causes error as x is not sent in from the host side
  }
}
// only sends in Y variable, x is not sent in.
```

Listing 8-6. Ouput of the Code in Listing 8-3

```
offload error: unexpected number of variable descriptors
offload error: process on the device 0 unexpectedly exited with code 1
```

This macro is only defined by the compiler while compiling coprocessors code. It is undefined when you use the `'-no-offload'` compile switch. If you use the `'-mmic'` command line option, which instructs the compiler to build for the coprocessor only, this macro is defined. This macro will be true for all future MIC architecture. If you want to build for Intel Xeon Phi architecture but not for any future architecture, you may want to use the __KNC__ macro. The **__INTEL_OFFLOAD** macro is used when the code should not be built when the target is host processor only executable. It is defined by the compiler when building offload code for the host processor and the coprocessor but undefined when you use the `'-mmic'` or `'-no-offload'`c ompiles witch.

Intrinsics

Intrinsics allow you to use C/C++ functions and variables for readability instead of assembly codes in your source code. These are necessary where there are no corresponding C/C++ language constructs to perform the same work as intended. When used inside a code, they are inlined by the compiler, thus removing the function call overhead. New intrinsics that correspond to Xeon Phi coprocessors instruction set (Intel Initial Many Core Instructions) have been defined on top of existing intrinsics implemented in Intel Compilers. These intrinsics for Xeon Phi architecture enable you to use the vector processing capabilities of Xeon Phi processors.

There are two versions of these intrinsics: one for the nonmasked and the other for masked operations of the corresponding vector operations. The intrinsics are defined in immintrin.h and need to be included in your source file where you want to use them.

Xeon Phi intrinsics operate on vectors. There are 32 vectors (v0-v31), each having 512 bits corresponding to underlying hardware registers of Xeon Phi coprocessor. These vectors are represented by the new proprietary __m512 (single precision vector), __m512i(int32/int64 vector), and __m512d (double precision vector) data types. The compiler aligns __m512 local and global data types to 64-byte boundaries on the stack. Note that you cannot operate these data types through arithmetic instructions such as +, −, and so forth. You must use these on either side of an assignment, a return value, or as a parameter in a statement. These can only be used with the intrinsics defined for these data types. You can use the data type as a union to access individual elements.

These instructions operate on the same memory address space as the standard Intel 64-bit instructions, using the vectors for packed data sources and results. Vector mask support is provided by eight vector mask registers and allows conditional execution over 16-SP or 8-DP elements in a vector instruction.

Intel compiler also provides a set of intrinsics for Xeon Phi coprocessors that are vector variants of the corresponding scalar math operations. These are referred to as the Short Vector Math Library (SVML). They take vector elements and perform scalar math operations on each element of the source vectors. The result of the operation is returned in a vector. The supported SVML operations include the following for both single precision, double precision, and integers where applicable:

- Division operations: quotient of a division, reminder of division operation

- Error function operations: inverse cumulative distribution, error functions, complementary error function, inverse error function

- Exponential operations: Exp10, Exp2, Expe, exponential value of one argument raised toa nother

- Logarithmic operations: Log10, Log2, Log-natural logarithm, calculate the signed exponent

- Rounding operations: ceiling (ceil), floor, round off to nearby integer, round off to nearest even integer, truncate to nearest integer not larger in the absolute value

- Square root and cube root operations: sqrt, invsqrt, hypotenuse, cuberoot

- Trigonometric operations: various categories of sines, cosines, tans, and their inverses

Please refer to the Intel C++ Compiler XE users and reference guide provided with the Intel Composer XE package for details on the available intrinsics.

C++C lassL ibraries

In addition to the intrinsics defined above, C++ class libraries have been defined to abstract the 512-bit vector operations on Xeon Phi for several math routines. These libraries provide similar functionality to that provided by Intel C++ libraries for SSE2 instructions on Intel Xeon processors. The following C++ classes are implemented to support operations on Xeon Phi vectors objects and declared in the micvec.h header file:

- F64vec8: 8 elements of 64-bit signed double precision vector class

- I64vec8: 8 elements of 64-bit-long integer vector class

- F32vec16: 16 elements of 32-bit single precision float vector class

- I32vec16: 16 elements of 32-bit integer vector class

- Is32vec16: 16 elements of signed 32-bit integer vector class

- Iu32vec16: 16 elements of unsigned 32-bit integer vector class

For example, if you want to add two 16-element 32-bit SP vectors and generate a 16-element 32-bit vector, you can use the following code:

```
F32vec16 A,B,C;
// initialize the vector elements
C = A + B; // results addition of A and B to get the results in C
```

Application Programming Interfaces

Intel Compiler implements a set of application programming interfaces (APIs), which are equivalent to host processor APIs but targeted toward the coprocessor and can be executed inside the code running on the host to set the coprocessor runtime environment. Each of these APIs take two additional arguments: target_type, which can be TARGET_NONE, TARGET_MIC, or TARGET_HOST, and target_number, which is a signed integer and interpreted as defined in the pragma offload section earlier in this chapter. You can set the target_type to DEFAULT_TARGET_TYPE,w hich is set to TARGET_MIC, and target_number to DEFAULT_TARGET_NUMBER, which is set to 0. For example, omp_set_num_threads(num_threads) is an OpenMP API to set the number of execution threads for OpenMP applications. There is an equivalent API for Xeon Phi called omp_set_num_threads_target(target_type, target_number, num_threads) to set the number of coprocessor threads.

A set of offload APIs provides control and memory allocation during runtime on the coprocessors. These APIs include _Offload_number_of_devices, _Offload_get_device_number, _Offload_get_physical_device_number, _Offload_shared_malloc, _Offload_shared_free, _Offload_shared_aligned_malloc, _Offload_shared_aligned_free, _Offload_signaled, _Offload_report, omp_set_device_num,a nd omp_get_device_num. There are many more APIs that are not covered here. These APIs are defined within the offload.h header file shipped with the Intel Compiler.

Environment Variables

Once an application is built with offload extensions and run on a host with Xeon Phi coprocessor, its behavior can be controlled and logged with the help of environment variables on the host. For example, you can set the number of threads running on the coprocessor using the environment variables presented in the following sections, which may be different from what is set on the host.

MIC_ENV_PREFIX

The execution environment on the coprocessor itself can be modified in the same way it can be done on the host environment. For example, you can set `OMP_NUM_THREADS` to set the number of OpenMP threads to be run on the host and coprocessor. The problem may arise if you want to set the number of threads differently on the host and the coprocessor. `MIC_ENV_PREFIX` provides such a facility to differentiate between the host and coprocessor environment variables. By default all environment variables set on the host are passed to the coprocessor. Using `MIC_ENV_PREFIX`, you can set the prefixes so that the environment variables with this prefix are only passed to the coprocessor runtime environment. For example, setting `MIC_ENV_PREFIX=MIC` will allow you to set `MIC_OMP_NUM_THRADS=240` and `OMP_NUM_THREADS=16`. This allows you to run OpenMP applications with different numbers of threads on the host processor and the Xeon Phi coprocessor. The environment variable that is set on the coprocessor will have the MIC prefix removed, that is it will be set to `OMP_NUM_THREADS` on the coprocessor.

When you have multiple coprocessor in a host and you want to specify environment variables specific to a coprocessor, you can do so by using `mic_prefix_card_number_var=value`. For example, to set the number of OpenMP threads on coprocessor 2 to 60 instead of 240, you can set the environment variable on the host to `MIC_2_OMP_NUM_THREADS=60`. Other environment variables supported by Intel Compiler to support coprocessor execution are listed in the sections that follow.

OFFLOAD_REPORT

Outputs offload execution time and bytes exchanged between the host and coprocessor. This environment variable is equivalent to using the `_Offload_report`A PI.

The supported values are:

- 1: Produces a report about time taken for offload work

- 2: Produces time taken and bytes transferred

- 3: Add details of offload activity

- None:N oo utputp roduced(default)

MIC_LD_LIBRARY_PATH

Specifies the location for a target-shared object on the host. This is required by the compiler runtime to discover the dependent dynamic library files for the offloaded code to be sent over to the coprocessor for successful execution. This is set by default when you set up the Composer XE environment variable through compilervars.sh.

MIC_PROXY_IO

Because MIC devices are not directly connected to the I/O devices on the host, they are to be proxied by the compiler runtime environment. This environment variable enables (1) or disables (0) the proxy of stderr or stdout to the coprocessor. If enabled, which is the default setting, the "printf" and other outputs to stdout or stderr devices will be reflected on the host from the code executing on the coprocessor.

MIC_STACKSIZE

This environment variable is used to specify the stack size of the main thread for the offload. It corresponds to ulimit -s (BASH shell) or limit stacksize (C shell) on the host Linux environment.

Syntax: `MIC_STACKSIZE = integerB|K|M|G|T`, where the integer is the value of the stack size requested and B, K, M, G, and T stand for bytes, kilobytes, megabytes, gigabytes, and terabytes, respectively. The default stack size on the coprocessor is 12M.

OFFLOAD_DEVICES

This environment variable restricts the offload process to coprocessors listed as comma-separated list values of this environment variable. The devices are numbered from 0 to the number of devices on system-1. Setting OFFLOAD_DEVICES=0,2 will restrict offloading to device number 0 (first) and device number 2 (3rd) coprocessor in a system with three or more coprocessors.

OFFLOAD_INIT

Specifies the runtime and when to initialize the coprocessors in a system. The values are on_start, where all the coprocessors are initialized upon entering the main, on_offload, where specific coprocessors are initialized immediately before the offload to those specific coprocessors, and on_offload_all(default), where all available coprocessors, regardless of whether code will be offloaded to them or not, are initialized immediately before the first offload in an application.

Compiler Options

Because the same code can be used on hosts with or without Xeon Phi coprocessors, Intel compiler defined various compiler switches to control the compilation of the code for the coprocessors. For example, you can turn off the offload compilation portion of the source code with a switch. Also the compiler can provide various diagnostic messages related to offload extensions and their behavior with appropriate switches, as follows:

- -mmic: This compiler switch is used to cross-compile the source for Xeon Phi targets. Binary code produced with this switch runs natively under the coprocessor OS.

- -no-offload: This allows you to build the source ignoring pragmas related to Xeon Phi offload. Thus you can make sure the code generated runs only on the host processor.

- -offload-attribute-target: This causes the compiler to make all the file scope functions and the data objects in the source file available for execution on Xeon Phi. This achieves equivalent functionality by using offload attribute target(mic) with all of these functions and data in the sourcec ode.

- -offload-option: Provides options to be used for building Xeon Phi specific codes.

- -opt-report-phase=offload: Allows you to generate an optimization report during offload specific compilation. It prints out the input and output variables the host sends to the offload target and variables that the host receives from the target.

CreatingO ffloadL ibraries

You can use xiar or 'xild –lib' to create static libraries with offload code to be used in offload applications. In order to do so, you need to first create a library using –offload-build option with xiar or 'xild –lib'. This will create two versions of the library: one for the CPU, lib.a, and one for the MIC, libMIC.a. For example, xiar -offload-build rcs libtest.a obja.o objb.o will create two libraries: libtest.a containing obja.o, objb.o, and libtestMIC.a containing objaMIC.o, objbMIC.o objects. When linking in these libraries with your application, use the –ltest option, which will cause the compiler to link in appropriate libraries for the host and Xeon Phi.

Intel Fortran Composer XE

Intel Fortran compiler allows you to write code that runs natively on Intel Xeon Phi coprocessor or build host code with part of execution offloaded to Xeon Phi coprocessor. Many of the supports described in the C/C++ compiler for Xeon Phi are also available on the Fortran compiler, which are relevant to Fortran language programmers. Because the semantics are the same for Fortran as they are for C++, you may refer to the C/C++ sections earlier in this chapter for detailed descriptions of these constructs.

Directives

Directives are equivalent to C/C++ pragmas. Please refer to the Intel Compiler XE users and reference guide installed with the compiler for syntax of these directives. The explanations of these directives are the same as those described in the C/C++ section earlier and will not be covered here. Data exchanges with these offload directives are scalars, arrays, and Fortran-derived types, which are bitwise copyable.

A brief description of the directives supported by Intel Fortran compiler follows:

ATTRIBUTES OFFLOAD directive: This directive is used to specify the variables and procedure that should be made available on the coprocessor. All procedures called from the procedure marked with ATTRIBUTES OFFLOADs hould also be defined with the same directive so they are available on the coprocessor. The compiler will issue warnings for procedures and data referenced in the offload section that are not marked with the ATTRIBUTE OFFLOADdir ective.

OFFLOAD directive: This directive transfers data and executes the statements and directives following this directive on the coprocessor. The statement following the OFFLOAD directive must be one of the following, which are executed on the coprocessor:

- An OpenMP PARALLEL, PARALLEL SECTIONS or PARALLEL DOdir ectives

- A CALLs tatement

- An assignment statement where the right-hand side only calls a function

OFFLOAD_TRANSFER/OFFLOAD_WAIT directive: Used for asynchronous data transfer between the host and the coprocessor. Usage is the same as defined in the C/C++ section above.

OFFLOAD BEGIN and END OFFLOAD directive: Causes a group of statements bracketed by these directives to execute on the coprocessor. This is similar to the OFFLOAD directive but allows you to offload a block of code. However, you cannot have OpenMP directives inside the code block within these two directives, where you would need to use the OFFLOADd irectiveo nly.

Macros

Intel Fortran compiler also supports __MIC__, __KNC__, and __INTEL_OFFLOAD macros defined in the C/C++ section earlieri nt hisc hapter.

Application Programming Interfaces

The APIs are provided as part of the mic_lib.f90 file. These functions allow you to deal with multiple coprocessors, calling functions on the CPU to modify the coprocessor's execution environment.

Environment Variables, Compiler Options, and Creating Static Libraries

Please refer to corresponding sections described earlier in this chapter related to C/C++ compiler.

Third-Party Compilers Supporting Xeon Phi

There are few third-party compilers that support the Xeon Phi coprocessor. The main issue with compiler support for Xeon Phi is the lack of standards for supporting offload compilation. With the standardization of OpenMP 4.0, more compilers will support the Xeon Phi coprocessor.

CAPSC ompiler

CAPSc ompilers[1] OpenCL backend supports code generation for Xeon Phi coprocessor through OpenHMPP and OpenACCd irectives.

Debugging Xeon Phi Applications

There are two solutions available for debugging applications with code running on Xeon Phi coprocessors:

1. Intel Debugger with Eclipse IDE (integrated design environment) and command linei nterface

2. GNUd ebuggerf orX eonP hic oprocessor

Intel Debugger

Intel debugger (IDB) has been extended to support Intel Xeon Phi architecture for debugging C++ and Fortran programs in the command line or graphical user interface (GUI) running on the host system. IDB allows you to debug both the offloaded as well as the native applications. For native applications, you need to attach to a process running on the coprocessor.

The debugger for Xeon Phi coprocessor support is modified to consist of two loosely coupled debuggers. The *host debugger*(idbc) component runs on the host. It launches and debugs the offload application built with Xeon Phi support. Under the GUI environment the *target debugger*(idbc_mic) is launched by the host debugger when it encounters an offload directive to start executing on the coprocessor by attaching to the offloaded process. For applications that run natively on the Xeon Phi, you can use the target debugger by attaching to the process running natively on the coprocessor, or you can start the application with the target debugger. The auto-attach feature is not available when using the command line version of the debugger. Under Eclipse IDE, when debugging offload code, the debugger automatically switches to view and control code running on the Xeon Phi coprocessor. The behavior of the IDB for debugging the offload code can be describes as follows:

1. The host debugger starts the main application process.

2. When an offload pragma or declaration is encountered in C++ or Fortran, the offload process gets launched on the coprocessor.

---

[1]http://www.caps-entreprise.com/products/caps-compilers/

3. The debugger remotely attaches to the offloaded process running on the Xeon Phi through a debug agent downloaded to the coprocessor, and it communicates to the host debug process through the TCP/IP.

4. Once the offload process finishes, the view changes to host process.

5. Once the host process has finished, the offload process is removed and the debugger detachesf romt heo ffloadp rocess.

Please refer to the Intel debugger users and reference guide for the details on using Intel debugger for debugging Xeon Phi applications.

Third-PartyD ebuggers

There are several third-party debuggers that support debugging codes built for Intel Xeon Phi coprocessor. Some of thema red iscussedb elow.

GNU Debugger

The GNU debugger (GDB) supports the Intel Xeon Phi coprocessor and is provided as part of the MPSS package. The support for Xeon Phi is provided through native and cross-remote debug versions. It supports C/C++ and Fortran and Parallel Debug Support (PDBX). There are three components to the GDB for Xeon Phi. Two of the components are for host-based debugging, that is you start the debugging session on the host, and the other one is for Xeon Phi native debugging. The host-based debugging components are the debugger (x86_64-k1om-linux-gdb) and the debug server (gdbserver) running on the Xeon Phi. The native debugger is gdb.

The debugger allows you to run gdb commands on the coprocessor so you can obtain coprocessor-related information. For example, you can view all the vector registers and masks using the command "info registers zmm." Listing 8-7 is the output of such a command executed in the gdb running natively on Xeon Phi coprocessor.

Listing 8-7. Output of "info registers zmm" Command in Xeon Phi Native Version of GDB

```
(gdb) info register zmm
k0              0x0     0
k1              0x0     0
k2              0x0     0
k3              0x0     0
k4              0x0     0
k5              0x0     0
k6              0x0     0
k7              0x0     0
zmm0            {v16_float = {0x0 <repeats 16 times>}, v8_double = {0x0, 0x0, 0x0, 0x0, 0x0, 0x0,
0x0, 0x0}, v64_int8 = {
    0x0 <repeats 64 times>}, v32_int16 = {0x0 <repeats 32 times>}, v16_int32 = {0x0 <repeats 16
times>}, v8_int64 = {0x0,
    0x0, 0x0, 0x0, 0x0, 0x0, 0x0, 0x0}, v4_uint128 = {0x00000000000000000000000000000000,
    0x00000000000000000000000000000000, 0x00000000000000000000000000000000,
0x00000000000000000000000000000000}}
```

TotalView

TotalView by Rogue Wave Software is a popular commercial debugging tool for single and multithreaded application and provides support for debugging Intel Xeon Phi coprocessor.[2] It supports OpenMP and MPI debugging.

Distributed Debugging Tool

The Distributed Debugging Tool (DDT) is a commercial debugging tool developed by Allinea software that supports Intel Xeon Phi.[3] The tools support OpenMP and MPI debugging in addition to scalar code debugging. It can be used forc lusterd ebuggingp urposes.

Optimization Tool: Intel Vtune Amplifier XE

Intel Vtune Amplifier XE provides a GUI and command line tool for understanding an application runtime profile and allows you to detect the critical code sections, also known as hot spots, and optimize the code for better performance on the Xeon Phi coprocessor. It can also provide you with critical information such as bandwidth used by your application during its runtime, threading behavior, load imbalance, and so forth to help detect possible performance bottlenecks.

Intel Xeon Phi hardware implements performance monitoring hardware to allow low overhead profiling of the runtime execution behavior of applications.[4] The Vtune Amplifier XE comes with a sampling driver that gets installed on the Xeon Phi coprocessor OS. This driver is responsible for communicating with the Xeon Phi hardware performance monitoring unit and collecting hardware events corresponding to applications executed on the coprocessor. You can start the event collection process from the host using the GUI or command line interface provided by the Vtune Amplifier XE tool. The help documentation installed is a good guide on how to use the Vtune Amplifier XE. Here I will provide only a rough outline on how to use the tools for profiling the Amplifier XE binaries.

In order to collect performance data for applications running on Xeon Phi, you need to take following steps:

1. Set up a project on the Vtune Amplifier XE that is responsible for executing application that will run on the Xeon Phi coprocessor. Because the application is executed from the host, you need to make sure the scripts called from the project set-up target specification performs the necessary upload of the executable with the needed dependent files and executes the application on the Xeon Phi. You also need to build your binary with the appropriate debug symbols (-g –debug inline-debug-info), so the tool can point you to the source location of the hotspots located by the tool. Then you can specify the search directories using the set-up screen so that the source files are locatable by the tool. You may also need to add the Composer XE library path containing mic libraries (e.g., /opt/intel/composer_xe_2013/lib/mic) and the vmlinux (typically /lib/firmware/mic) to locate symbols related to these runtime libraries.

2. Start the performance event collection. You start this event collection analysis by clicking the 'New analysis' ('>') button on the toolbar. This will open an analysis window, where you can select various predefined analysis types include 'Lightweight hotspot.' The "Lightweight hotpot" profile is a good starting point to get an initial understanding of the application runtime profile on the coprocessor. Default collection happens on coprocessor '0.' For other processors, you can enter the value or comma-separated values

---

[2]http://www.roguewave.com/products/totalview.aspx
[3]http://www.allinea.com/intel-xeon-phi/
[4]http://software.intel.com/sites/default/files/forum/278102/intelr-xeon-phitm-pmu-rev1.01.pdf

in the field "List of Intel Xeon Phi coprocessor cards." Click the Start button to begin the collection process. The default "Lightweight hotpot" collects CPU_CLK_UNHALTED and INSTRUCTIONS_EXECUTED events. You can create a custom event for the Xeon Phi coprocessor by clicking the "Create New Analysis type" (showed using symbol $\Lambda+$) button on the Analysis type toolbar. From the drop-down list, select "New Knights Corner Event-based Sampling Analysis." This will bring up the Custom Analysis window, as shown in Figure 8-1, where you can add custom events available for the Xeon Phi processor by clicking the "ADD" button in the dialog box. Note that the Add custom analysis dialog box may be small and may need to be stretched by grabbing the lower right corner before you cans eet heb uttons.

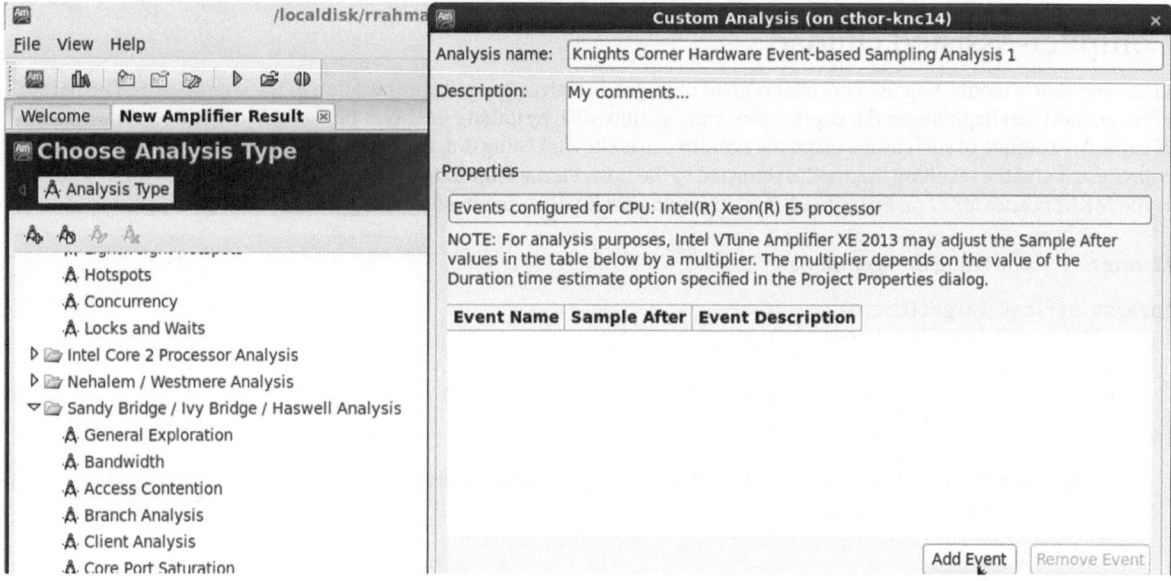

Figure 8-1. *Vtune Custom Analysis for Xeon Phi*

3. View and interpret the results. This is the analysis phase, which is similar to any other Intel platform performance analysis. Here you look at the application hotspots and use your hardware knowledge of the Xeon Phi coprocessor, as discussed in Part 1 of this book, to understand what the possible issues are. Using application knowledge and tuning expertise, you may be able to modify code, user compiler switches, and pragmas to optimize the performance of the whole application.

Libraries

Intel provides the Intel Math Kernel Library (MKL) optimized for Xeon Phi. It provides technical computing applications for extracting performance from Xeon Phi coprocessors for commonly used math functions. MKL can be included in your code in two primary ways. You can use the Xeon Phi version of the library to link to the native version of the code or call the MKL routine from the offloaded version of the code.

Native or Symmetric Execution

Native execution occurs when the application runs completely in the Xeon Phi coprocessor under the coprocessor OS. This requires minimal changes to the application and may benefit some code where the processes can execute in parallel with host processes, such as in symmetric mode. To build an application that runs natively, you need to use the –mmic switch, as discussed earlier in this chapter on compiler usage. You also need to link in the Xeon Phi version of the MKL. The native version of the MKL library is by default installed in the /opt/intel/composer_xe_2013/mkl/lib/mic folder in your build system. Once built and linked this way, you can execute this code under the native OS or use the binary as part of an MPI run in symmetric mode. I cover the MPI execution details later in this chapter.

Note that you need to send all the necessary dependent libraries to Xeon Phi for execution and set the runtime environment appropriately for dynamically linked libraries.

Compiler-Assisted Offload

In this execution model, you use compiler offload or target directives to send computation to the coprocessor. The part of the execution that happens on the coprocessor can call into MKL by linking the Xeon Phi version of MKL to that section of code. An example of such usage using the sgemm call is shown Listing 8-8. Here matrices A, B, and C are sent to the coprocessor and the resulting matrix C is returned to the host. Please refer to Intel MKL Library users guide on how to link in the MKL libraries for Xeon Phi offload. It is similar to host linking except a different path is used to get the libraries.[5]

Listing 8-8. Code Using the sgemm Call

```
#pragma offload target(mic:0) \
    in(A: length(matrix_elements) ) \
    in(B: length(matrix_elements) ) \
    in(transa, transb, N, alpha, beta) \
    inout(C:length(matrix_elements) )
    {
        sgemm(&transa, &transb, &N, &N, &N, &alpha, A, &N, B, &N,
                &beta, C, &N);
    }
```

Using the Automatic Offload Version of the MKL Library

In this case, the MKL library runtime executing on the host processor detects the presence of a coprocessor and can automatically offload some of the processing to the coprocessor to take advantage of additional computing power provided by Xeon Phi. This usage model enables you to link your application to the MKL as you would normally do on the host OS, however, using an environment variable or a function call, thus providing performance improvement with fewer changes to the code than compiler-assisted offload. MKL determines the best division of work between the host and the coprocessors. However, you can specify custom work division using the environment variable of utility functions provided by MKL. You need to set MKL_MIC_ENABLE to 1 or call mkl_mic_enable() in your code to activate automatic offload of MKL computations to Xeon Phi coprocessor. Other relevant environment variables and APIs are:

> MKL_HOST_WORKDIVISION: Its value is a floating point number between 0.0 and 1.0 and specifies the fraction of work that will be done by the host processor. For example, a value of 0.2 will indicate 20 percent of the work is done on host processor and 80 percent is offloaded to coprocessors in the system. Note that corresponding API is mkl_mic_set_workdivision().

---

[5]Intel MKL provides a link line advisor (http://software.intel.com/en-us/articles/intel-mkl-link-line-advisor) to help with writing a file to link in MKL.

MKL_MIC_WORKDIVISION: Indicates the fraction of work to be performed on the Xeon Phi coprocessors. This divides the work among all the coprocessors available in the system. If you want to target specific coprocessors, you can use MKL_MIC_<coprocessor_number>_WORKDIVISION. The corresponding API is mkl_mic_set_workdivision().

MKL_MIC_MAX_MEMORY: Specifies the maximum coprocessor memory that can be used by automatic offload in all coprocessors. Specific coprocessor can be designated by MKL_MIC_<coprocessor_number>_MAX_MEMORY. Memory size is in kilobytes (K), megabytes (M), gigabytes (G), or terabytes (T). The equivalent API is mkl_mic_set_max_memory().

Third-PartyM athL ibraries

There are several other libraries available for application development on Xeon Phi coprocessor that you may make use of. Some are summarized in the following sections.

Magma

Magma MIC was developed by the Innovative Computing Laboratory at the University of Tennessee. It provides dense linear algebra library routines ported to Xeon Phi. It is available at http://icl.cs.utk.edu/magma/software/index.html.

ArrayFire

ArrayFire by AccelerEyes is an OpenCL library that supports Xeon Phi coprocessors and Xeon processors. The library contains various math, financial, and image-processing functions of use to various technical computing and other computational domains.

Intel Cluster Tools

Intel Cluster tools help you to build applications that can be run and analyzed in a cluster environment containing Xeon Phi coprocessors. Because Xeon Phi is mainly expected to be used in technical computing or high-performance computing applications, these tools are critical to support such application enabling. For the Xeon Phi coprocessor environment, the tool includes the MPI library that helps you create an MPI-based application that runs natively in a Xeon Phi coprocessor, a node with a Xeon Phi processor in symmetric mode, or a cluster of nodes with Xeon Phi coprocessors. The toolset also includes Intel Trace Collector and Analyzer, which allows you to understand how the messages are exchanged between various MPI processes (ranks) and how the computation and communication overlap.

Chapter 7 on system software explained that the Xeon Phi coprocessor provides extensive support for the Intel MPI library. The usage model for Xeon Phi is the same as that of the host except you need to link in the Xeon Phi version of MPI with your application binary targeted toward execution on the coprocessor OS. For native applications running solely on Xeon Phi, you can link in the Xeon Phi version of the MPI library with the code and set up the library path and binary path so that the executable can locate the MPI drivers (i.e., mpiexec.hydra, mpirun). The execution is similar to that of an MPI application execution on host processor environment on Linux OS.

For symmetric execution, you need to build two sets of binaries, one for Xeon and the other for Xeon Phi. The Xeon Phi binary should be cross-compiled with the –mmic switch so it can execute native on Xeon Phi. For example, say you have built two MPI-based binaries, test.mic and test.host. You can place the necessary Xeon Phi binary on the card, in the /tmp directory, with all the relevant libraries. In this case, a symmetric execution will be invoked as follows:

```
mpirun -n 1 -host localhost /tmp/test.host : -n 1 -host mic0 /tmp/test.mic
```

This will cause the test.host and the test.mic to start on the host and mic0 coprocessor as two MPI ranks of a single application test, and they can communicate with each other through the MPI messages to perform its task. Note that the MPI tasks can use OpenMP underneath to make use of the processor and coprocessor cores for its execution. You can set the type of fabric used by the MPI by setting the I_MPI_FABRICS environment variable. For example, to use RDMA for MPI communication between the host and Xeon Phi, use `I_MPI_FABRICS=shm:dapl`.[6]

Third-PartyC lusterT ools

In addition to the tools provided by Intel Cluster, there are other third-party tools available for cluster development and management with support for Xeon Phi coprocessors. Some of these are listed in the sections that follow.

PBS Professional

PBS Professional by Altair is a cluster job scheduling software that supports the Xeon Phi coprocessor for cluster job scheduling, management, and monitoring.[7] This is done by native integration of the coprocessor as a resource for job scheduling in the PBS scheduling manager. The tool can log the coprocessor usage, such as the number of coprocessors or number of cores in a coprocessor, to help the management process.

Bright Cluster Manager

Bright Cluster Manager by Bright Computing allows you to install, manage, and monitor clusters with Xeon Phi coprocessors by native integration of the coprocessor as a computing resource.[8] The tool accounts for Xeon Phi resources in its scheduling and management process of HPC clusters.

Summary

This chapter looked at various tools and libraries developed by Intel and third parties to help develop, debug, and tune applications on hosts containing the Intel Xeon Phi. It is important to learn to use these tools properly to get the benefits from the Intel Xeon Phi.

The next chapter will cover the application development considerations on Xeon Phi coprocessor using the tools and libraries described here. These considerations are necessary to get optimal performance on Xeon Phi coprocessors.

---

[6]There is a wealth of information on Xeon Phi cluster runs and set up at `http://software.intel.com/mic-developer`, in addition to the general Xeon Phi development topics and blogs.
[7]`http://www.pbsworks.com`
[8]`http://info.brightcomputing.com/intel-xeon-phi/`

PART 3

Applications: Technical Computing Software Development on Intel Xeon Phi

CHAPTER 9

■ ■ ■

Xeon Phi Application Design and Implementation Considerations

Parallel programming on any general-purpose processor such as Intel Xeon Phi requires careful consideration of the various aspects of program organization, algorithm selection, and implementation to achieve the maximum performance on the hardware.

One of the key challenges in developing a parallel code for the Xeon Phi coprocessor is to develop and parallelize offload computations on as many as 244 threads to exploit the massive parallel computing power provided by the coprocessor. To achieve that degree of parallelism, application developers often face the following challenges:

- *Parallelization overhead*: OpenMP overhead to start and stop threads can kill the performance if there are not enough computations to amortize thread creations.

- *Load imbalance*: Load imbalance can reduce parallel efficiency drastically. If one or more of the cores are given more workload than other cores in the system, these cores will become the bottleneck as the rest of the system waits for these cores to finish processing before the whole program can end.

- *Shared resource access overhead*: Because so many threads or processes are working in parallel, they can easily be bottlenecked by concurrent memory or ring bus access latency and bandwidth.

- *Data and task dependency*: The large number of tasks and data divided among the cores causes dependencies and serialization that may not be present in the original serial version of the code. By Amdahl's law, discussed in the next section, these dependencies add to the serial component of the application execution time.

In order to counter these issues, the application developers need to manage data across the threads with minimal sharing, align data structures for vector operations for optimal compiler code generations, select algorithms to exploit higher flops or bytes, and balance workloads across MIC or Xeon and Cluster for load balancing.

Figure 9-1 shows various considerations you need to take into account to develop code for Intel Xeon Phi. These are broadly categorized as:

- *Workload considerations*: You must determine what size and shape of the workload fits into Xeon Phi and how to divide it among the computing devices, such as the host processor and one or more Xeon Phi coprocessors, so they can complete the job in minimal time.

- *Algorithms and data structures*: Parallel algorithm development needs a very different mindset in thinking about expressing the computational problem. Although our brains function in parallel, our thought processes as traditional programmers have developed in a serial fashion to be tractable. Parallel programming needs different ways of thinking about expressing the same problem we ordinarily express serially. The algorithm that has been optimized for serial operation may not perform as well in parallel and may require a very different algorithm and data structure to solve the same task.

- *Implementation*: Massively parallel implementation on Xeon Phi needs support from programming languages, tools, and libraries. Because there are various way to parallelize, choosing the right parallel language suitable for programming the hardware for a specific problem will depend on the programmer, the problem at hand, and the specific library supports to perform optimally on the hardware. You can use *single program multiple data* (SPMD), loop structure, or thread fork joint models to do the parallel code implementation.

Considerations for Application Development on MIC

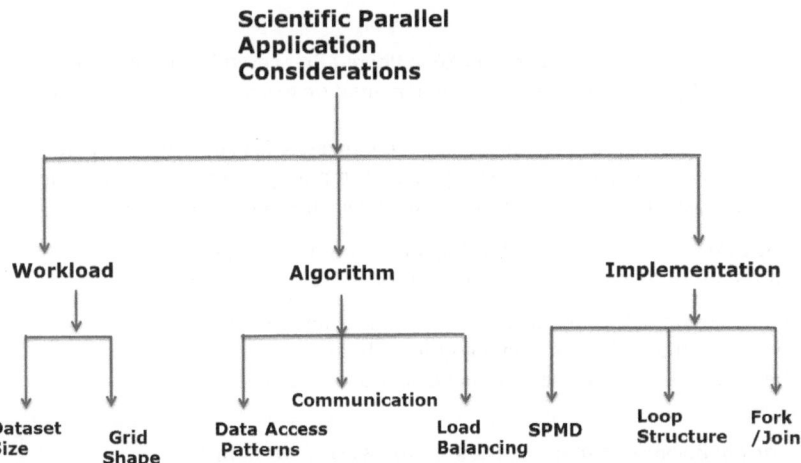

Figure 9-1. *Scientific parallel application development considerations*

This chapter will explain each of these broad categories and share some ideas on how to handle each challenging issue. These aspects of programming can in themselves fill up a book, but the goal here is to introduce the possible aspects of software development on Xeon Phi so you can pursue them further on your own.

Workload-Related Considerations

The first step toward thinking about, developing, and running applications on a parallel computer is to think about the size of the problem that will be run on the machine. Amdahl's law, which is familiar to many parallel application developers, states that the amount of parallelization that can be achieved by parallelizing an application is limited by the fraction of the code that runs serially during the whole application execution period.[1] Serialization is necessary when starting up the program, using a common resource such as writing to a single file and data consistency.

---

[1]Gene Amdahl, "Validity of the Single-Processor Approach to Achieving Large-Scale Computer Capabilities." *AFIPS Conference Proceedings* 30, 1967, pp. 483–485.

Amdahl showed that the speedup that can be achieved by a parallel program on N number of processors can be given by the expression $(s + p)/(s + (p/N))$, where s is the serial portion, p is the parallel fraction, and N is the number of parallel processors. If we use single processor runtime to normalize, which is the total runtime on a serial computer, we can define speedup as:

$$Speedup = 1/(s + (p/N))$$ [Eq. 9-1]

Equation 9-1 indicates that the serial portion s will dominate in massively parallel hardware such as Intel Xeon Phi, limiting the advantage of the manycore hardware. According to the formula, as N tends to infinity, the parallel portion of the computation can be completed in no time. So the application cannot be made infinitely fast by throwing more computing resources at the problem or by adding more computational cores. This was a big concern for computer scientists, and there was a prevalent feeling at that time in academia and industries that it is not a good return on investment to create parallel computers with more than 200 general-purpose processing nodes.

In 1985, Alan Karp of the IBM Palo Alto Research Center challenged the scientific community to demonstrate a speedup of at least 200 times on a general-purpose *multiple instructions and multiple data*(MIMD)m achineo n three scientific apps. John L. Gustafson and his colleagues showed that it is possible to achieve such performance on parallel computers.[2] The solution boiled down to better understanding of the problem characteristics that will be solved by these types of computers. Such problems follow Amdahl's law, but the problem size gets bigger on larger machines, such that the parallel portion of the workload keeps on increasing with the addition of more processors. This causes the serial section to become smaller and smaller, hence maintaining scalability. Gustafson et al. proposed a scaled speedup that represents scientific computing problems where data size is not fixed. As more processors are thrown into the mix, even larger problems can be solved.

Amdahl's law predicts the speedup curve as a function of the serial fraction, as shown in Figure 9-2, so that a maximum speedup of 24x is achieved with a serial fraction of only 4 percent.

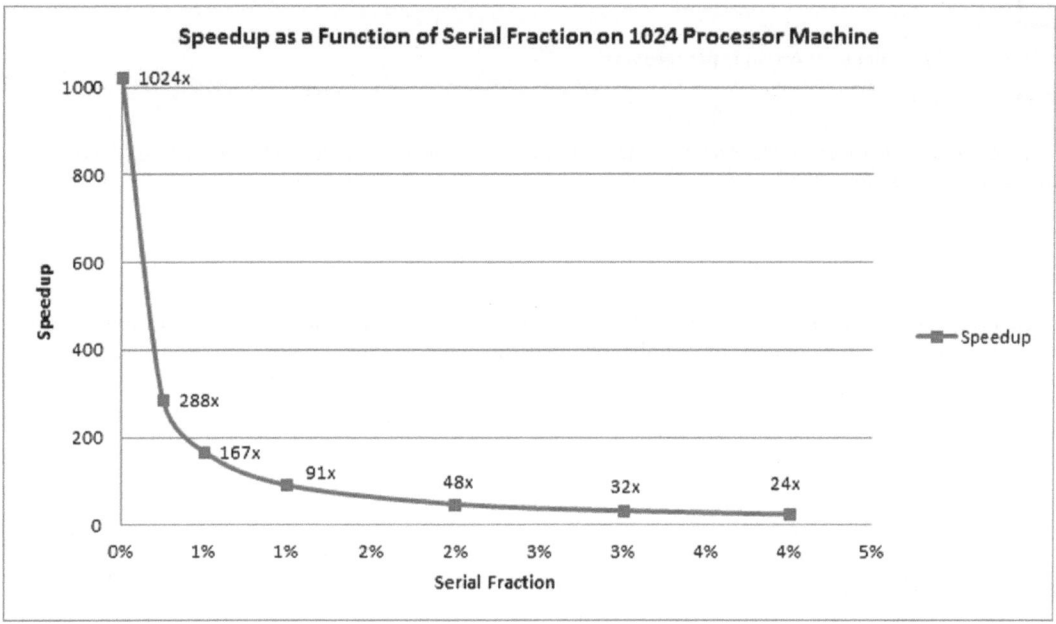

Figure 9-2. *Amdahl's law applied to a 1024 processor parallel MIMD machine*

---

[2]John L. Gustafson, Gary R. Montry, Robert E Benner, and C. W. Gear. "Development of Parallel Methods for a 1024-Processor Hypercube." *SIAM Journal on Scientific and Statistical Computing* 9(4), 1988, pp. 609–638.

We might infer from the highly parallel workload associated with a 4 percent serial fraction that it would be wasteful to build any machine with a 1024 processor. To understand how Amdahl's law may be misleading if generally applied to all parallel computing problems, let's apply it to a general scalability problem and see how Gustafson's law can provide a clearer idea of the value of parallel computation. The next section discusses further the important consideration identified by Gustafson and his team for understanding and practicing parallel application performance on these massively parallel machines.

Gustafson'sL aw

Gustafson and his Sandia colleague Edwin H. Barsis provided a speedup model that removed the barrier against parallel computation posed by Amdahl's model.[3] Gustafson showed that, for three practical applications with serial fraction ($s = 0.4 - 0.8$), his team was able to achieve more than 1,000x speedup on 1024 MIMD machines. In fact, the parallel portion of the "work done" in real applications scales with the number of processors, causing the overall serial fraction to be greatly reduced. Barsis proposed an inversion of Amdahl's model. Instead of asking how long a serial program will take to run on a parallel machine, he asked how long it will take a parallel program to run on a serial machine, and he came up with the definition of scaled speedup, which is given in the next section and shown in Figure 9-3.

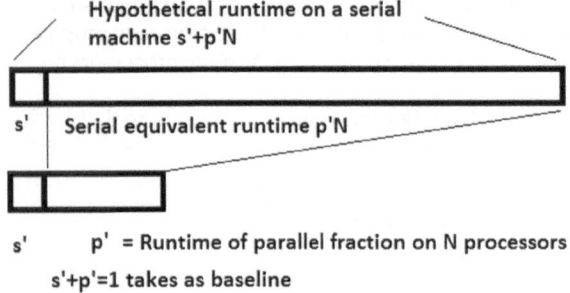

Figure 9-3. Scaled speedup definition by E. Barsis. (Adapted from John L. Gustafson, "Reevaluating Amdahl's Law." Communications of the ACM May 1988.)

ScaledS peedup

If we use s' and p' to represent serial and parallel time spent on the *parallel* system, then a serial processor would require time $s' + p' \times N$ to perform the task, where N is the number of processors. This reasoning yields Gustafson-Barsis's counterpoint to Amdahl's law (Figure 9-3):

$$Scaled\ speedup\quad = (s' + p' \times N)/(s' + p')$$

$$= s' + p' \times N = s' + (1 - s') \times N$$

$$= N + (1 - N) \times s$$

where $s' + p' = 1$ is the time spent on parallel computer taken as baseline.

---

[3]John L. Gustafson. "Reevaluating Amdahl's Law." *Communications of the ACM* 31(5), 1988, pp. 532–533.

As shown in Figure 9-4, Gustafson's law indicates that the scaled speedup is a line with moderate slope of $1 - N$, where N is the number of parallel processors. Thus, increasing the number of processors can still provide fairly good performance for practical applications to be solved by such computers. Figure 9-4 shows that you can achieve 983x speedup on a 1024 core processor using Gustafson's model for a 4 percent serial fraction of the workload.

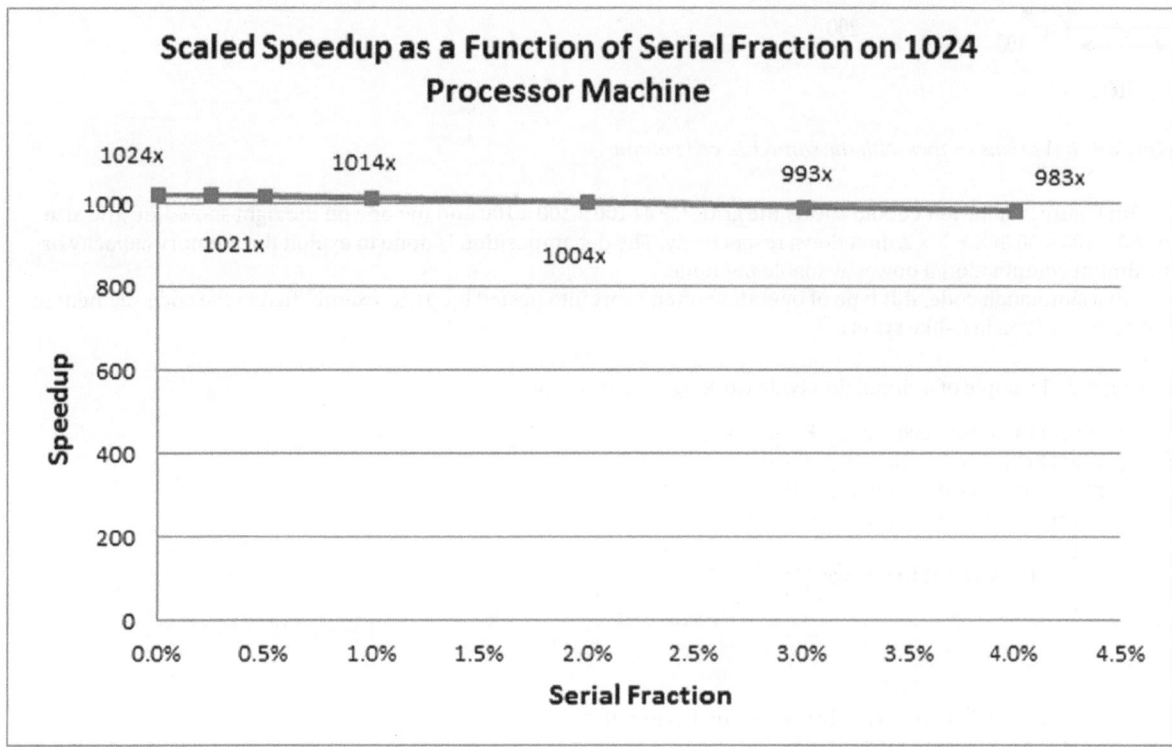

Figure 9-4. *Scaled speedup based on Gustafson's model*

Effect of Grid Shape on Performance

Technical computing applications often need to discretize the dataset into grids as part of the numerical representation of the problem. The grid size can sometimes drastically affect the performance of these apps on vector-based machine architectures, such as Intel Xeon Phi, as it dictates the memory access patterns. Often a developer or user has flexibility in picking the block shapes for simulation if they are aware of the advantage of one shape over the other.

As an example, let's look at two different shapes with the same volume, as shown in Figure 9-5. Both of these represent some simulation area—say, a region of earth where the weather patterns will be simulated.

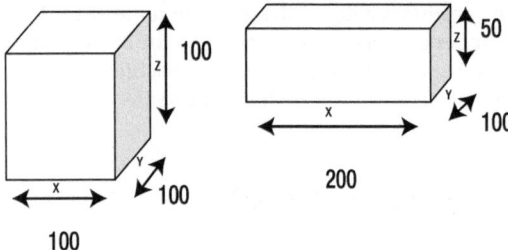

Figure 9-5. *Various shapes with the same 1 M cell volume*

In Figure 9-5, the left cuboid shows the grid size as 100 × 100 × 100 and the one on the right shows the grid size of 200 × 100 × 50 in X × Y × Z directions, respectively. The decomposition is done to exploit the memory capacity or maximum computational power available per node.

In a simulation code, this type of operation often turns into nested loops, as exemplified in the code segment in Listing 9-1 written in C-like syntax.

Listing 9-1. Example of a simulation code working on a 3D array

```
//Loop execution for cuboid in Figure 9.5
for ( z=zstart; z <zstart+100; z++){
    for(y=start;y<ystart+100;y++){
        for(x=start;x<xstart+100;x++)
        {
            Do simulation steps();
        }
    }
}

//Loop execution for rectangular cube in Figure 9.5
for ( z=start; z <zstart+50; z++){
    for(y=ystart;y<ystart+100;y++){
        for(x=start;x<xstart+200;x++)
        {
            Do simulation steps();
        }
    }
}
```

It needs to be recognized that if a big chunk of data is divided up among the cores of Xeon Phi, only the X dimension access for a pair of y and z values is expected to be in consecutive locations so that the processor can stream the data in for a given pair of y and z values. Once we move to a different pair of y and z values, the x start may be in a different memory page altogether. However, consecutive memory access for data elements along the x axis is consecutive if laid out properly.

This property will let the compiler vectorize the inner loop so that the memory access will be unit stride, allowing maximum memory access bandwidth in Xeon Phi's cache-based system. Having a longer x axis (say, 200 elements vs. 100 elements) allows the processors to do more work between resetting the X start address for the next pair of y and z values.

You can see the correlation between the innermost loop performance in the simulation computation and the X direction length of the volume being processed. In many cases, where the problem admits the flexibility of dividing the input dataset into different volume shapes, it may be possible to achieve high performance by doing so.

In internal experiments with similar data shapes for a simulation, we are able to achieve around a 35 percent boost in performance by changing the simulation grid shape to make vectorized code be more efficient.

Workload Consideration 1

- Choose the right problem size that will benefit from the Intel Xeon Phi.
- Amdahl's law can be misleading in designing for parallel performance.
- Gustafson's law is a better representation of parallel scientific computations.

Workload Consideration 2

- Choose a grid shape that is rectangular cuboid by making the unit stride dimension of the inner loop long enough.
- For better use of cache lines, map the unit stride long dimension to the inner loop in nested loop iterations.

AlgorithmC onsiderations

In order to get optimal parallel performance on Xeon Phi, you need to identify algorithms and data structures that may need modification from the serial version of the code. It is often found that the existing parallel machines are limited by memory bandwidth rather than compute bandwidth for most of the applications, while the serial codes are often limited by the compute bandwidth of the single core. So the algorithm has to be redesigned or a different algorithm may need to be used to achieve high performance on the Xeon Phi manycore architecture.

An example of change in the choice of algorithm appropriate to solve a problem as we move from a sequential to parallel machine is the common data-sorting algorithm. We know that Quicksort is the algorithm of choice for serial computation for many applications because of its optimal average performance. But Quicksort involves walking over the array elements in the first step to divide them into two parts based on the pivot element and requires the step to be performed in a single processor, which seriously limits the performance. Computer scientists have proven that bucket sort, a seemingly simple algorithm, may be more appropriate in the parallel world.

The optimal performance algorithm chosen should match the practical hardware-supported flops-to-bytes metric. This metric provides the ratio of peak floating-point operations the processor can perform to peak bytes of data the hardware is able to sustain for the duration of computation. If you know the peak flops and peak bandwidth of a piece of hardware, this metric can be easily computed. The physical limit of Phi hardware determines the work-to-memory access ratio supported and influences the type of algorithm chosen to work optimally on a piece of hardware.

Many applications of practical importance nowadays are *memory bound*, that is, the compute waits on the data to arrive. In these cases, if F represents the algorithms compute-to-data ratio (flops/bytes) and B represents the maximum bandwidth (BW) bytes/sec of the platform, then the maximum performance achievable on such a platform is equal to $F*B$ flops. However, you need to use the appropriate BW for the platform, taking into account that some of the data may reside in the cache line.

Take, for example, an optimized DGEMM routine working on the L1 cache for its computation. Assuming that an optimized DGEMM routine can deliver a 3 flops/bytes ratio and the L1 cache can sustain 300 GB/sec BW on Xeon Phi, a DGEMM routine can achieve 3 × 300 = 900 GFlops/sec. On the other hand, the stream triad benchmark works on three double-precision numbers and performs two floating-point operations on them, providing a flops-to-bytes ratio equal to 2 / (3 × 8 = 24) = 0.083. So the highest achievable flops for this benchmark is 0.083 × 180 = 14.9 GFlops, limited by the memory interconnect bandwidth of approximately 180 GB/sec.

Parallelizing algorithms introduces issues that may not be present in the serial version of the code. As stated by Amdahl's law, once the application has been parallelized, you need to examine the sequential portion of the algorithm to reduce the serial fraction of the algorithm for optimal performance scaling and reap the benefit of parallel processing. This includes the communication overhead introduced by the parallel algorithm, which may not be present in the serial version of the code.

Communication and synchronization between the threads and processes introduced by parallelizing the algorithm usually show up as big overhead during the runtime of an application running on Xeon Phi. Experiments have shown that 30 percent of runtime overhead can in some cases be attributed to OpenMp or MPI communication and synchronization overhead. We would need to determine, for a given programming model, how to divide the task to minimize the communication-to-computation overhead. There are various patterns for parallel program and algorithm development available for programmers to design their applications optimized for their needs.[4] Intel provides a parallel programming library, the Intel Threading Building Blocks (TBB), and Intel Cilk plus language support and runtime to help reduce parallel overheads.

Our development experience with Xeon Phi has shown that the data-parallel design and algorithm patterns work well for Xeon Phi architecture. As Xeon Phi has a cache-based vector architecture, data-decomposition algorithm patterns result in better memory reuse and require less memory per core (as needed by task-parallel codes), because the total dataset does not need to be replicated to each individual node and can work on a subset of the total dataset. Having access to data to be worked on in parallel is a necessary condition for vector processing architecture.

Another side effect of data-parallel applications is less communication between the parallel processes, except in boundary exchanges. The data-parallel pattern allows the developer to focus on organizing data and can lead to better cache utilization and vector code generation by the compiler, resulting in better performance. However, some of the parallel applications that have been shown to perform well on Xeon Phi, such as ray tracing, are inherently task-parallel and do not need to be forced into data-parallel mode.

Data Structure

Another important consideration in achieving optimal performance on Xeon Phi is the data structure used by the algorithm. As a cache-based vector coprocessor, Intel Xeon Phi is heavily dependent on data layout and data access patterns for optimal performance. In designing the data structure for an algorithm, you need to give careful attention to the memory access patterns expected from or influencing the algorithm. The goal here is to maximize the reuse of data already residing in the L2 and L1 caches. The hardware consists of physical components that limit how fast the data can be accessed from the different levels of the memory hierarchy. For a given designed flops rate and bandwidth limit, there is a physical limit to the floating point-to-data bus bandwidth of these processors.

As an example of data structure selection, consider an algorithm working on an array of structures where structure elements are only partially accessed at one time. In the code segment in Listing 9-2, the position structure contains the x, y, and z coordinates of the object. Keep in mind that such data structures are more complex in real-world applications, with many more attributes added to them.

If the object is to move along the x-direction, we need to update the x-positions of the objects by accessing the objectPosition array of structures for the x position and updating them. Although we need only the x elements, owing to cache behavior the whole cache line containing the objects' position structure and consecutive object position

---

[4]T. Mattson, B. Sanders, and B. Massingill. *Patterns for Parallel Programming.* Reading, MA: Addison-Wesley Professional, 2004.

structures will be pulled into the cache. In addition to unnecessary data related to y and z elements polluting the cache line, it also wastes valuable interconnect bandwidth by using only the x component of the structure in the computation while reading all three x, y, and z values from memory, as shown in Listing 9-2.

Listing 9-2. Inefficient data structure layout for the given computation

```
typedef struct position
{
    double x;
    double y;
    double z;
}POSITION;

POSITION objectPositions[NUMOBJECTS];

Foo()
{
    // move the object along X direction by DIST amount
    for(int i=0;i<NUMOBJECTS; i++){
        objectPositions[i].x += DIST;
    }
}
```

If, however, the data structure is laid out such that the x-positions of all the objects are kept together, we will make optimal use of the data cache and bandwidth by pulling in x elements only, as shown in Listing 9-3. This common technique for parallel processors is known as the *Array of Structures-to-Structure of Arrays*(AoS-to-SoA) *transformation.*

Listing 9-3. AoS-to-SoA transformation

```
typedef real POSITION;
POSITION objectPositionsX[NUMOBJECTS], objectPositionsY[NUMOBJECTS],
objectPositionsZ[NUMOBJECTS];

Foo()
{
    // move the object along X direction by DIST amount
    for(int i=0;i<NUMOBJECTS; i++){
        objectPositionsX[i] += DIST;
    }
}
```

OffloadO verhead

Because Xeon Phi is an attached coprocessor on a host system, the computational data have to be sent back and forth between the card and host memory to perform the computation. The algorithm must be chosen so that the data communication between the host and the card is minimized, be it an MPI or OpenMP or other threading-based application. The offload overhead can be considered part of the communication overhead of the algorithm for analysis purposes. When exporting computations to the Xeon Phi card, the data and computation code have to be exported to the card using the offload programming model.

Algorithms that allow asynchronous execution of various steps provide better parallelization and may reduce offload overhead by overlapping phases of computation and communication. Another aspect of algorithm design is to choose algorithms that allow for load balancing of computational tasks by dividing them between the host cores and the Xeon

147

Phi coprocessor cores. This can often be achieved with an algorithm using a pipelining technique to do its computation and creating a cost model for each of the computational pipeline stages. For example, in Linpack computation on a node with a Xeon Phi processor, you can design the algorithm so that the factorization, broadcast, and update of the matrices happen asynchronously. This will allow pipelining, the overlapping of various computational phases between the host and the coprocessor and prioritize performance-critical tasks to allow dependent tasks to progress.

LoadB alancing

One of the key differentiating factors between a good and bad parallel algorithm when implemented is how well they divide the work among parallel processing units so that they are equally loaded. Load imbalance can lead to major performance loss. *Load balance* can be defined as the ratio between the average time to finish all of the parallel tasks (T_{avg}) and the maximum time to finish any of the parallel tasks (T_{max}). For a perfectly balanced load, the time spent by each of the processing units is equal and the load balance equals 1.

Load balance limits the parallel efficiency achievable by an algorithm on a piece of hardware. It can be shown that parallel efficiency is less than or equal to load balance for an algorithm on a piece of hardware.[5]

There are various algorithm patterns that result in load-balanced works, such as the "nearest neighbor" algorithm.

Algorithm and Data Structure Considerations

- Parallel algorithms that allow vectorization (such as data-parallel algorithms) are preferable. It is possible to gain 8x/16x for DP and SP code respectively, over nonvectorized code if fully optimized.

- Understand the loops and data layout in algorithms for optimal performance for Xeon Phi hardware.

- Try to maintain load balance for optimal performance.

Implementation Considerations

After the design and algorithm development for Xeon Phi, you need to look at the implementation issues. This involves understanding the hardware microarchitecture, the language constructs to implement the algorithm, the parallelization libraries, and the code optimization techniques to maximize underlying hardware efficiency.

MemoryM anagement

Memory hierarchy enforces different optimizations for different parts of the code. Use of software prefetches and scatter gathers to get data to the L2 cache, where the hardware prefetchers are not effective, is one way to solve the issue. Hardware prefetchers in Xeon Phi will not be able to prefetch data into the cache if the data access is random or crosses page boundaries. Carefully experiment with software prefetching when necessary. Hardware prefetch helps on predictable strides and only prefetches data to the L2 cache. So use software prefetches to get data to the L1 cache, even in cases where the hardware prefetcher may be active. Sometimes you can use loop unrolling to work on multiple data items in the innermost loop, hiding instruction latencies and improving the flops-to-bytes ratio.

---

[5]L. R. Scott, T. W. Clark, and B. Bagheri. *Scientific Parallel Computing*. Princeton, NJ: Princeton University Press, 2005.

Figure 9-6 shows various memory latency considerations in optimizing the code. It shows estimated nonload latencies in different cache hierarchies on a Xeon Phi processor. It can be seen that there are 600 to 1,000 cycle latencies for getting data to the L2 cache line, so although a vector instruction can execute at four cycles, any stall due to data not available in the L2 cache line will incur hundreds to thousands of cycle latencies. It is important to have the data available in the cache line with some form of linear or scatter gather prefetches. This type of cache miss often happens when the data are accessed randomly from memory, and only the developer may have some way to prefetch the data in place for a given application. Figure 9-6 also shows that the fetching from L2 can itself cause tens of cycles if not already put into the L1 cache. So for latency-sensitive code, it may be necessary to further prefetch the data into the L1 cache with L1 prefetch instructions.

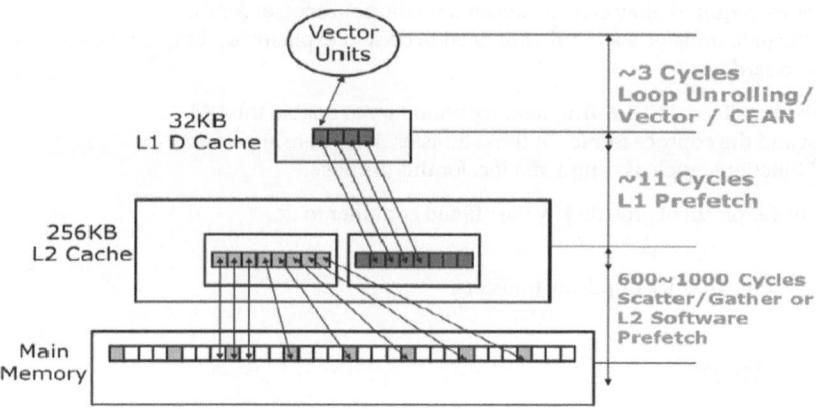

Figure 9-6. *Memory latency considerations during code optimization in selecting prefetch distances*

Mixed-PrecisionAr ithmetic

Mixed-precision arithmetic indicates the use of single- and double-precision mathematics in a computation. Many problems can be reformulated using mixed precision with no loss in the final precision of the resulting value. Using lower precision—say single-precision instead of double-precision numbers—can result in a large speedup thanks to reduced memory traffic, because single-precision data are half the size of double-precision data, thus providing a better flops-to-bytes ratio. As explained in the architecture sections, there is hardware support in Xeon Phi that allows you to use single-precision transcendental functions in computations, also providing significant speedup. Some examples include iterative solvers, such as the Richardson iterative solver—where using single precision in the approximation step does not result in loss of computational accuracy but may in some cases improve performance. The Richardson iterative process seeks a solution to the matrix equation $Ax = b$, where A and b are given. It starts by approximating x values to x_k. The first step is to compute the residual using double-precision arithmetic. The second step finds a delta value to approximate the next x value until it converges. Because this is an approximation, it is possible to use single-precision arithmetic in this case, as shown in step 2 of the loop (Listing 9-4). This can yield substantial performance improvement.

Listing 9-4. Richardson's Iteration

```
While (|r_k| > e){
    r_k=b-Ax_k     <- DP SpMV -------- (step 1)
    p_k=A^-1r_k    <- SP approximation (step 2)
    x_{k+1}=x_k+p_k   <- DP
}
```

Similar mixed-precision arithmetic can be used in preconditioned Krylov solvers. The preconditioner can use single precision and the outer solver can use double precision without have much effect on the solution, while achieving a performance gain over default implementations.

Optimizing Memory Transfer Bandwidth over the PCIe Bus

Because Xeon Phi is an attached coprocessor, the input dataset has to be sent to the coprocessor of the PCIe Gen2 bus, which connects it to the core. A challenge we often face is how to get the maximum data transfer BW out of this communication channel. Use the following techniques to optimize the data transfer BW:

1. If the scratch-data buffers are required, they can be allocated on the coprocessor for the offload model to reduce the data transfer, so they do not need to be sent explicitly as they are already available on the card.

2. Align the data buffers to be transferred to the 4KB memory boundary to enable the DMA transfer between the host and the coprocessor for optimal transfer BW. There are several language constructs and functions, such as __mm_malloc, for this purpose.

3. Use the asynchronous transfer protocol provided by the offload compiler to do thetr ansfer.

4. Use persistent data on the card to reduce duplicate transfers.

DataA lignmentC onsiderations

One of the key performance benefits may be achieved by ensuring that the data are aligned to the cache line boundary on the host and Xeon Phi and that the algorithm works on cache line sizes. This allows better code generation from the compiler and low latency memory access. But keep in mind while creating such data access patterns that each individual thread is able to access aligned data. This often slips one's attention, but alignment of the overall dataset does not necessarily imply that each thread working on it will have aligned access. Because each thread accesses a part of the data structure, individual access to shared data structure may not be aligned. Remember to let the compiler know that the data are aligned by using the aligned pragma. Often the compiler cannot figure this out by itself, so conveying such information, where you have carefully laid out the data structure, will allow the compiler to generate optimal code. This will allow vector units throughput to be maximized without waiting for memory load latencies caused by unaligned access.

Communication

Once a program has been converted to a parallel version, there is often a need for various parallel components to work together and communicate with each other to finish a task. Some of the communications are at the startup phase, where the data/tasks are communicated to processes/threads by broadcast or one-to-one communications during runtime exchange information, such as the boundary condition between the threads or processes by one-to-many or one-to-one communication, and at the end to reduce and gather the results in the final output of the tasks through some sort of reduction method. Because communication could contribute to the serial part of a program, it is necessary to reduce the communication overhead. The hardware architecture as well as the algorithm play a big role in what type of communication needs to be done between the cores and processes.

Depending on the hardware architecture, you often need to decide between shared memories vs. the message-passing mode of communication. Although the shared memory system has much less overhead than message passing, access to shared resources can impose a high overhead owing to the need of synchronization. If you have a lot of communication and fewer shared resources, OpenMP may be better than MPI or vice versa. If you are using an offload programming model to communicate with Xeon Phi coprocessors, asynchronous data transfer often leads to a lower communication overhead than that of synchronous transfers. The same is true for message-passing algorithms.

File I/O

There are three ways to perform file input/output (I/O) on a Xeon Phi–based system. The coprocessor native I/O uses card memory for the file system. This consumes valuable GDDR memory space but is faster than other solutions. The second option is to use proxy I/O. In this configuration, you set MIC_PROXY_FS_ROOT to point to the host directory where you want the files to be proxied to. MPSS proxy I/O manager manages the I/O from the coprocessor file system to the proxied host file system. The third method is mounting a *network file system* (NFS) directory to the Xeon Phi coprocessor. In this case, all the writes from the coprocessor are written to the host-exported NFS directory.

The proxied and NFS-based file I/O are slower, as they have to transfer I/O data over the PCIe bus, but they do not consume any valuable memory resources. For optimal I/O performance and memory usage balance, it is beneficial to store smaller scratch files or performance-sensitive files on the coprocessor RAM drive and other files on the NFS-mounted or proxy file system. Proxy file I/O is based on NFS and, as such, does not provide any performance benefit over the NFS-mounted file system.

Implementation Considerations

- Use array vector notation and elemental function to help vectorization.

- Do some code restructuring for optimal vectorization.

- Used mixed-precision arithmetic where possible. Exploit hardware transcendental functions.

- Select proper parallelism constructs, OpenMP, MPI, and others to reduce communication to computation overhead.

- Strike a balance between native RAM file system and NFS or proxy file system for optimal file I/O performance without wasting coprocessor memory for file storage.

Summary

This chapter has looked at the various considerations that developers must take into account in designing and developing code for the Intel Xeon Phi coprocessor in order to extract maximum performance out of the hardware. You have seen the importance of selecting the proper workload to make full use of the raw compute power. You have also seen that the algorithm and data structure developed for bigcore processors such as Intel Xeon needs to be adjusted for the manycore architecture of Xeon Phi. Finally, you have seen that, even if proper design choices are made in the first two steps, implementation issues such as communication overhead may play a big role in application performance.

The next chapter looks at specific optimizations you can incorporate in your code to make it perform well on aX eonP hic oprocessor.

CHAPTER 10

■ ■ ■

Application Performance Tuning on Xeon Phi

This chapter explains how to tune the performance of applications developed for Xeon Phi. The work of achieving optimal performance starts by designing your application with proper consideration to application design and implementations, as discussed in Chapter 9. Once an application has been developed, you can tune it further by optimizing the code you have developed for the Xeon Phi coprocessor architecture. The tuning process involves the use of tools such as VTune, compiler, code structuring, and libraries in conjunction with your understanding of architecture to fix the issues that cause performance bottlenecks. The "artistic" aspect of the tuning process will emerge incrementally during the course of your hands-on work with the hardware and the application as you figure out how to apply various tools efficiently to optimize the code fragment that cause the bottleneck. This chapter will provide the *best-known methods* (BKMs) to start optimizing code for the Xeon Phi coprocessor. I will assume in this chapter that you have already parallelized the code as part of your algorithm design, as discussed in Chapter 9.

The optimization process can be broken into two main categories:

- *Node-level optimization*, in which you optimize the code for a single node.

- *Cluster-level optimization*, in which you optimize the performance at the cluster level.

The node-level optimization cycle consists of the following steps:

1. Set up a benchmark and baseline for the application you will be tuning for a single node.

2. Create a profile of the application and locate potential performance bottlenecks using a single node profiling tool such as VTune or a cluster-profiling tool such as Intel Trace Collector or Intel Trace Analyzer.

3. Set the target performance. From the application profile, you can try to estimate the application performance on the hardware. This process involves getting some estimate of the hardware performance using a common benchmark such as STREAM[1] or Scalable Heterogeneous Computing (SHOC) Benchmark[2] to measure the various performance metrics of Xeon Phi hardware. For example, if your application is bandwidth-bound,

---

[1] John D. McCalpin, "STREAM: Sustainable Memory Bandwidth in High Performance Computers," a continually updated technical report (1991-2007), available at http://www.cs.virginia.edu/stream/.
[2] Anthony Danalis, Gabriel Marin, Collin McCurdy, Jeremy S. Meredith, Philip C. Roth, Kyle Spafford, Vinod Tipparaju, and Jeffrey S. Vetter, "The Scalable Heterogeneous Computing (SHOC) Benchmark Suite," Proceedings of the 3rd Workshop on General-Purpose Computation on Graphics Processing Units, March 14, 2010, Pittsburgh, Pennsylvania. Xeon Phi version of the benchmark available at https://github.com/vetter/shoc-mic.

you can use the stream number to predict how much headway you have. VTune can tell you how much bandwidth you are using, so that you can see what headroom you have for your application if it is memory-bound.

4. Experiment with applicable system-level configurations, such as transparent huge page settings, to address the performance issues.

5. Use compiler switches, pragmas, and code restructuring to go around the performance issues pointed to by VTune or other profilers.

6. If the code uses common math functions that are available in the MKL libraries, use instead the libraries that are optimized for Xeon Phi.

7. If the threading overhead is high, look for ways to reduce the threading imbalance or threading constructs to be more efficient. Try playing with such parameters as the thread affinity and the number of threads.

8. For symmetric applications, make sure you have load balance between the host and coprocessor components of your application.

9. Collect the new performance numbers and repeat from step 2 till you are satisfied with the codep erformance.

Once you are happy with the node-level optimization, proceed to cluster-level optimization as follows:

1. Use cluster-profiling tools such as Intel Trace Collector and Intel Trace Analyzer to see whether you have load imbalance.

2. Optimize the MPI parameters for lower message overhead. You may need code restructuring for optimal MPI performance.

3. Optimize OS, MPSS, and network configuration for best performance.

This chapter will explain each of these steps for extracting extract good performance out of the Xeon Phi coprocessor-based system.

Getting Baseline Data

It is important to set up a performance discipline that will let you know whether the optimization work you do has any benefit. Not all optimization efforts will provide performance gains. Indeed, some optimization strategies that seem good choices on theoretical grounds may even degrade performance. That is why it is important to take a disciplined approach to performance measurement. You need to set up a tracking process—perhaps an Excel spreadsheet where you log the system setup details such as the host processor and the Xeon Phi coprocessor specifications, the BIOS configuration of the host such as hyper threading on/off, the memory size, and setup such as the ECC status, the tools and library versions used, cluster configuration, and so forth—that will allow you to reproduce the benchmark results on a different machine if need be or provide run-to-run consistency.

Once you have set up a discipline, you will need to get a baseline performance number for your application. A timer is used to measure the performance of your application. It is important that you use the same timer on the coprocessor OS or host processor (if measuring offload code) when measuring application performance over time to be able to assess the effect of optimizations that you incorporate in the codebase. The coprocessor OS supports two hardware-based timers: the *elapsed-time counter*(ETC)a ndt he *timestamp counter* (TSC) as a clock source. So if your application calls the gettimeofday() routine, the time values will be provided by the coprocessor OS based on the source you select as a timer source. It is important to make sure you keep the timer source constant in run-to-run measurements, as the resolutions are different between the timers, and that you select the proper timer for accuracy.

There is one ETC for the whole coprocessor chip and it is independent of chip power management. It has a high consistency as it is not affected by power management, but its access time is approximately 100x slower than that of TSC when using the gettimeofday function call. It is always a good idea to have your code timed at high granularity—say, by increasing the number of iterations timed to make the timer overhead negligible to time spent in the code execution that you are trying to time.

The TSC timer is faster to access, but it is affected by the power management. So if you are measuring performance with TSC, you need to make sure the chip power management in turned off. You can check which clock source is being used by looking at /sys/devices/system/clocksource/clocksource0/current_clocksource on the coprocessor.

Timing Applications

Timers are functions or tools that allow you to time the execution of a code fragment you are trying to optimize. For example, the coprocessor BusyBox utility supports the time command, which allows you to time the total runtime of the application at a coarse level. It will output the real time, user time, and system time after the application run completes. The *real time* is the elapsed wall clock time that you can measure with a stop watch. The *user time* is the sum of all processor time spent in user mode code. Note that for parallel applications, the sum of the time spent in each user process can be larger than the elapsed time. The *system time* accounts for time spent in the kernel for the process being timed.

Sometimes you will need a finer resolution timer than provided by the Linux time command. For example, in Xeon Phi–based code optimization, the focus is often on the part of the code that is offloaded to the coprocessor or of interest in native or symmetric runs. In such cases, you will need to have some function calls in your code that allow you to time specific sections of the code.

In Fortran, you can use the RTC, DTIME, and ETIME functions to time sections of the code. These functions are supported by the Intel Fortran compiler. In the C/C++ compiler, you can use clock, times, getrusage, gettimeofday(), or other functions to time your code. Code Listing 10-1 shows how you can use gettimeofdayin your code to measure time. Here you can call elapsed time before and after a code segment you want to measure to collect time spent in your code.

Code Listing 10-1. Timing Routine Returning Time Value in Seconds

```
#include <sys/time.h>

extern double elapsedTime (void)
{
    struct timeval t;
    gettimeofday(&t, 0);
    return ((double)t.tv_sec + ((double)t.tv_usec / 1000000.0));
}
```

If you are interested in cycle-level timing, there is an intrinsic __rdtsc() (read time stamp counter) which reads from a 64-bit register and counts the number of cycles since the last reset. You need to use the core frequency to convert these cycles to second units. This counter is affected, however, by the power management on the core and it has to be used carefully.

Remember to find the timer resolution you will be using to measure a section of code segment. The resolution should be high enough to make the measurement relevant.

Detecting Application Execution Bottlenecks

Once you have your baseline data, you are ready to investigate whether there are opportunities for code optimization. At this step, you will use some sort of profiling tool such as Intel VTune Amplifier XE to locate the hotspots in your code. In general, *hotspot* refers to a code section where the code is spending most of its time. For technical computing applications, you should locate the top ten functions where more than 95 percent of the time is being spent. The fewer the number of functions showing up in your top 95 percent of execution, the better your chance of being able to optimize the code to get better performance with minimal effort. The greater the number of hotspot functions in your applications, as is often the case for flat-profile applications, the greater the effort and time required to get better performance out of those applications.

First, you need to resolve system-level issues, such as whether your offloaded code is being limited by the PCIe data transfer bandwidth. Using your timing routine, you can see whether or not the PCIe data transfer bandwidth is acceptable. To get a baseline, you can run some open source benchmark such as SHOC to get your estimated PCIe bandwidth. Once you are happy with the system-level performance, you can use VTune to profile the code running on Xeon Phi using performance monitoring hardware counters. The hardware is a black box to software developers with respect to how the instructions flow through the pipeline as the code executes. One way the hardware communicates with the software users is though these performance monitoring counters implemented in the coprocessors. These counters expose how the instructions are flowing through the cores, what type of cache hits and misses are happening, and how memory bandwidth is consumed for reading and writing data using the knowledge of cores and uncores in the coprocessor. Hardware architects usually build these counters to help with this bottleneck detection process.

The performance monitoring works by the hardware supporting various *performance events*r elatedt oc ore execution and methods to configure and capture those events. VTune allows you to select which performance event you are interested in and lets you choose how often the hardware event is sampled. When an application is running, you can select to monitor its effect on the hardware instruction flow pipeline to locate what type of issues you are facing. I will not be covering this topic in this chapter, but you can find details in the Intel Xeon Phi Coprocessor Performance Monitoring Units documentation.[3]

Performance events are associated with various architecture features that were discussed in Chapters 3 through 5. Most of the performance monitoring counters that were available on Pentium processor core are available on Xeon Phi. In addition, new counters appropriate to a multicore processor with a new MIC instruction set and features are added to Xeon Phi to expose the new architectural behavior for code execution.

Using these events, you can gather some interesting architectural behavior while executing your application. From the data for these events, you can create useful metrics for memory access performance, such as various levels of cache miss rate (miss/references); for core execution issues, such as vector unit usage efficiency; for parallel overhead, which can be discovered by the percentage of time spent in noncomputational code such as OpenMP or MPI library code; and for many other areas of architectural behavior.

From these metrics, you will be able to figure out whether the hotspot code is getting limited by memory access issues such as bandwidth, latencies due to cache miss, floating-point execution issues, integer execution issues, and so on. Equipped with such knowledge, you will be able to apply the various tuning techniques discussed in this chapter. VTune can also show you whether your code is spending too much time in MPI/OpenMP or parallel constructs that are provided to make use of the cores in parallel but that do not do any of the useful computational work needed by your application. Your goal is to increase the ratio of useful task to parallel overhead in Xeon Phi architecture. This can be accomplished by increasing the *effective computation*—that is, the actual computation that your threads in thread-level parallelism or MPI tasks are doing compared to communication/synchronization overheads.

---

[3]Intel Xeon Phi Coprocessor (codename: Knights Corner) Performance Monitoring Units, Document Number:327357-001 http://software.intel.com/sites/default/files/forum/278102/intelr-xeon-phitm-pmu-rev1.01.pdf.

Some Basic Performance Events

Although there are many performance events that are supported in the Xeon Phi coprocessor, not all of them are needed in the initial phase of performance root cause. I have listed some of the events that may be useful in your exploration process. These events, together with VTune profile analysis feature, can be useful in detecting your application issues related to execution bottleneck, data fetching overhead such as latencies or bandwidth limitations, and parallelization overhead.

Locating Hotspots

The most important events that you need to collect in order to locate hotspots are CPU_CLK_UNHALTED, which gives you the number of cycles executed in the core, and INSTRUCTIONS_EXECUTED, which gives you the number of instructions executed by the core. Using these two events, you will be able to pinpoint the code fragments and functions that are taking most of your code's execution time. Although software developers have a tendency to associate *cycles per instruction* (CPI) to performance, it is important to note that you are interested in reducing the total number of cycles taken by your application, not necessarily the CPI value. If you are executing mainly vector instructions, you might have a higher CPI than if you were executing scalar instructions, because vector instruction latencies might be 4 cycles compared to some scalar operations. Using vector instructions will, however, reduce the number of instructions by up to 16x for floating-point operations, so overall runtime will be lower.

Code Execution Issues

Once you have located the hotspots, you may want to proceed to investigate the vectorization efficiency of the hotspot sections of your code. As discussed in Chapter 3, utilizing vector units efficiently is key to achieving high performance on Xeon Phi. You can use the ratio of VPU_ELEMENTS_ACTIVE, the number of elements in a VPU register that were not masked out and actively participated in the vector execution to VPU_INSTRCUTIONS_EXECUTED, so signifying the number of vector instructions executed by the thread, to get the approximate vector efficiency. The theoretical maximum for single-precision arithmetic, for example, is 16, because there are 16 elements that can be acted on per vector instruction. This is only an approximate indicator because the VPU_INSTRUCTIONS_EXECUTED includes vector loads, masks manipulation instructions, and so on—so the ratio may be lower than the actual vector execution efficiency. To make an assessment of how good the metric is as applied to your code, look at the corresponding assembly code block. You will learn in this chapter how to improve the vectorization of your code by applying the compiler and tools.

In addition to vectorization inefficiencies, too many branches might lower your code's performance. You can use the performance events, VPU_INSTRUCTIONS_EXECUTED, and INSTRUCTIONS_EXECUTED, to figure out what percentage of executed instructions is vectorized. However, not all vectorized instructions are efficient because the usage of masks may prevent the vector unit from working on all vector elements at the same time. Sometimes the compiler will generate vector code even for scalar operations. To see how many average vector elements are active with each VPU instruction executed, you can use the VPU_ELEMENTS_ACTIVE/VPU_INSTRUCTIONS_EXECUTEDr atio.

Data Access Issues/Stalls

The next step is to look at the cache hit rate. You might have good vectorization efficiency, yet your data are arriving late. Most of the issues in Xeon Phi optimization are related to accessing memory efficiently. You can approximate the average clock cycle spent in executing the vector instructions in a code segment by dividing EXEC_STAGE_CYCLES by VPU_INSTRUCTIONS_EXECUTED to estimate the instruction latencies. If you find that this metric is higher than expected for an efficiently vectorized loop—say, more than the latencies for each instruction—you will need to root-cause the stalls happening in the processing the loop. Possible reasons why the memory subsystem may be having an issue delivering application data to the execution units on time include:

- Missing L1/L2 caches for data access

- MissingT LBe ntries

- Saturating the number of data streams that the hardware is able to fetch simultaneously

Recognizing Memory Access Latencies

To get the L1 miss ratio, divide the per thread events DATA_READ_MISS_OR_WRITE_MISS (the L1 references that missed the cache) by DATA_READ_OR_WRITE (the total number of L1 cache accesses). It should be high (> 95%) to achieve good results. If you are missing the L1 and L2 cache by too much, you may be stalled trying to access the memory.

Recognizing TLB Issues

TLB misses are another possible source of data access issues. As discussed in Chapter 4, TLB misses can lead to delay in the memory load, which may in turn cause reduced performance. This phenomenon is often seen in technical computing applications where the memory access lacks locality and jumps across page boundaries many more times than the number of TLB entries available for a given page size within a tight loop. This effect can be measured using the L1 TLB miss ratio, which is obtained by dividing the DATA_PAGE_WALK events (the number of L1 TLB misses) by the DATA_READ_WRITE events (the number of read-write operations). You can also calculate the L2 TLB miss ratio by dividing the LONG_DATA_PAGE_WALK events (the number of L2 TLB misses) by the number of DATA_READ_WRITEe vents (the total read-write operations performed by the application). For a 4K page, if sequentially accessed, this number should be 1/64 since there are 64 cache lines in a 4K page. So anything near 1 indicates that there is a heavy miss in the TLB due to a capacity or associativity conflict, which needs to be looked at carefully in the code. In this case, you can restructure the code and data structure to ameliorate this issue.

Recognizing Bandwidth Saturation

You also need to find out whether the code is saturating the memory by measuring the bandwidth used by your application. The VTune analyzer contains a custom profile for Xeon Phi to help with the process using uncore events. If you are saturating the memory bus, you will need to restructure the code or modify the algorithm to put less pressure on the memory subsystem and increase data reuse using cached data. If you are not saturating the memory bus, you may be able to insert proper prefetches to reduce the L1 and L2 misses. If the bus is saturated, you may be able to restructure code and data to reduce bus pressure.

Parallel Execution Overhead

Finally, you want to reduce the parallel overhead by balancing your workload and increasing the work for each core. Parallel execution overhead will show up in the profile as CPU_CLK_UNHALTED in OpenMP/MPI or other parallelization constructs. If you look at the parallel execution profile that shows up as a timeline in VTune, you will recognize the imbalance in the thread execution that may be causing the high OpenMP overhead. For MPI processes, you can use the cluster checker/profiler tool to recognize the parallel execution imbalance and overhead in the application.

Setting Target Performance

After recognizing that the code is memory bandwidth-, memory latency-, or compute-bound, you need to set a target performance for your application. Your application performance may also be bound by the PCIe bus bandwidth. The first step to setting the performance target is to use some standard Xeon Phi-optimized benchmarks or microbenchmarks to set the expected optimal performance of the Xeon Phi hardware you will be using. The SHOC benchmark that has been optimized for MIC can be used as a starting point. For example, the components of the SHOC benchmark, *BusSpeedDownload* and *BusSpeedUpload,* allow you to see the bandwidth and latencies of data transfer over the PCIe bus for various data sizes. You can use these benchmarks to estimate the performance of your application if it is PCIe bandwidth-bound. Once this is set, you can use various methods to reduce the bottleneck to change your code to go around the bottleneck. Similarly, you can run the Xeon Phi-ported STREAM benchmark to see and set the possible GDDR memory bandwidth achievable on your applications. Sometimes, because there is a limitation on the number of outstanding read buffers that the hardware provides, if your application has more streams of data being accessed than the hardware is capable of supporting, you may see a drop in achievable bandwidth. In this case, you may want to modify the STREAM or create your own microbenchmark to view the performance when the number of data streams you access is more than that used in the STREAM benchmark. Similarly, you may be able to use the peak achievable floating-point operation for single and double precision measured with the SHOC MaxFlops benchmark.

As for memory latency-bound applications, experience shows that the optimization of these workloads converts to bandwidth-bound applications. This is due to the fact that the optimization of such workloads includes prefetching of data in addition to other algorithmic or code restructuring work. Predicting the performance of such code is possible by using the bandwidth achievable by such applications when properly optimized.

Once you know the theoretical limit, a simple method for estimating your performance is to use the following equation:

$$P_T = P_C \times B_A/B_C$$

where

P_T = *target code performance*

P_C = *current code performance*

B_A = *achievable performance of bottleneck metric. This will be the peak achievable bandwidth, flops, and so forth for the benchmark condition.*

B_C = *current performance of the bottleneck metric for the code segment under optimization.*

It is extremely important to set a target performance for better understanding of the hardware performance as well as your code. This also guides you as to how much headroom there is for you to optimize a section of the application code and thus plan accordingly. It might also be possible for you to recognize that the code may not be suitable for optimization on Xeon Phi at this stage. For example, if the code works on byte-sized data (8-bit units) as the basic part of computation and cannot be cast into the basic vector units of Xeon Phi, which are 32-bit units, this may not be suitable for utilizing vector units properly and may require a fundamental change in the algorithm/data structure to make the code fit the architecture.

Optimizing Code

Once you have set a target performance, it is time to use various tools to optimize out the hotspots. The first step is to determine the tool to use. If you are looking at some math functions, it is best to see whether these are supported by any math library that has optimized code for Xeon Phi. This will help you get the maximum benefit out of the optimization work done by the library developers to achieve performance in a short time. The next step might be to use a compiler to optimize the code. This is a fairly involved process and requires understanding how the code compiler does some code transformations and their effect on bottlenecks.

Compiler-DrivenO ptimizations

To begin with, it may be possible to play with various compiler switches that help you generate a code stream based on the knowledge you have for the application. Optimization engineers have figured out ways to restructure your code so that it can get around various bottlenecks. Table 10-1 lists such optimizations and their effect on the various types of bottlenecks already discussed. Many of the code changes listed in the table can be done by modern compilers such as Intel Compiler automatically or through pragmas without requiring manual changes to code.

Table 10-1. *Code Restructuring Techniques to Reduce Specific Performance Bottlenecks*

Optimizations	Bottlenecks					
	VectorIn struction Generation and Execution	Branch Issues	TLBIssu es	Data Access Latencies	Memory Bandwidth Issue	Parallel Overhead
Prefetching				+	–	
Dataa lignment	+			+		
Removingp ointer aliasing	+					
StreamingS tore					+	
Usingl argep ages			+	–		
Loopi nterchange			+	+		
Loopf usion	+			+	+/–	
Loopf ission	+					
Loopp eeling		+				
Cacheb locking			+	+		
Unroll	+					
Unrolla ndj am					+	
Using Intel Cilk Plus array notation	+					+
OpenMP/CilkP lus/ TBB Optimization						+
Usingc ompiler supported classes/ elemental function/ libraries (memset/ svmlclasses)	+				+	

Note: + indicates reduces the bottleneck; – indicates may add to bottleneck.

Prefetching

Prefetching is a technique that can be used for reducing memory load latencies, but it may increase the GDDR memory bus bandwidth. Prefetching the data needed by a vector computation can reduce the data latencies and thus improve the vector performance. The Xeon Phi coprocessor supports a hardware prefetcher to prefetch L2 data when it recognizes certain data access patterns. But you will need to use software prefetches to get data to the L1 cache and for cases where the hardware is not able to recognize the access patterns. Intel Compiler provides compiler options and pragmas to help with software prefetching. Since the coprocessor fetches a cache line at a time, a single prefetch is needed to get 16 single-precision or 8 double-precision consecutive numbers in a cache line. Prefetching data helps when the data are not in the cache and is used in the subsequent computation before being evicted by a subsequent data load without being used. It is important that you use the proper prefetch distance so that the data fetch is timed properly to be used by the intended instruction. Prefetching uses bandwidth, so untimed or unnecessary data fetch may cause a loss of useful bandwidth, cache lines, and consequently the application performance.

Prefetching is turned on by default in the Intel Compiler at an optimization level at and over '-O2' and issued for regular memory access inside a loop. You can use the compiler report option "-opt-report-phase hlo -opt-report 3" to see the prefetching the compiler generates for each loop. You can use '-no-opt-prefetch' to turn off prefetching. Here 'hlo' stands for *high-level optimization*. Often this helps in testing whether compiler-generated prefetching is helping or hurting your application performance.

Intel Compiler can also generate prefetches for pointer access where addresses can be predicted in advance. Intel Compiler generates two prefetches: VPREFETCH1 from memory to L2, and VPREFETCH0 from L2 to L1 cache for each memory access. The prefetch distance is determined by the compiler heuristics but can be controlled by the compiler option -opt-prefetch-distance=d1[,d2], where d1 is the prefetch distance for vprefetch1 and optional d2 is for vprefetch0. The prefetch distance is expressed as the number of loop iterations after the loop is vectorized. If you want to prefetch only from L2 to L1, you can set d1 to 0 in the above compiler option.

You can also use compiler supported intrinsics to add your own prefetch instructions to the code. This is especially useful for indirect accesses like a[index[i]]. The Xeon Phi hardware prefetcher does not kick in if the software prefetch is successful.

Intel Compiler supports two C++ compiler pragmas and corresponding Fortran directives—pragma prefetch var:hint:distance and pragma noprefetch—to turn on or off the prefetch for a specific loop or function. If there are a lot of L2 misses, software prefetching is critical for the Xeon Phi coprocessor as this indicates that hardware prefetching is ineffective. In this case, it is critical to play with the software prefetch intrinsics, pragmas, and compiler switches for improving application performance. You can also provide clues to the compiler by using "loop count" directives to help the compiler with the software prefetch code generation.

DataA lignment

Data alignment is a technique that can be used to improve vector code generation and reduce memory load latencies. Aligning your computational data and letting the compiler know that the data being accessed are aligned to the 64-byte boundary can help the compiler generate efficient vector code for the Xeon Phi coprocessor. If the compiler knows that the array element accessed in a vectorized loop is aligned to the 64-byte boundary, it can avoid generating some prologue code needed to deal with non-cacheline-size-aligned arrays.

You can define an array to be aligned to a certain bytes' boundary by using __attribute__((aligned(Byte_aligned)) in C++ and !dir$ attributes align:Byte_aligned in Fortran.

For example, to allow the compiler to align array X to the 64-byte boundary, you can say float X[1000] __attribute__(aligned(64)). You can also use the compiler switch '-align' to allocate all arrays to certain byte boundaries.

For dynamic array allocation to aligned boundary, you can use __mm_malloc() and __mm_free() functions in the C++ compiler.

To communicate to the compiler that an array or pointer is aligned so that it can generate efficient vector code, you can use the pragma or directive "vector aligned" in Intel Compiler or attribute "aligned" with OpenMP4.0 directive omp simd or omp declare simd.

To declare that a specific data element is aligned to a certain byte boundary, you can use the `__assume_aligned` (`data, byte_aligned`) macro in C++ or the `ASSUME_ALIGNED data:byte aligned` directive in Fortran.

Once a loop is vectorized with aligned memory, there may still be some remainder loop to help with data access at the end of the loop that is less than the cache line size. In this case, you can pad your array with extra bytes to make them a multiple of cache lines. You can use a compile time switch `-opt-assume-safe-padding` to tell the compiler to assume that the arrays are padded properly to make their length a multiple of the cache line size. This will allow the compiler to remove the reminder/epilogue loop and reduce your code path length and hence potentially improve performance.

Data alignments also help data transfer over the PCIe bus. If you align data to the cache line boundary, the compiler may be able to DMA application data directly over the PCIe bus from the host to the Xeon Phi coprocessor or vice versa.

RemovingP ointerA liasing

Removing pointer aliasing is a technique that can be used for vectorizing code. Intel C/C++ Compiler assumes that more than one pointer in a code segment may point to the same location and thus uses caution when optimizing these codes, often resulting in nonvectorized code generation. Even though Fortran language supports pointers, the language definition assumes that the pointer is not aliased by default, unlike the C language definition.

To let the compiler know that your code adheres to the ISO C aliasing rule, use the `-ansi-alias` compiler switch. This allows aggressive optimization of the code, and you will often find the code to be vectorized by the compiler compared to the case where the switch is not used. You can also use the `-restrict` option together with the C `restrict` keyword to express pointer nonaliasing of the function parameters.

Streaming Store

Steaming store is a technique that can be used for reducing GDDR memory bus bandwidth pressure. In general, the Xeon Phi memory write includes a memory read to get the data from the memory into the cache line. However, this causes unnecessary waste of bandwidth if the data are write-only. Xeon Phi implements special instructions `vmovnrngoaps` and `vmovnrngoapd` for the case in which the write is a streaming store and the data need not be read into the cache. These instructions are useful when you have unmasked cacheline-aligned vector writes. By default the compiler should generate these instructions using its own heuristics, but you need to make sure this happens if the code generated by the compiler does not contain these special instructions. To help the compiler generate streaming store for a loop, you first need to make sure that the array is aligned by using the pragma or directive "vector aligned" for the data array and specifying "#pragma vector nontemporal" or "!DEC$ vector nontemporal" for the data element. You can also force the compiler to use streaming store by using the switch "-opt-streaming-store always".

You can use the compiler reporting mechanism "-vec-report6" to see whether or not the compiler generated streaming stores for a loop.

Using Large Pages

The *page size* is a block of virtual address space that the coprocessor OS uses for memory management. For example, if the page size is 4K, 4MB of the page requested by an application will use 1000 pages. The Xeon Phi coprocessor's memory management unit supports page sizes 4kB and 2MB. A TLB is used to cache the virtual to physical page address mapping so that when applications try to access a physical page, depending on a virtual address, the TLB entry can be used to locate the physical memory location quickly. When a mapping is not cached in the TLB entries, the translation is done manually by walking a four-level table structure, which is kept in memory. The walking of the table structure involves pointer-chasing code and is time-consuming, especially on low-frequency cores such as that of the Xeon Phi coprocessor. Sometimes when an application is accessing memory sequentially and the page misses are too high, it may be beneficial to use larger page sizes so that more address space mapping is available through the TLB structure of the coprocessor, thus reducing the number of TLB misses. With 8 TLB entries in 2MB pages, you can cover 16 MB of memory address spaces, whereas with 64 entries for 4kB pages you can only cover 248 kB only. On the other hand, if you are randomly accessing pages (say, larger than 2MB) all over the virtual address space and you do not use much data out of that page, it may be more beneficial to use 4kB pages as they provide more TLB entries than 2MB pages and thus could reduce the number of TLB misses on Xeon Phi. Another problem with using 2MB pages is the possibility of allocating more memory than needed—if, say, only 1 byte per 2MB pages is touched, you may want to use 4kB pages. The goal is always to reduce the TLB misses.

The Xeon Phi coprocessor OS supports *transparent huge pages* (THP). The THP support automatically promotes or demotes page sizes on the Xeon Phi coprocessor OS. You can control the huge page support in Xeon Phi by using the "/sys/kernel/mm/transparent_hugepage/enabled" file in the coprocessor OS virtual file system.

To disable the THP, do:

```
echo never > /sys/kernel/mm/transparent_hugepage/enabled
```

To enable the THP, do:

```
echo always > /sys/kernel/mm/transparent_hugepage/enabled
```

To be able to control the THP programmatically, do:

```
echo madvise > /sys/kernel/mm/transparent_hugepage/enabled
```

The madvise is used when you do not want to waste page memory by enabling the THP system wide but want to do that for specific memory region. In this case, you can use the system call int madvise(void *addr, size_t length, int MADV_HUGEPAGE); to set the address range where the THP support is to be enabled for the applications.

Always play with this option in the Xeon Phi coprocessor, as it could have significant impact on code performance one way or the other.

Loop Optimizations

Intel Compiler provides various high-level loop optimizations that relieve the programmer from having to do them manually. Some of these are discussed below. In general, you should let the compiler perform the optimizations and do them manually only when the compiler is unable to perform them as required. Manually performing these transformations causes the code to be hard to read and maintain and may make them specific to a hardware architecture.

Loop Interchange

Intel Compiler can interchange loop indices to provide efficient memory access. This optimization is used to increase single stride references and thus make better use of cache lines and fewer TLB misses for large memory access.

Consider, for example, the following loop in C language.

Code Listing 10-2. Example of Loop Interchange before the Modification

```
for(j=0; j< LENGTH; j++){
    for(i=0; i<LENGTH; i++){
        data[i][j] = 0.0;
    }
}
```

Since the 'C' arrays are 'row' major, to access consecutive bytes, you need to increment the 'j' index inside the inner loop to make use of cachelines more efficiently. This can be done by interchanging these for loops and bringing the 'j' loop inside, as shown in Code Listing 10-3.

Code Listing 10-3. Example of Loop Interchange for Optimal Performance

```
for(i=0; i< LENGTH; j++){
      for(j=0; j<LENGTH; j++){
          data[i][j] = 0.0;
      }
}
```

This is done by Intel Compiler and can be detected if you turn on `-O3 -opt-report-phase HLO` in compile time options. It may look something like the following code.

Code Listing 10-4. Compiler Output Reporting Loop Interchange

```
LOOP INTERCHANGE in loops at line: x y z
Loopnest permutation ( 1 2 3 ) --> ( 2 3 1 )
```

Loop Fusion/Fission

Loop fusion is the process of fusing or merging two separate loops into a single loop to increase the data reuse or remove unnecessary data movement. Often in technical computing applications, one loop runs through a data stream, does some computation, and creates a secondary array, which is scanned again in a second loop immediately following the given loop to do some more computations. In such cases, it may be beneficial to merge the loops to make better use of bus bandwidth and increase the flops/byte ratio. Intel Compiler can perform loop fusion at optimization level O3. You can determine whether or not the compiler is fusing loops by turning on the *high-level optimization* (HLO) report. Sometimes you may want to tell the compiler not to fuse a set of loops, as they may hurt performance due to lack of enough hardware resources. For example, source codes with multiple memory read streams distributed across different loops may perform worse with loop fusion due to limits on the number of read buffers. In this case, you can use `#pragma nofusion` to prevent the compiler from fusing the loops that may cause performance degradation.

Loop fission is the opposite of loop fusion, distributing large loops into two smaller loops. It is useful when vectorization or software pipelining cannot take place due to high register pressure—that is, the code generator runs out of register to be able to vectorize the code. Intel Compiler supports pragma/directive "`distribute point`,"which allows programmers to do loop fission without manual restructuring. If placed before a loop, the compiler will try to use heuristics to fission the loop. You can also place the directive inside the loop to explicitly tell the compiler where to perform the loop fission.

Loop Peeling

Often conditional statements are put inside a loop to handle boundary conditions, memory alignment, and so on. This may prevent vectorization, as the code inside the loop may become complex. In this case, it is possible to simplify the loop by peeling out the conditional case—say, the unaligned data access case outside the loop—and performing operations on the aligned data inside the loop, thus allowing vectorization of the loop.

This is another optimization that Intel Compiler performs and can be detected in the HLO report before implementing it manually.

Cache Blocking

Cache blocking is a very useful optimization for the Xeon Phi coprocessor to make optimal use of cache data. Since memory access is often the main bottleneck in many technical computing applications, it is a common optimization applied to such code. The optimization involves restructuring the data access in a loop so that they fit in the L1 or L2 cache. This is done by breaking the large array into smaller blocks of memory area, pulling the memory fragments into the cache, and working on them before moving to the next block of data. By controlling the data cache locality, the application can benefit from a high cache hit rate and thus improve performance.

The effectiveness of such optimization depends on the data block size, the cache size, and the reuse of the cache block. Intel Compiler applies cache blocking at the –O3 optimization level and is reported by the HLO compiler optimization report.

If the compiler is not able to perform this optimization, it is often possible to perform this manually to get performance improvement on Xeon Phi applications.

Loop Unrolling

Loop unrolling is another common loop optimization performed by the Intel Compiler. By unrolling a loop, you provide more work to the coprocessor for each loop iteration, reducing the branches and the number of cache misses. For example, you can convert the loop in Code Listing 10-5 to something like that in Code Listing 10-6.

Code Listing 10-5. Loop Performing Data Copy

```
for(i=0; i<SIZE;i++){
   x[i] = y[i];
}
```

Listing 10-6. Loop Unrolled by 4

```
int lastBlock = 4*SIZE/4;
for(i=0; i<lastBlock;i+=4){
   x[i] = y[i];
   x[i+1] = y[i+1];
   x[i+2] = y[i+2];
   x[i+3] = y[i+3];
}

for(i=lastBlock;i<SIZE;i++){
   X[i] = y[i];
}
```

Fortunately, Intel Compiler performs these transformations for you, so you do not need to do them manually. It is often a good idea to let the compiler do the unroll optimization, because performing it manually may hurt other optimizations that the compiler may be able to perform if the original loop was maintained.

Intel Compiler supports the pragmas/directives "pragma unroll," "pragma unroll(n)," and "pragma nounroll" to control loop unroll optimization.

Unroll and Jam

Unroll and jam refers to unrolling the outer loops and jamming them together into a new loop. This technique helps increase the flops/bytes ratio of the computations performed in the loop and is an important optimization for Xeon Phi architecture. Keep in mind, however, that this optimization increases the register pressure as the amount of unrolling is increased and may cause performance drop if the loop runs out of registers causing register spill and fill. Intel Compiler supports the pragmas/directives "pragma unroll_and_jam" and "pragma nounroll_and_jam"to controlthisoptim ization.

Using Intel Cilk Plus Array Notation

Intel Cilk Plus array notation is a C/C++ language extension implemented by Intel Compiler to express a data-parallel operation on array objects. Expressing array operations in this notation helps Intel Compiler map these operations to Xeon Phi-implemented vector data and instructions.[4]

For example, you can express an array multiply and add of three arrays a, b and c of the same dimensions as follows:

```
c[:] = a[:]*b[:] + c[:];
```

This notation not only removes the explicit loop needed to operate on these arrays as done in conventional C program but also helps the compiler to map these array operations directly to the Xeon Phi vector FMA operations described in Chapter 3. This notation is a very useful and an easy way of expressing vector operations in code that can also provide a good performance gain.

Parallelizing Code with OpenMP/Cilk Plus/TBB

Intel Compiler supports OpenMP constructs and may help you parallelize your code easily to maximize the core utilization and performance on the Xeon Phi architecture. You can use the -openmp-report compiler switch to see the sections of the code/loop with OpenMP pragmas that the compiler is able to parallelize. Parallelization with low parallel runtime overhead and vector unit utilization is a must for Xeon Phi performance. In addition, runtime for OpenMP contains various functions or environment variables to control and improve OpenMP performance on Xeon Phi. In order to get optimal application performance, you need to make sure the load is balanced and can use various OpenMP scheduling schemes to enforce them. You can also play with the number of threads that provides optimal performance on your workload.

In order to get good performance, you need to make sure that the OpenMP threads are affinitized to hardware cores on the Xeon Phi coprocessors. You can use the "KMP_AFFINITY" environment variable to do so. You can determine, depending on how the data are shared among the threads, whether to place them in compact, scattered, balanced, or explicit modes. You can also use the environment variable KMP_PLACE_THREADS to place threads on the subset of the coprocessor cores, and it is easier to use than using explicit values in KMP_AFFINITY. Another useful environment variable is KMP_SETTINGS. When this variable is set, the OpenMP runtime will print out various OpenMP variable settings being used by the runtime. This will allow you to debug and tune the OpenMP execution.

A useful optimization with OpenMP is the *loop collapse* directive. In order to efficiently use all the cores, it is important that each core gets enough task to amortize for the OpenMP thread start/stop and synchronization overhead. In multiple nested loops, it may be possible to collapse loops so that each loop gets an increased amount of work between synchronization points. This is done through the OpenMP directive omp parallel for collapse.

OpenMP barriers implicitly used at the end of loops for thread synchronization can be a large overhead in Xeon Phi due to the sheer number of threads involved. You need to look for opportunities to remove such barriers by using the nowait clause where possible.

One of the drawbacks of OpenMP is the lack of *composability*. This means that if you are calling into a library—say, MKL—which may itself be using OpenMP parallelism, you may end up oversubscribing the cores of Xeon Phi processor, thereby causing degraded performance. This is the result of the OpenMP runtime for your code spawning a certain number of threads and the MKL library itself creating another set of threads. Users of OpenMP should

---

[4]For detailed syntax of Cilk Plus array notation, see *Intel® C++ Compiler XE 13.1 User and Reference Guide*. Document number: 323273-131US. (http://software.intel.com/sites/products/documentation/doclib/iss/2013/compiler/cpp-lin/).

carefully play with OpenMP threads for their applications and underlying libraries that use OpenMP to control oversubscription. For example, MKL provides its own environment variable to tell it how many threads to spawn to perform its tasks. Cilk Plus[5] or TBB[6] parallel constructs do not have these problems, because the parallelization in these libraries is based on the "work stealing" concept, whereby the number of threads is kept constant for the applications and, depending on the availability of idle cores, tasks are executed as needed. Note that OpenMP is available in both C++ and Fortran languages, whereas Cilk Plus is mainly C/C+, and TBB is purely a C++ language-basedi mplementation.

Using Xeon Phi Optimized Class, Elemental Function, and Libraries in Intel Compiler

Intel Compiler provides various utility libraries and classes to allow users to make use of optimized code. The Short Vector Math Library (SVML) is supported by Intel Compiler and provides various vectorizable math functions. Intel Compiler may detect use of these functions in your code and use the SVML library to vectorize the code. Thus calling these routines in your code can help in producing vector code and thus providing optimal performance. The SVML includes transcendental functions such as cos, sin, tan, exp, log, erf, and so forth. The Intel Compiler reference guide for SVML lists these functions and their corresponding intrinsics.

Elemental function allows you to write data-parallel functions. This in turn allows the compiler to vectorize code at the function call site. So if you call such functions from inside a loop, the loop can be vectorized by the compiler.[7]

Intel Compiler has various default options that allow it to recognize certain constructs and apply optimized library calls instead of generating compiled code for those constructs. For example, it can recognize a matrix multiplication loop nest and use an optimized matrix multiplication library instead. You can use the compiler switch -no-opt-matmul if you want to use your own code. The compiler also has its own implementation of dynamic memory usage routines such as _intel_fast_memcpy, _intel_fast_memset, and _intel_fast_memcmp. These can be used by the compiler instead of generic memcpy, memset, or memcmp routines at the –O3 optimization level.

Vectorization with Intel Compiler

Intel Compiler provides strong support for vectorization using auto-vectorization and pragma-driven vectorization. It is a must to have efficient vector code running in order for Xeon Phi to provide performance, and Intel Compiler plays a big role in it. The steps for vectorization with Intel Compiler follow.

Step 1: Using Compiler Report

The vector report of Intel Compiler can tell you which loops are vectorized and which are not. The report will give you some clue as to why it did not vectorize specific loops. The –vec-report levels (0 to 6) control emission of the following vectorization report messages:

```
LOOP WAS VECTORIZED
loop was not vectorized: << reason >>
Reason, dependence information: dependence from xx to yy
```

---

[5]http://software.intel.com/en-us/intel-cilk-plus
[6]http://software.intel.com/en-us/intel-tbb
[7]For detailed syntax of Cilk Plus array notation, see *Intel® C++ Compiler XE 13.1 User and Reference Guide.* Document number: 323273-131US.(http://software.intel.com/sites/products/documentation/doclib/iss/2013/compiler/cpp-lin/).

Step 2: Vectorizing Code

There are various techniques to vectorize a code if it does not autovectorize. The first step is to use the *guided autoparallelization* (GAP) feature in Intel Compiler. This is activated by using the –guide switch. It will provide advice on code changes, applying certain pragmas in your code and adding command line options to help vectorize the code.

The second method is to use the Cilk Plus array notation discussed in this section. Try to maintain unit stride array access for optimal code performance. You can apply other techniques shown in Table 10-1 that help with vectorization. For example, using the SVML can help vectorize the code using the random number generator inside a loop. It would also make sense to define your functions as vector elemental functions if they are called from inside a loop, which would help vectorize the loop that otherwise might not be vectorized.

Sometimes you will see that you vectorize a code yet it does not show any performance gain. Such failure might be due to inefficient vector code generation—as in the case of using scatter/gather instruction, which is not very efficient in Xeon Phi implementation. In such cases, you may want to restructure the code to let the compiler generate unitstr idecode .

Using the Math Kernel Library

Many technical computing applications may benefit from the MKL ported to Xeon Phi. If your application uses any library function available in the MKL, try using them for Xeon Phi. You can use following coding techniques to extract maximum performance out of the MKL on Xeon Phi processor:

1. MKL routines perform well when 2MB page sizes are used to hold the input/output data to MKL function calls. So make sure to play with THP support or other methods to utilize 2MB pages in MKL-based applications.

2. Align data to a 64-byte boundary.

3. Specifying `MKL_MIC_MAX_MEMORY` to set aside memory that can be used by MKL automatic offload can enhance MKL routine performance, as this allows the math routines to reserve and keep memory allocated on the coprocessor for optimized performance.

4. It may be beneficial to use suggested memory affinity for OpenMP when using certain MKL routines.

    For BLAS, LAPACK, and Sparse BLAS routines, set OpenMP affinity to:

    `KMP_AFFINITY= compact, granularity=fine`

    ForF FT:

    `KMP_AFFINITY=scatter, granularity=fine`

    ForF FT:

    - Set OMP_NUM_THREADS to the power of 2.

    - Set the number of threads to 128 if the total size of input and output data is less than 30MB, the approximate size of last level cache. Otherwise set to 4* (number of Xeon Phi cores).

    - For 2D or higher FFTs and for single-precision use, leading dimensions should be divisible by 8 (half the vector length), not 16; and for double precision—the leading dimensions should be divisibleb y4,not8.

The section "Parallelizing Code with OpenMP/Cilk Plus/TBB" discussed how to detect and reduce threadingo verhead.

Cluster-Level Tuning

MPI can be used to develop and run applications on Xeon Phi in three different models. In the *coprocessor-only model*, all MPI ranks run on Xeon Phi natively and communicate with other Xeon Phi on the host or other cards in the cluster. In the *symmetric model*, the MPI ranks run on both hosts and Xeon Phi in a cluster. In the *offload model,*e ach MPI rank can run on the host and perform offload.

In all of these programming models, the MPI overhead on Xeon Phi may become a serious bottleneck and need some sort of debugging/profiling tools to resolve the issues. The Intel cluster tools Trace Collector and Analyzer[8] may help you with the cluster-level optimization of code running on a cluster of the Xeon Phi processor. This is a two-level process in which you first detect and resolve any MPI issue at the node level, where the Xeon Phi card looks like a separate node to the host. You use the Trace Collector and Analyzer to detect node-level issues. Here you can fix the load imbalance between the host code and the coprocessor code to achieve optimal node performance by optimizing the computation-to-communication ratio.

Remember that since the compute power is different between the host and Xeon Phi, you need to carefully think through how the work must be divided between the host and coprocessor for balanced execution. It is important to minimize the MPI communication between the host and the coprocessor in a node and across the node. You also need to think carefully about the MPI rank topology and use a mix of MPI+OpenMP on Xeon Phi to improve the computation-to-communication overhead within a node and across the nodes. Usually it is better to use the least number of MPI processes on Xeon Phi for communicating with other MPI processes on the host or other nodes in a cluster. This can be achieved with the hierarchical MPI or MPI+X (OpenMP or another threading mechanism) programming model.

Another option that may be used for cluster-level programming with the Xeon Phi coprocessor is to apply the offload model to use Xeon Phi from the MPI ranks running on each host node in the cluster. This MPI+offload model reduces the number of MPI communications between the nodes and thus reduces the cluster-level complexity during programe xecution.

Summary

This chapter reviewed the optimization techniques and processes for code development for the Xeon Phi processor. It looked at how Intel Compiler pragmas provide alternatives to manual code changes to achieve performance improvements. It also explained how to deploy various libraries such as the MKL and SVML to improve code performances.

The next chapter will discuss various case studies and techniques for optimizing a category of applications on XeonP hi.

---

[8]http://software.intel.com/en-us/intel-trace-analyzer

CHAPTER 11

■ ■ ■

Algorithm and Data Structures for Xeon Phi

Algorithms and data structures appropriate for Xeon Phi are active fields of research and deserve a book on their own. This chapter will touch only on some common algorithm and data structure optimization techniques that I have found useful for common technical computing applications. These algorithms will definitely evolve as we gain more experience with the hardware. This chapter does not derive the algorithms but rather focuses on optimization techniques to achieve good performance on Xeon Phi. For example, I assume familiarity with Monte Carlo simulation techniques and the algorithms used in financial applications and instead focus on those components of the algorithms that be optimized to make the most effective use of Xeon Phi architecture capabilities.

This chapter looks at how the Xeon Phi architecture affects the design of the algorithm and data structures that are targeted for this coprocessor. Although existing algorithms optimized for Intel Xeon processors will work on Xeon Phi, not all algorithms will scale by reason of the following differences in the cores:

- Xeon Phi has a much higher number of threads (240) compared with the 24 threads supported on the typical Intel Xeon processor core. Moreover, the single-threaded performance of Xeon Phi is much slower than that of the Xeon processor. As a result of these two characteristics of the Xeon Phi coprocessor, the part of an algorithm that depends on single-threaded performance will be adversely affected and need modification. The low serial performance causes thread synchronization primitives to take on a higher percentage of the overall runtime and may require a fundamental change in the algorithm to reduce the parallel overhead.

- Xeon Phi has a larger vector length than Xeon: 512 bits vs. 256 bits. Loops that benefit from a 256-bit vector length may not perform well on 512 bits due to insufficient loop counts.

- The total flops achievable on the 60-core Xeon Phi coprocessor is 2 petaflops (PF) single precision vs. ~1 teraflops (TF) on a two-socket Xeon E5-2670 processor running at 2.6 GHz. This is achieved by using all the cores and all the vector operations efficiently. On the other hand, the practical memory bandwidth per core on Xeon Phi is less than that on Xeon. The lower flops/byte supported by the Xeon Phi coprocessor compared to the Xeon processor may require different algorithms to solve the same problem.

- The amount of memory per core, ~266 MB per Xeon Phi core vs. 4 GB per core on a 24-core Xeon two-socket system with 96 GB memory, will in many cases require changes in the algorithm to accommodate core scheduling changes to handle a large number of tasks with a small work size per task.

These data points show that the only way to achieve better performance on Xeon Phi is to have the algorithms exploit the massive flops available on the Xeon Phi and mostly running from cache. The Xeon Phi coprocessor will also need to be paired with the Xeon processor capabilities of large memory and high single-threaded performance to achieve this goal. Since the vector sizes are wide, the data to be vectorized will need to be wide enough to make use of the vector capabilities. Key to achieving high performance on Xeon Phi architecture is implementing an efficient algorithm paired with an appropriate workload size.

Algorithm and Data Structure Design Rules for Xeon Phi

To exploit the power performance efficiency of Xeon Phi processor, an algorithm should conform to the following rules:

- Rule 1. *Scalable parallelization*: The code should be able to scale to all the cores and preferably all the threads. Not only will you need to vectorize at the thread level, but you must also scale the algorithm to a large number of threads.

- Rule2. *Efficient vectorization*: The code should be able to efficiently use 512-bit vectors on Xeon Phi. This requires that the input dataset be large enough to provide enough work for the coprocessor such that:

  - The input array size is long enough.

  - The working dataset residing on memory is properly aligned for optimal vector load and store.

  - The working dataset accessed is coalesced so that, when filling the cache line, the consecutive bytes come from consecutive regions rather than needing to be gathered fromm ultipled atal ocations.

- Rule3. *Optimal cache reuse*: Maximum reuse of the cache should overcome the memory bandwidth limitation and increase sustainable flops/byte.

Rules 1 and 2 require that the problem size match the machine size, which is defined as the (vector length × number of cores). For a 60-core Xeon Phi, the machine size is (64 bytes × 60 cores) = 3.8 kB. To fully utilize the hardware, the algorithm will need at least 3.8 kB of data to work on.

Each algorithm should go through the following high-level steps to perform optimally on the Xeon Phi coprocessor:

1. Divide the data equally among the cores and threads within a core.

2. Divide the data so that each portion of working dataset can fit in the L2 cache of each core.

3. Work on the data using vector primitives.

4. Merge the results back using vector and optimal reduction algorithms.

Each data structure should possess the following characteristics for optimal cache reuse and minimal pressure on memory interconnects:

1. If needed and possible, convert the array of structures to an aligned structure of arrays for single-stride access for all threads running on the coprocessor.

2. Block the data structure. The data should be blockable so that they can fit in the cache and bew orkedo n.

Let's look at the logical thinking behind some common algorithms to see how they can be implemented to run efficiently on Xeon Phi architecture.

General Matrix-Matrix Multiply Algorithm (GEMM)

General matrix-matrix multiplication (GEMM) is one of the most commonly used algorithms in technical computing applications and is available in the basic linear algebra library (BLAS) in the form of the routines SGEMM or DGEMM for single-precision and double-precision dense matrix-matrix multiply operations. xGEMM, where x can be 's' for single precision and 'd' for double precision, computes the new value of matrix C based on the matrix product of matrices A and B and the old value of matrix C, formulated as:

```
C = alpha*op(A) * op(B) + beta*C
```

where `alpha` and `beta` are scalars and `op` indicates a possible transpose of the matrices.

The general operation is a triple-nested loop:

```
for(i=0; i<M;i++)
  for(j=0;j<N;j++)
    for(l=0;l<k;l++)
        C(i,j) = C(i,j) + A(i,l)*B(i,j)
```

The problem with this triple-nested loop algorithm is that it:

- Will not vectorize by the compiler because the compiler is unable to resolve aliasing among arrays A, B, and C.

- Has in general a very large memory footprint to fit in the L2 cache of each core.

- Demands a lot of memory bandwidth, requiring three memory accesses to A, B, and C to performa nF MAo peration.

Rules 1 and 3: Scalable Parallelization and Optimal Cache Reuse

In order to optimize this algorithm for Xeon Phi, make use of the blocked dense matrix multiply method. It can be shown that if A, B, and C matrices are divided into blocks with conformable block sizes, the blocked matrix-matrix multiplication can be done like a regular matrix-matrix multiplication.[1] This property enables you to utilize the same triple nested loop algorithm described previously to work on blocks of matrices instead of individual elements and arrive at the same result as multiplying the whole matrices. This method allows you to break up the work among the cores of Xeon Phi and optimize cache reuse.

You will need to break up the dataset so that you can perform multiple GEMM operations in parallel on each available thread on the coprocessor and work out of the cache. For illustration's sake, assume that we are using two cores of the Xeon Phi. Figure 11-1 shows how input matrices for op() set to no-transpose, A, B, and C are broken into blocks of a certain size to be distributed between these two cores. The blocks of matrices B and C that are colored black will be worked on by core 0 till finished with all the blocks, and the blocks of matrices B and C that are colored light gray will be worked on by core 1. The dark gray blocks of matrix A will be needed by each core and will be replicated in the respective L2 caches of each processor. The results will be the desired output once all the tasks distributed to all the cores are finished and the destination memory is updated. The block size depends on the L2 cache size. It should be chosen such that the multiple blocks fit in the L2 cache (512 kB) of each core and the most commonly used A and B blocks also fit the L1 cache (32 kB) to provide fastest access.

---

[1] Howard Eves, *Elementary Matrix Theory*.D overB ooks,1980.

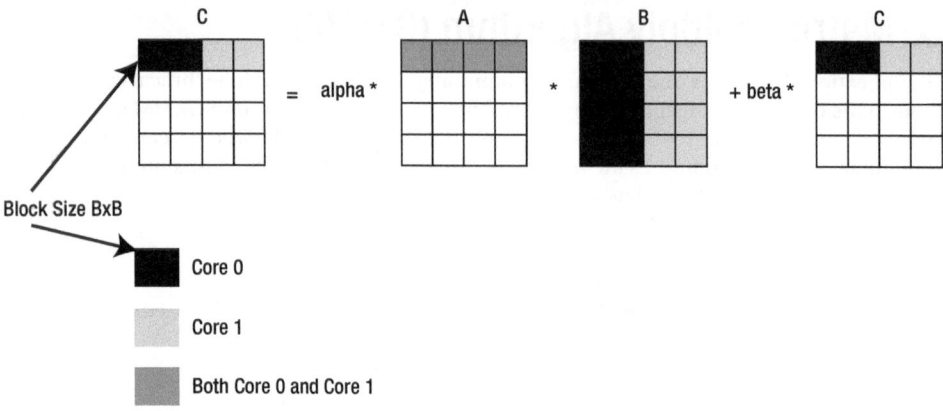

Figure 11-1. *xGEMM parallelization using blocked matrix*

Rule 2:E fficientV ectorization

The blocks submitted to each core are worked on by multiple SMT threads in parallel on each core (Figure 11-2). For sGEMM (single precision), each block is broken into 16x16 subblocks aligned to the cache line boundary. The 16-element width of the subblocks is chosen to match the vector width of the Xeon Phi coprocessor. The subblocks of C can be aligned loaded into 16 vector registers (16x16 register blocking). Each row of B subblock (16x1) is loaded into another vector register by memory-aligned load. (In Xeon Phi, there are 32 vector registers per thread.)

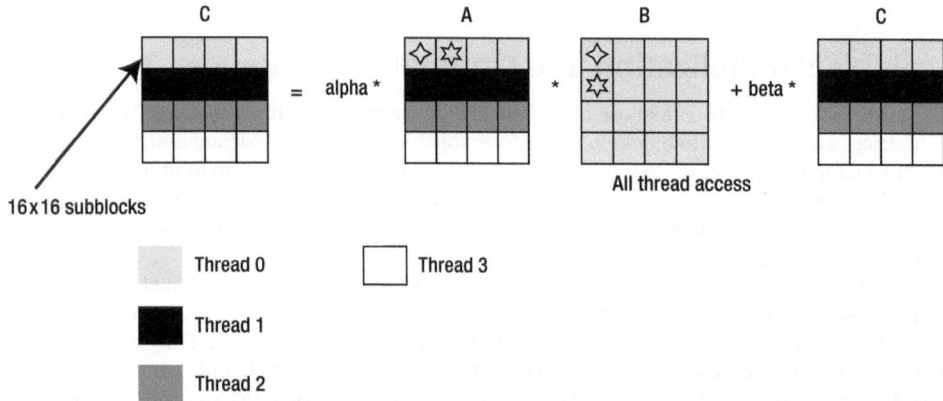

Figure 11-2. *Per core operation on a matrix block. Here A, B, and C represent blocks of the original matrix in Figure 11-1 assigned to a core*

In Figure 11-2, to compute a subblock of C, a column of A coming from the L1 cache can be multiplied by a row of B and accumulated into 16 vector registers holding C. To illustrate the process, think about a 2x2 square matrix A, B, and C. By sketching on a sheet of paper, you will see that the first components of C11, C12, C21, and C22 can be obtained by multiplying A11 × B11, A11 × B12, A21 × B11, and A21 × B12, which is obtained by multiplying a column of A (A11, A21) by a row of B (B11 and B12). Assuming a 2-wide vector register, you load and broadcast A11 in one register and multiply with a register loaded with a row of B to update C registers holding C11 and C12 values (first components) of the matrix multiplication. This can be extended to the 16x16 matrix subblocks discussed here.

Using the cache blocking and software prefetch, you can get the values of the matrix blocks into cache levels L2 and L1 to achieve good efficiency with this algorithm on Xeon Phi.

It can be verified that this algorithm conforms to all three design rules of an optimal algorithm for the Xeon Phi coprocessor. It satisfies Rule 1 by dividing the input matrices into smaller chunks to be able to distribute them equally among the cores and threads within a core. The algorithm satisfies Rule 3 by fitting the data into the L2 and L1 caches and including prefetches to reduce data access latencies. And it satisfies Rule 2 by working on the data unit by vector instructions. At the output generation step, the output is done in parallel by each core and individual threads within a core without contention by working on the disjoint area of array C.

The simple square matrix multiplication example considered in this section is an artificial example. Implementing matrix multiplication in practice requires handling various shapes and boundary conditions for optimal performance. I highly recommend that you make use of off-the-shelf libraries such as Intel MKL for such operations. These libraries implement various BLAS and Sparse BLAS routines and make it easier for users to optimize for Xeon Phi coprocessors.

Molecular Dynamics

Molecular dynamics (MD) are a subset of the broader class of applications known as the *particle dynamics* or *n-body applications*. The goal of these applications is to simulate the interaction between particles using the Newtonian equations of motion caused by force fields defined by the underlying physics. In the MD problem, the goal is to determine the molecular movement over a period of time till the molecules and atoms involved in the simulation get to a steady state. The forces and potential energy involved are defined by molecular mechanics and used to compute the velocities and movement of the atoms and molecules. The MD algorithm is used in many fields besides classical mechanics, including material science, biochemistry, and biophysics.

The basic algorithm of MD simulation is very simple and straightforward. It is a time-stepped simulation where, at each time step, the application calculates the forces between the atoms. The forces may be bonded or non-bonded forces. Using the calculated forces, the atoms' positions are updated. The time step is repeated till either steady state is reached or a certain number of time steps have been performed.

The molecules and atoms are represented by an array of data structures containing the forces, velocities, and positions of each particle. The most time-consuming computation of MD code is computing the nonbonded force field, which requires computing the force exerted on a particle by every other particle in the system. This computation consumes almost 80 percent of execution time for practical workload sizes. A common optimization is to set a cutoff distance for the neighbor list of interacting molecules and to calculate forces only among them. MD code can also benefit from spatial sorting of the neighbor list to help optimize the force calculation. This section looks at the time-consuming force-computation component of MD applications on Xeon Phi. Other computations such as the neighbor-list build and sort may be done on the host processor.

In general, MD code can compute various types of forces between the molecules. Code Listing 11-1 shows the pseudocode for a *Lennard-Jones force calculation* in an MD kernel.[2] The Lennard-Jones potential is widely used in MD code to describe interactions between the molecules or atoms being simulated.

Code Listing 11-1. Lennard-Jones Force Calculation

```
// loop over all the atoms
for (int i = 0; i < numAtoms; i++)
{
    //Get position info for a given atom
    POSITION ipos = position[i];

    neighList = getNeigborList(i);
    numNeighbors = neighList.getCount();
```

---

[2]A similar implementation of this code can be found in the SHOC benchmark for Xeon Phi. https://github.com/vetter/shoc-mic

```
// loop over all the neighbors of the given atom
for(int j = 0;j < numNeighbors;j++)
{
    int jidx = neighList[j];
    // get position of the nrighbor jidx
    POSITION jpos = position[jidx];

    double delx = ipos.x - jpos.x;
    double dely = ipos.y - jpos.y;
    double delz = ipos.z - jpos.z;

    // compute distance between the neighbors
    double r2inv = delx*delx + dely*dely + delz*delz;

    // if the distance is less than cutoff distance
    if (r2inv < cutsq) {

        // calculate the force
        r2inv = 1.0f/r2inv;
        double r6inv = r2inv * r2inv * r2inv;
        double force = r2inv*r6inv*(lj1*r6inv - lj2);
        // accumulate the force value for this atom
        Force[i].x += delx * force;
        Force[i].y += dely * force;
        Force[i].z += delz * force;
        Force[jidx].x -= delx * force;
        Force[jidx].y -= dely * force;
        Force[jidx].z -= delz * force;

    }
  }
}
```

The goal here is to show how this code could be optimized for the Xeon Phi coprocessor. The code behaves as follows:

1. The code goes over each atom one at a time.

2. The code loops over all the neighbors of the atom.

3. The code gets the positions of the neighboring atoms and calculates the force using the distance between the atoms.

4. If the distance between the atoms is less than the cutoff distance, the code updates the force for this atom and the interacting atoms.

Rule 1:S calableP arallelization

In order to run this code for Xeon Phi in accordance with the rules for optimal algorithms, I make the modifications shown in Code Listing 11-2. The first rule dictates that the code should be scalable to all the threads. In this case, I use OpenMP parallel and dynamic schedule to achieve this scalability. Since the amount of work for each atom depends on the neighbor size and may not be equal, dynamic scheduling will prevent load imbalance in the overall force computation task on Xeon Phi. This modification is provided in line 1 of Code Listing 11-2. Since in general MD code will have millions of atoms to be simulated per node, this will provide enough work for each thread.

Code Listing 11-2. Xeon Phi Lennard-Jones Force Calculation

```
// loop over all the atoms in parallel
#pragma omp parallel for schedule(dynamic)    ----- line 1
for (int i = 0; i < numAtoms; i++)
{
    POSITION ipos = position[i];
    neighList = get NeigborList(i);
    numNeighbors = neighList.getCount();
    // loop over all the neighbors of the given atom
    for(int j = 0;j < numNeighbors;j++)
    {
        int jidx = neighList[j];
        // prefetch position array to cache level 1 and level 2
        // Note you need to prefetch 16 elements to help with the
        //gather - just shown 2 for clarity
        __mm_prefetch(&position[j+offset], _MM_HINT_TO);  -- line 15 // prefetch to LO cache
        __mm_prefetch(&position[j+offset], __MM_HINT_T1;  -- line 16 // prefetch to L1 cache
        // get position of the nrighbor jidx
        POSITION jpos = position[jidx];
        double delx = ipos.x - jpos.x;
        double dely = ipos.y - jpos.y;
        double delz = ipos.z - jpos.z;

        // compute distance between the neighbors
        double r2inv = delx*delx + dely*dely + delz*delz;

        // if the distance is less than cutoff distance
        if (r2inv < cutsq) {
            // calculate the force
            r2inv = 1.0f/r2inv;
            double r6inv = r2inv * r2inv * r2inv;
            double force = r2inv*r6inv*(lj1*r6inv - lj2);
            // accumulate the force value for this atom
            Force[i].x += delx * force;
            Force[i].y += dely * force;
            Force[i].z += delz * force;
            Force[jidx].x -= delx * force;
            Force[jidx].y -= dely * force;
            Force[jidx].z -= delz * force;
        }
    }
}
```

Rules 2 and 3: Efficient Vectorization and Optimal Cache Reuse

Rules 2 and 3 for optimization of algorithms for Xeon Phi are hard to meet for MD problems, which by their very nature entail that the neighbor atoms be distributed randomly in the memory address space. This property constrains that the bytes accessed by the vector code not be unit-stride, which results in inefficient vector gather/scatter operation and the possibility that the various arrays being operated on, such as force arrays, may not be properly aligned. Moreover, the neighbor list needs to be updated from time to time as the atoms may move out or enter the neighbor list. This is why MD code may not be able to exploit the full computational potential of Xeon Phi architecture unless it is reorganized by data structure to allow efficient vector unit usage of the hardware. You can improve the vectorization efficiency by the following techniques:

1. Since the different data structures such as position and force in the code are accessed using the vector gather/scatter instruction, which results in path length increase and memory access latencies, a big performance gain may be obtained by inserting prefetch as shown in lines 15 and 16. If successfully prefetched into the cache level, the inefficiency due to scatter gather code is vastly reduced, thus providing good performance.

2. Data structures such as positions and the neighbor list can be aligned to cacheline boundaries when allocating the data structures and padded to be multiples of cache line size.

3. Since the gather operation works in a loop where each iteration brings in a cache line, it might be possible to have more neighbor data in a cache line if the neighbor position matches the memory layout of the neighbor list. This can be effected by spatial sorting of the neighbor list so that particle orders in the sorted neighbor list are in the nearby cache-friendly memory region.[3]

4. Divide the nonbonded force compute between the host and Xeon Phi using asynchronous computations.

5. In some cases it may be possible to utilize mixed-precision arithmetic—such as computing force and position in single precision and accumulating in double precision—to achieve higherp erformance.

Stencil Operation

Stencil operations are commonly used in many technical computing applications for simulating diffusion in fields such as computational fluid dynamics, electromagnetics, and heat propagation. These problems are associated with structured grids and use mathematical finite difference representation of differential operators—such as Laplacian $(u_{t+1} \leftarrow \nabla^2 u_t)$ operators, divergence, and gradient—to find answers to the problems formulated. *Stencil* refers to the predetermined set or pattern of nearest neighbors including the element itself. The stencil can be used to compute the value of various elements in an array at a given time-step based on its neighbors' values computed from previous time-steps. The algorithm in general steps in time with some given initial conditions over all the elements to simulate the diffusion or other physical process in time.

Figure 11-3 graphically represents a stencil operation performed on an element in a 3D array for a Laplacian operator. This particular stencil is denoted the *13-point stencil* because its computation involves 13 elements. Equivalent code can be written as shown in Code Listing 11-3. The fout[z,y,x] element is the center element shown in Figure 11-3 and has value based on neighboring elements f[], as shown in Figure 11-3.

---

[3]S. Meloni, M. Rosati, and L. Colombo, "Efficient Particle Labeling in Atomistic Simulations," *Journal of Chemical Physics*, Vol. 126, No. 12, 2007.

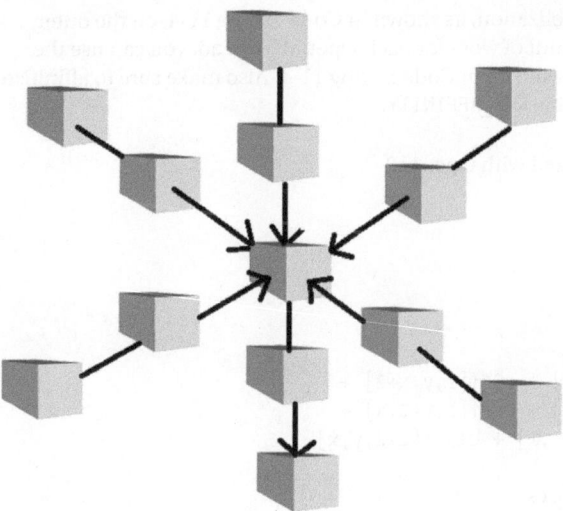

Figure 11-3. *Graphical representation of a 3D stencil operation*

Code Listing 11-3. Stencil Operation Pseudo-code

```
for(t=0; t<numTimeSteps;t++){
   for(z=2; z<NZ-2; z++){
     for(y=2; y<N2; y++){
      for(x=2; x<NX-2; x++){
       fout[z,y,x] = c1*f[z,y,x] +
        c2*f[z,y,x-2] + c3*f[z,y,x-1] + c4*f[z,y,x+1] + c5*f[z,y,x+2] +
        c6*f[z,y-2,x] + c7*f[z,y-1,x] + c8*f[z,y+1,x] + c9*f[z,y+2,x] +
        c10*f[z-2,y,x] + c11*f[z-1,y,x] + c12*f[z+1,y,x] + c13*f[z+2,y,x]
   }}}
   double *tmp = fout; fout = f; f=tmp; //switch buffers
}
```

The constants $c1$-$c11$ represent the weighted contribution of the various neighboring elements of the given cell value being computed and defined by the physics of the problem. In this code you are working with one input and one output array and switching between them in every time step. For other operators, such as gradient and divergence, the number of input and output arrays may be multiple and you may need simultaneous access to multiple arrays. In addition, the physics of the problem may impose formulations with more data arrays to be read per grid point computation, increasing the data traffic even more.

The code sweeps through the input 3D array $f[\ ]$, which is usually larger than the L2 cache of the Xeon Phi hardware. This causes low flops/byte for this operation, in turn causing performance to be memory bandwidth-bound. Having more arrays to work on puts more pressure on the memory subsystem of Xeon Phi, causing a further performance drop.

Rule1 :S calableP arallelization

In the stencil-based application, parallelization happens by naturally breaking up the larger 3D grid into smaller ones per card. The boundary (*halo*) exchange may happen between neighboring cells at every time step to exchange the boundary data. Within a card, because this is a structured grid, a parallelization technique is often used to divide the contiguous blocks allocated to Xeon Phi card equally among the cores so that the threads in a core share one block.

To parallelize the loop, you can do OpenMP-based parallelization, as shown in Code Listing 11-4, on the outer two loops and vectorizing the inner loop. To increase the amount of work for each OpenMP thread, you can use the OpenMP loop collapse construct on the outer loops as well, as shown in Code Listing 11-4. Also make sure to affinitize the code to the Xeon Phi core to make optimal cache reuse using `KMP_AFFINITY`.

Code Listing 11-4. Stencil Calculation Pseudo-code Parallelized with OpenMP

```
for(t=0; t<numTimeSteps;t++){
#pragma omp for collapse(2)
   for(z=2; z<NZ-2; z++){
     for(y=2; y<NY-2; y++){
       for(x=2; x<NX-2; x++){
        fout[z,y,x] = c1*f[z,y,x] +
          c2*f[z,y,x-2] + c3*f[z,y,x-1] + c4*f[z,y,x+1] + c5*f[z,y,x+2] +
          c6*f[z,y-2,x] + c7*f[z,y-1,x] + c8*f[z,y+1,x] + c9*f[z,y+2,x] +
          c10*f[z-2,y,x] + c11*f[z-1,y,x] + c12*f[z+1,y,x] + c13*f[z+2,y,x]
   }}}
   double *tmp = fout; fout = f; f=tmp; //switch buffers
}
```

You can now execute the code in parallel on all the available Xeon Phi cores to attain better performance compared with that of the serial version of the code.

Rule 2:E fficientV ectorization

The stencil methods have a high degree of parallelism but usually are not friendly to vector architectures such as Xeon Phi. To start with, the compiler is unable to vectorize the inner loop in Code Listing 11-4 due to the possible alias between the two c pointers: `fout[ ]` and `f[ ]`. In order to vectorize this code, you need to tell the compiler to assume the array pointers point to the disjoint location by using `#pragma vector always` or `#pragma ivdep`. This pragma will vectorize the inner loop, but the vectorization is inefficient due to memory access issue, as you will see shortly. To help vectorize the code more efficiently, you can remove the prologue and epilogue of the vectorized code by aligning the array data to the cacheline boundary and padding the arrays so that the innermost dimension is a multiple of the cacheline size. Aligning the data will also help with cache-way oversubscription in some scenarios. Once the data are aligned, you can use `pragma vector aligned` to tell the compiler to assume aligned vectors. Finally, you don't want to waste BW when writing to the `fout[ ]` array, which causes output data to be read, to complete the read for ownership operation. This can be done by indicating to the compiler that `fout` is a nontemporal write and thus not to waste valuable BW needed to read the data in.

The compiler-generated code created by the above changes and directives will be inefficient. Inefficient vectorization happens because you are adding shifted versions of data elements such as `f[z,y,x-2] .. f[z,y,x+2]` in the same computing statement. This inefficiency is known as *stream alignment conflict* and refers to the fact that the vectors needed to perform the computation from the same data stream but are not aligned to one another, thus requiring extra data manipulations. In this case, the compiler generates code that requires redundant load and inter-register shifts following a load operation. To get around this problem, you will need to use a data structure transformation such as dimension-lifted transposition.[4]

---

[4]T. Henretty, K. Stock, L. N. Pouchet, F. Franchetti, J. Ramanujam, and P. Sadayappan, "Data layout transformation for stencil computations on short-vector SIMD architectures," *Compiler Construction*: Lecture Notes in Computer Science, Vol. 6601, 2011, pp. 225–245. http://link.springer.com/chapter/10.1007/978-3-642-19861-8_13#page-1

Rule3 :O ptimalC acheR euse

Cache use can be improved by using cache-blocking in the X and Y directions.[5] By blocking the code, you can increase the temporal locality. The goal of cache-blocking is to render those elements that are needed by the stencil code available in cache as the code works along the column of the Z-axis. This is shown in the hypothetical example in Code Listing 11-5 and graphically represented in Figure 11-4. If threads in the same core work on the same block or neighbor blocks, data reuse would be higher and balanced affinitization would enable better performance.

Code Listing 11-5. Stencil Pseudo-code Optimized with Blocking and Vectorization

```
for(t=0; t<numTimeSteps;t++){
#pragma omp for collapse(3)
   for(yy=2;yy<NY-2;yy+=By)
   for(xx=2;xx<NX-2;xx+=Bx)
    for(z=2; z<NZ-2; z++){
     for(y=yy; y<min(NY-2,yy+By-2); y++){
#pragma vector aligned //indicate no alising
#pragma vector nontemporal (fout) // indicate fout can be streaming store
      for(x=xx; x<min(NX-2,xx+Bx-2); x++){
       fout[z,y,x] = c1*f[z,y,x] +
        c2*f[z,y,x-2] + c3*f[z,y,x-1] + c4*f[z,y,x+1] + c5*f[z,y,x+2] +
        c6*f[z,y-2,x] + c7*f[z,y-1,x] + c8*f[z,y+1,x] + c9*f[z,y+2,x] +
        c10*f[z-2,y,x] + c11*f[z-1,y,x] + c12*f[z+1,y,x] + c13*f[z+2,y,x]
   }}}
   }}}
   double *tmp = fout; fout = f; f=tmp; //switch buffers
}
```

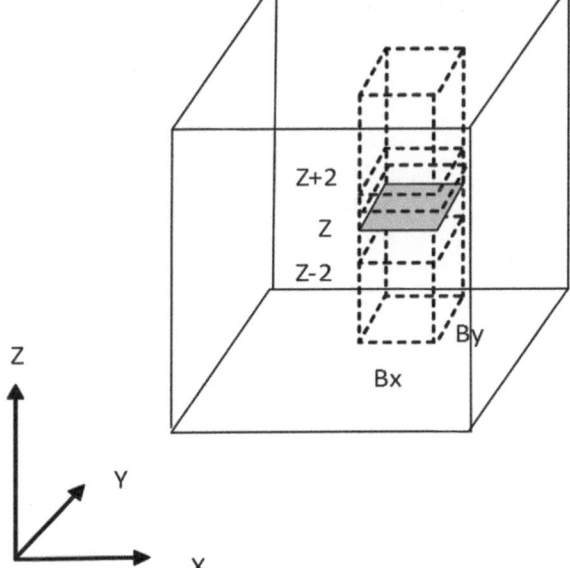

Figure 11-4. *Graphical representation of blocking optimization on cache reuse*

---

[5]G. Rivera and C. Tseng, "Tiling optimizations for 3D scientific computations." In *Proceedings of SC'00*, Dallas, TX, November 2000.

You need to pick the block sizes in Bx and By such that the XY planes formed by these blocks fit in the cache for the values calculated along the Z-axis. Since for each z iteration the fout[x,y,z] requires 5 planes of size Bx*By block of data to be residing in cache, the condition for selecting block sizes is 5*(Bx*By) < L2 cache size. The number **5c** omes from the fact that there are five Bx*By planes corresponding to Z-1, Z-2, Z, Z+1, and Z+2 in the cache for the calculated stencil for all the points in that subblock shown in gray in Figure 11-4. You may improve the cache hit by pulling in the cache lines using software prefetch for z iterations.

European Option Pricing Using Monte Carlo Simulation in Financial Applications

Monte Carlo simulation is a computational method widely used in the financial sector to model option prices[6] of an underlying stock. This section looks at optimizing the Monte Carlo algorithm used for European option pricing on the Xeon Phi coprocessor.

Figure 11-5 is a simplified illustration of the basic step of Monte Carlo simulation of European option pricing. It suggests how such simulation can be optimized for Xeon Phi coprocessors. The general Monte Carlo process of option pricing starts by generating a set of random numbers (Step 1 in Figure 11-5). The simulation process takes a batch of queries to set option prices of the underlying security by specifying their input parameters, such as current stock price, option strike price, expiration date, and so forth. At Step 2, for each of these options to be calculated, the computation generates a block of possible stock price at the expiry date using a solution to the stochastic process that simulates underlying stock prices over time. The solution to the stochastic process for each random variate x generated in Step 1 results in a function that is of the form:

```
S(T) = S(0) Exp2(f(x,T))
        where:
        S(T) = Stock price at maturity.
        S(0) = Stock price at the option issue date.
        Exp2(f(x,T)) = exponential of a function of variate 'x' and time T
```

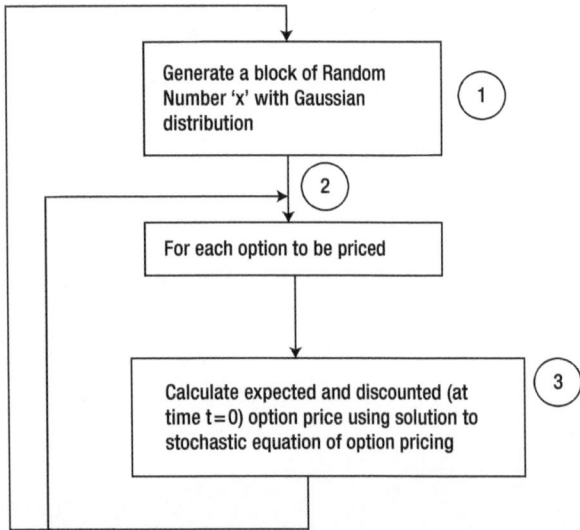

Figure 11-5. *Monte Carlo simulation of option pricing*

---

[6]Phelim P. Boyle, "Options: A Monte Carlo Approach," *Journal of Financial Economics*, Vol. 4, No. 3, pp. 323-338, May 1977.

Profiling of the Monte Carlo simulation shows that the most compute-intensive part of the computation is evaluating the S(T) price in Step 3.

Rule1 :S calableP arallelization

The Monte Carlo simulation is a highly parallel process involving the evaluation of thousands of options at a time. So it is easily distributed across Xeon Phi threads such that each thread can work on a subset of options to be evaluated in parallel with dynamic load balancing. This can be easily implemented by inserting the OpenMP 'parallel for' construct in the code at Step 2 of Figure 11.5. The high-degree parallelization of this compute-bound algorithm can exploit a large number of cores in Xeon Phi, giving good speed up.

Rule 2:E fficientV ectorization

The code can be vectorized efficiently using vectorized versions of random number generators and transcendental functions. The MKL's vector statistical functions contain vector random number generators with various statistical distributions, including the Gaussian distribution needed by Monte Carlo simulation. Functions such as vsRngGaussian or vdRngGaussian from the Intel MKL can be used to generate vectorized single- and double-precision random numbers.[7] The loop at Step 2 in Figure 11-5 is vectorized by the compiler by using vector transcendental functions. For single-precision arithmetic, high-throughput transcendental instructions such as vexp223ps are implemented in Xeon Phi hardware and can provide an excellent boost in performance by vectorizing the key calculation at Step 3 in the loop. In my experiments, the Intel Compiler was able to vectorize such loops. For double-precision computation, you can use the Intel short vector math library to vectorize the computation as well. The biggest benefit and performance gain can be obtained by using the fast hardware-implemented transcendental functions provided the algorithm can handle the lower precision of these functions.

Rule3 :O ptimalC acheR euse

Monte Carlo simulations are compute-bound applications and the data usage easily fits in the L2 cache. So cache reuse is fairly optimal and not a concern for this algorithm.

Conforming to all three rules for optimal algorithms—scalable parallelization, efficient vectorization, and optimal cache reuse—Monte Carlo simulation is ideally suited to reap the potential benefits of the Intel Xeon Phi hardware.

Summary

This chapter looked at various common algorithms and their data structures and how they help and hinder performance while executing on Xeon Phi. You have seen that there are ways to restructure code and data structure so that they follow the three rules of scalable parallelization, efficient vectorization, and optimal cache reuse to achieve high performance on Xeon Phi. This chapter is in no way a comprehensive treatment of technical computing applications, but it does impart a sense of the vista of exciting possibilities now before you, as you prepare to leverage what you have learned in this book to develop new algorithms and data structures for the Intel Xeon Phi coprocessor.

---

[7]http://software.intel.com/sites/products/documentation/hpc/mkl/mklman/GUID-63196F25-5013-4038-8BCD-2613C4EF3DE4.htm

CHAPTER 12

Xeon Phi Application Development on Windows OS

So far we have looked at application development on the Linux OS for the Xeon Phi coprocessor. This chapter looks at what types of support are available on Windows OS for developing applications for Xeon Phi.[1] Some application domains such as computer-aided design (CAD) and other workstation applications that can benefit from the raw compute power of Intel Xeon Phi are mostly used on Windows OS. In such cases, you would be able to offload part of the computationally intensive code section to the coprocessor by using the offload programming model, such as that based on the OpenMP 4.0 standard. Most of the concepts in this chapter also apply to the Linux development environment on Xeon Phi.

The Xeon Phi development OS environment includes support for Microsoft Windows Server 2008 R2 SP1 (64 bit), Windows Server 2012 (64 bit), Windows 8 Enterprise (64 bit), and Windows 7 Enterprise SP1 (64 bit). Windows OS supports familiar tools, such as Microsoft Visual Studio IDE with Intel Compiler and tools to be used for your code development within the Windows OS. The Intel compilers and tools for Xeon Phi plug into the Microsoft Visual Studio IDE to enable such development.

The system configuration for the Windows host is similar to that for the Linux host. The card resides on a PCIe x16 bus. As discussed in Chapter 7, the coprocessor hosts a Linux-based coprocessor operating system. The same is true in the Windows environment. The Windows driver is responsible for loading the coprocessor operating system on Xeon Phi as it is for the Linux environment. However, the Windows configuration makes the available supported programming model narrower than that provided on the Linux host OS. Because the Windows platform was designed to leverage the investment made in the Linux development environment, you may see some syntax, such as compiler switches for offload compilation, that is same as that in the Linux environment. Most of the frequently used system management tools on Linux are also available on Windows to manage Xeon Phi.

The Windows OS supports both the offload and native programming models. You can use internet protocol–based tools such as the secured shell SSH for Windows to communicate with the coprocessor OS based on Linux. You may need to learn Linux operating system commands for application execution under native mode inside the coprocessor OS. You can also share file directories between the Windows host and the Linux coprocessor OS by virtue of its support for the standard *network file system* (NFS) protocol.

The Windows development environment consists of the Intel MPSS stack, the C/C++ and Fortran compilers that plug into Microsoft Visual Studio, the debugger, and VTune Amplifier XE for application analysis.

---

[1]This chapter describes the beta version of the Windows support for Xeon Phi.

MPSS

The Windows version of the MPSS installation requires administrative privilege and .Net Framework 4.0 or higher.[2] The GUI-based installation process is straightforward. If, once the driver installation is complete, the MPSS service is not started by the Windows trust manager, the administrator may need to configure the Xeon Phi coprocessor environment by using the command line tools provided as part of the MPSS installation.

The MPSS install package contains:

- Device drivers and OS software for Xeon Phi

- Tools to control Intel Xeon Phi and collect coprocessor status

- SDKs for developing coprocessor applications. The SDKs contain samples for *common offload infrastructure* (COI), SCIF, and virtual shared memory programming—*mine-your-ours*(M YO) interface. It also provides basic libraries to build applications for the coprocessor.

The user may choose either a custom-install configuration allowing selection of which components to install or the default install of all tools.

Figure 12-1 of the various system components in the Windows environment shows how the host side of the MPSS provides the Windows device driver to manage the Xeon Phi hardware and the necessary communication channel with the host applications. The coprocessor OS provides necessary supports to run native and offload applications on Xeon Phi hardware.

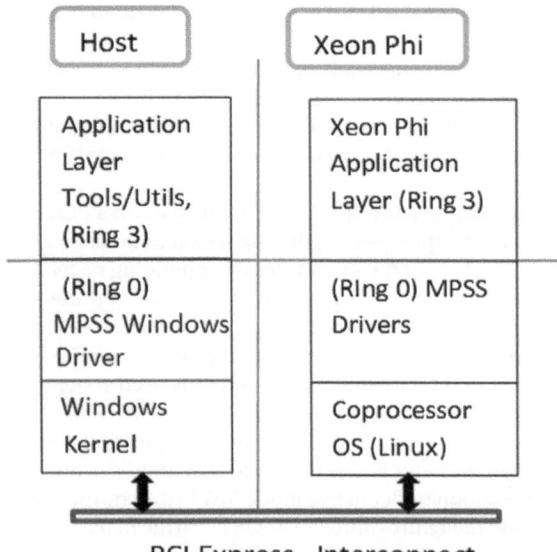

Figure 12-1. *System components in the Microsoft Windows environment*

The system software also provides important utilities for managing the coprocessor. The default install directory for MPSS is c:\Program Files\Intel\MPSS.

---

[2]For installation details for the Windows version of the MPSS, see the ReadMe document available with the MPSS stack.

The Windows driver is responsible for initializing the coprocessor OS and setting up the default file system layout. The coprocessor OS that is downloaded to the coprocessor during the Xeon Phi boot process resides on the Windows host file system and is by default installed in the c:\Program Files\Intel\MPSS\driversf older.

The docs folder in the MPSS install directory on the host contains descriptions and usage of the tools provided with the MPSS install.

MPSST ools

The tools installed on the host side in the default path c:\Program Files\Intel\MPSS\bini nclude:

1. MicInfo: Used to get information about the Xeon Phi cards installed on the system along with relevant information on the host system, the coprocessor OS, and the MPSS versions. The tool can be optionally invoked with following command line options:

   - -version: Displays tool version

   - –help: Displays command line help

   - –listDevices: Lists all the Xeon Phi devices detected on the host

   - –deviceInfo <deviceNum>[-group <groupname>]: Displays information about specific Xeon Phi devices numbered deviceNum. By default the utility dumps various groups of information about the card, OS, and MPSS together. However, you can use <groupname> to select only specific information to be displayed. The groupname may be one of the following:

   - Versions: Shows Flash and coprocessor OS versions

   - Board: Shows only coprocessor card-related information

   - Core: Shows Xeon Phi core-related information

   - Thermal: Shows fan and thermal-related data for the coprocessor card

   - GDDR:S howsG DDRm emory-relatedi nformation

2. MicSmc: Provides coprocessor status and utilization information in the status panel. This tool can execute in both GUI and command line mode. The GUI mode provides real-time monitoring of the coprocessor cards installed on the host. It is also used to change settings on the card, such as ECC on/off and Turbo on/off. The GUI mode is invoked by executing the micsmc utility without any parameters. In the GUI mode, you can see the list of all the Xeon Phi cards recognized by the driver and real-time information on core usage, core temperature, memory usage, power usage, total memory, and number of cores, either cumulatively on all cards or individually. The status panel in Figure 12-2 shows two cards on the system with a total of 122 cores and 32GB of memory. By enabling the display of mic0 and mic1, you can see the status and power consumption of the individual cards. In this case, I disabled power management to be able to use time stamp counterw ithout being affected by the power management feature of the core processor, which might affect the timing procedure. You can also choose between core histogram view and historical utilization view by selecting icons in the top right corners of the individual coprocessor windows. On the Advanced menu on the GUI of the tool, you can look at the error log, change card settings such as ECC and power management support, and get information about individual cards, such as their device driver versions.

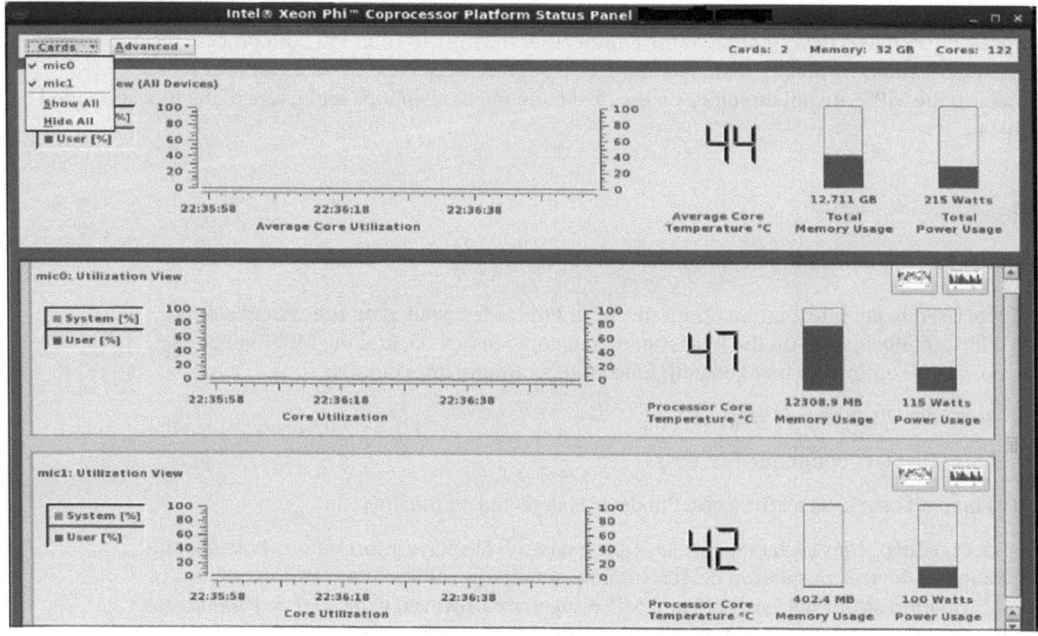

Figure 12-2. *MicSmc GUI mode execution with two cards available on the system*

ECC Mode Changes: Through MicSmc GUI, you can change the ECC settings of individual cards by using the Advanced ➤ Settings menu. This will put the card in maintenance mode, change the settings, and restart the coprocessor to make the changes effective. If an error condition is encountered, an error dialog will appear detailing the information. It will also be logged in the error log that can be viewed by the Advanced ➤ Error Log menu option. Similar setting changes can be done for Turbo and power management states. In addition, the LED mode setting is used to blink the LEDs on individual cards to identify the cards visually.

3. MicRas: A utility used on the host system to collect and log *reliability, availability,* a nd *serviceability* (RAS) events produced by Xeon Phi coprocessor. This utility is run as a Windows service and monitors any RAS event generated by the card. If it detects a fatal RAS event, it puts the card or cards in maintenance mode. MicRas logs messages into the file micras.log under the binary directory where it is installed. MicRas service depends on MPSS service. The command line invocation of MicRas can take optional parameters and can be as follows:

    - -help: Displays help information

    - -daemon: This option starts MicRas in the daemon mode and runs in the background. In this mode it can handle RAS events and logs the messages silently.

    - -loglevel [level]: Sets the category of messages. The level is a bitfield value with least 4 bits used to define the categories as follows:

        - Bit0 :L ogsi nformationalm essages

        - Bit 1: Logs warning messages

        - Bit 2: Logs error messages

        - Bit3 :L ogsc riticalm essages

The levels are defined to follow IETF RFC 5424 Syslog protocol standard.

4. MicFlash: A utility is used to program firmware on the coprocessor cards. This is done by updating the SMC boot loader as well as the flash on the card. The firmware and flash images are installed by default in the c:\Program Files\Intel\MPSS directory. Make sure you select the correct flash image to match the revision of Xeon Phi card you have. The flash update is done by putting the card in the ready state and then burning the new flash image by executing the following command (assuming default install directory):

    ```
    Command_prompt > MicFlash -update <path to flash file> -device all
    ```

5. micctrl: An important utility used to start, stop, and restart the coprocessor. You can use micctrl --start to start the Xeon Phi coprocessor, which performs the device initialization together with uploading the coprocessor OS and getting the coprocessor card to a usable stage. To stop the driver run, you can issue the command micctlr --stop. If you want to just reboot the coprocessor, a useful command is micctrl -b.

SDK (Binutils)

SDKs installed with the MPSS are a collection of tools and libraries that include files necessary to build and cross-compile Xeon Phi applications on Windows. These components are used by Intel Composer XE tools to build Xeon Phi applications. The utility install program comes with the MPSS install package and may be installed explicitly by using the provided binutili nstallb atchf ile.

Development Tools

The development tools for Xeon Phi on Windows include the C/C++ and Fortran compilers, debuggers, and VTune Amplifier XE application analyzers. The debugger and compiler are part of the Intel Composer XE 2013 for Windows package. These tools can recognize the code blocks to be offloaded to Xeon Phi and provide runtime support for executing offloaded code sections on Xeon Phi coprocessor(s). The language extensions for Xeon Phi in Windows are very similar to those of the Linux host OS.

The Composer XE installation comes with documentation and samples to get you started on programming the Xeon Phi coprocessor.

Language Extensions for the Xeon Phi Coprocessor

Composer XE for Windows provides two methods of offloading computation and sharing data between the host and the coprocessor: the nonshared memory model (*data marshaling*) and the virtual shared memory model, which is available only for C/C++ programs. Most of the features and language extensions for Xeon Phi that are available on Linux are still available on Windows. There are certain restrictions on the Windows offload model, which are valid in host-based Windows code and must be delineated by __MIC__ or __INTEL_OFFLOAD macros and may need to be placed in a separate file in certain cases, as follow:

*   Nos upportf or long and long doubled atat ypes

*   No bitfield support in data structure

*   No runtime type information (RTTI) support

- No structured exceptions handling in offloadc ode

  - For example, avoid code such as the following in the offload code:

    ```
    void f()
    {
      try {<statements>}
      catch[<error type>] { <statements> }
      finally {<statements>}
    }
    ```

- Nos upportf or #pragma pack

- No dll_import/dll_export such as __declspec(dllexport) void f(); in the offload code

- No pointer fields and only bitwise copyable object for nonshared memory model

- You may not use Windows calling convention __cdecl to declare an external callable function called from offload code

- Do not include Windows header #include <windows.h> in the offload code sections

Nonshared Memory Offload Extensions

Intel Composer XE 2013 for Xeon Phi supports proprietary extensions for nonshared memory program execution from the Windows host to the Xeon Phi coprocessor. The compiler also supports standard OpenMP 4.0 extensions for performing nonshared memory programming. Because the OpenMP 4.0 standard is still in progress, this chapter discusses only the proprietary Intel extension. The concept of the nonshared memory programming model is, however, very similar in the OpenMP 4.0 and Intel proprietary extensions.

These extensions provide the high-level syntax and runtime environment in C/C++ and Fortran to execute portions of the code on Xeon Phi. These methods use data marshaling techniques for transferring data between the host and the coprocessor and as such are appropriate for dealing with flat-data structures such as bitwise copyable structures, arrays, and scalars. On invocation of the offload code, the data are copied between the host and the card as indicated by the programmer. The data exchanged include data explicitly listed in the offload clause as well as implicitly defined data objects that are lexically referenced inside the offload code.

Virtual Shared Memory Offload Extensions (C/C++ Language Only)

The offload keywords _Cilk_shared, _Cilk_offload, and _Cilk_offload_to are defined for virtual shared memory programming support in Composer XE for Windows. These are useful when dealing with complex data structures such as linked lists, which need to be shared between the host and the Xeon Phi card.

Compiling and Running the Offload Programs

You can use either the command line option or Microsoft Visual Studio to build the offload programs for Windows. By default the C/C++ and Fortran compiler builds code for both the host and the Xeon Phi coprocessor. To compile and run in command line mode, start a command prompt with the proper environment variables set. You can start the command prompt as shown in Figure 12-3. The compiler detects the offload keywords and performs the offload compilation when encountered. The compiled binary is placed as designated by the Makefile and can be executed from the command line.

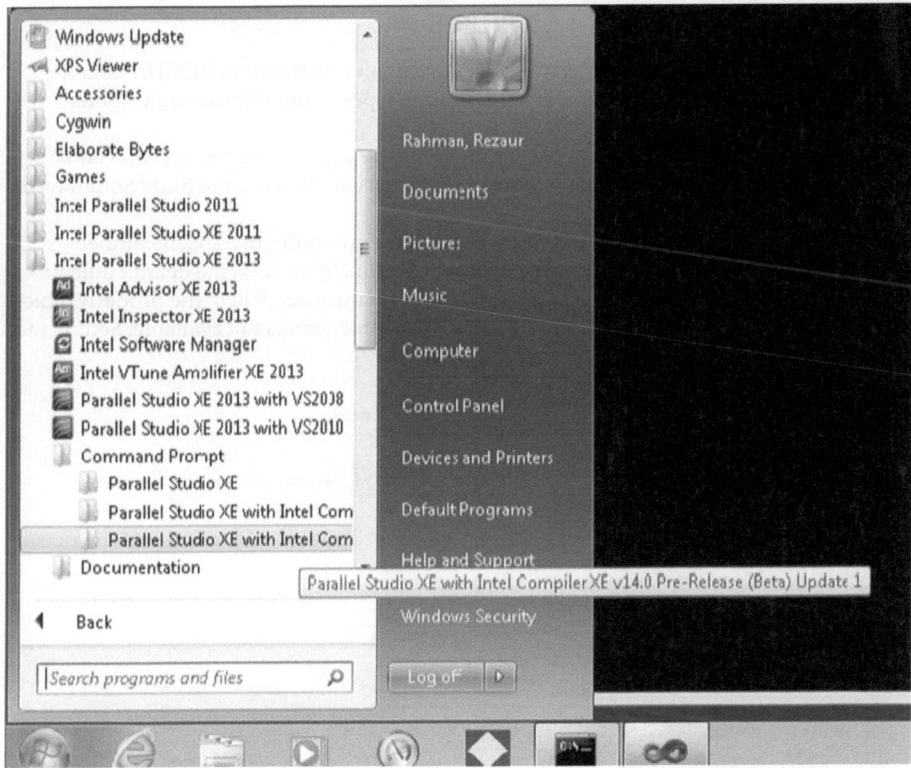

***Figure 12-3.** Starting command prompt on Windows to build Xeon Phi applications*

Note that offload code generation may not imply offload code execution. Offload code execution will depend on the presence and availability of the Xeon Phi coprocessor in the system. The offload may be designated as mandatory or optional by either of the following alternatives:

1. Usingt he mandatory, optional, and status clauses with offload pragmas or directives.

2. Using /Qoffload [none|optional|mandatory] command line options. The default is mandatory.

The clauses overwrite the compile time options.

For optional offload, if the offload request can be satisfied, the code is executed on the coprocessor; otherwise the code is executed on the host. If the status clause is used, the status variable can be queried for details of the offload. The status (var) clause may be used with offload, offload_transfer, and offload_wait directives. It sets the variable of type __Offload_status defined in offload.h in C/C++ or of type Offload_status for Fortran defined in mic_lib.f90. The status variable has a predefined member that can be queried for the success of the offload clauses during program execution.

In mandatory offload, if the offload clause can be satisfied, the code is executed on the coprocessor, otherwise the code is not automatically executed on the host. If the status clause is specified, the program continues and the user may examine the status code to take appropriate option. If the status variable is not specified, the application is terminated for mandatory offload case.

Using Visual Studio Integrated Development Environment

Intel Composer XE integrates into Microsoft Visual Studio Integrated Development Environment (IDE) by default during installation. Offload applications can use the same project and solution types as nonoffload applications except that they are limited to x64 release and debug configurations.

To compile and run an application, launch Microsoft Visual Studio and create appropriate projects and add source files to it. Alternatively, you can open an existing Visual Studio project. You can then use the Build Solutions or Projects page to build or run the application.

To control the behavior of offload compilation, you can set the configuration properties of a specific project. You can also set the behavior of offload constructs from the configuration properties. In Figure 12-4, the default offload behavior of the program is set to mandatory, as shown by the highlighted offload construct field of the property table. This tells the runtime environment to execute on the coprocessor or fail if the coprocessor is not available. Setting the option to None instructs the compiler to ignore all the offload constructs.

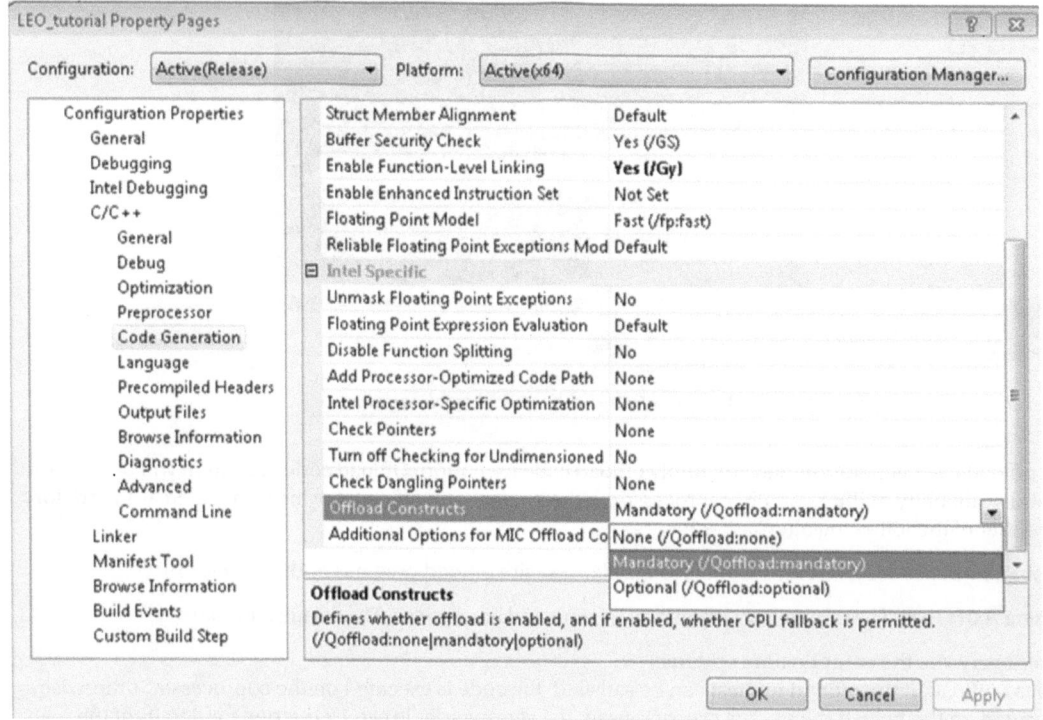

Figure 12-4. *Setting the behavior of offload constructs*

You can also provide additional options for the offload compiler by entering Linux-like command line options in the field "Additional Options for MIC Offload Compiler," shown in the next field below the highlighted field in Figure 12-4. For example, you can set the optimization level differently from your host compilation level.

Similarly options can be set specifically for the offload linker by entering the offload-specific link option in the dialog reached through the following navigation path: Projects ➤ Properties ➤ Configuration Properties ➤ Linker ➤ General ➤ Additional Options for MIC Offload Linker.

Compile Time Messages and Detecting Missing Symbols During Link Time

To differentiate between the compilation for the host and the coprocessor, the compiler prints out compile time messages with the special tag *MIC*, such as:

```
test.c(5): warning #120: *MIC* return value type does not match the function type
```

In the offload compilation model, the binaries are generated as Linux dynamic link libraries (files with the .so extension). Because the dynamic link libraries do not need to resolve the symbols during link time, the offload code may encounter runtime failure if the missing symbols are encountered during the runtime. You can use the following linker option for offload compilation to detect any missing symbols during compile time: /Qoffload-option,mic, link,"-Wl,-no-undefined".

OffloadE nvironmentV ariables

As with the Linux host OS execution environment, Windows also allows you to control offload execution using specific environment variables. The variable can be used to set the coprocessor OS execution environment from the Windows host. The environment variable MIC_ENV_PREFIX is used to distinguish variables that control the execution environment on the coprocessor. The variables are common between the Linux and Windows execution environment, except that you need to follow Windows conventions when specifying file system paths in Windows.

Debugging Offload Execution

Offload and native application debugging is supported only under Visual Studio (VS) 2012. This allows for seamless debugging under IDE for C++/Fortran code on multiple coprocessors. The debugger framework includes a debug engine and VS plugin that integrates GNU Project Debugger (GDB) for Xeon Phi into Microsoft Visual Studio 2012. These extensions are part of the Intel Composer XE 2013 SP1 and later products.

The offload debugging is started by a VS plugin when it detects a breakpoint inside offload region. The plugin spawns the debug engine which automatically connects to offload_main process running on the coprocessor. Debugging of offload applications requires specific PuTTY utilities, plink and pscp, and private key file id_rsa.ppk be installed on MPSS bin directory whose default path is c:\Program Files\Intel\MPSS\bin. You need to set up PuTTY so that you can access the Xeon Phi card from the host as explained in the next section.

Set up the debugger by the following steps:

1. Installr equiredP uTTYutil ities.

   a. Installi tu nder c:\Program Files\Intel\MPSS\bin for default installs or appropriately if the MPSS path is different.

   b. If PuTTY is installed in a separate directory, copy plink.exe and pscp.exe utilities from the PuTTY install folder to the c:\Program Files\Intel\MPSS\bind irectory.

2. Create key files private, public, authorized_keys under c:\Program Files\Intel\MPSS\bin.

3. The private key must correspond to the authorized_keys uploaded to Xeon Phi coprocessor. The private key must be renamed to id_rsa.ppk for recognition by Intel GNU GDBe xtensionf orW indows.

Logging into Xeon Phi Console using PuTTY

Because the Xeon Phi card hosts a Linux-based operating system, you can log in to the coprocessor OS as if it were a separate Linux node. After the MPSS is installed and running, you can directly log in to the Xeon Phi coprocessor OS for executing applications natively or for other purposes. To do so, you need to use standard SSH tools such as PuTTY.[3] To use SSH to log into the coprocessor, you need to have been added by the administrator as a user in the `micuser` group, and the admin needs to set up a public key for you on the Xeon Phi coprocessor OS to give you access, through `micctrl -addssh <username> <public-key>`, where `<username>` is your username and `<public-key>` is the public portion of the key pairs generated by you using a utility such as `PuTTY Key Generator (PuTTYgen)`. PuTTYgen can be used to generate authorized_keys, public keys, and private keys.

Once this is set up, you can log in to the coprocessor using the IP address of the Xeon Phi coprocessor card you are interested in. The default IP address is set to 192.168.1.100. You can use WinSCP to transfer files between the host andt hec oprocessor.

Using VTune Amplifier XE to Profile Offload Code on Windows

The VTune Amplifier XE tool can be used to understand performance issues on Xeon Phi execution on a Windows host, just as it is in the Linux environment. To be able profile and locate where in the source the issue is, the code to be analyzed needs to have debug symbols. Use the compile and link time option `/debug: full` to enable symbols.

Set up the VTune configuration so that the source and binary search path point to the relevant files. The VTune comes with predefined analysis types such as `Lightweight Hotspots`, `General Exploration`, and `Bandwidth` to help you get started with the profiling session. In many cases, these profiles point you to possible hotspots. You can add your own custom profile to enhance your VTune analysis.

Building and Running Xeon Phi Native Applications from the Windows Host

You can cross-compile code for Xeon Phi using Intel Composer XE from a Windows command prompt. To compile, start the Intel Parallel Studio XE 2013 command-prompt window for Intel 64 for a given VS configuration. Use the compile switch `/Qmic` to cross-compile the source for Xeon Phi native execution.

Because native programs build applications to run on the Xeon Phi Linux coprocessor OS, the binary code is a Linux application and the compiler takes Linux switches.

Once built, the binary and relevant dynamic libraries (.so) files need to be copied to the Xeon Phi coprocessor using pscp or similar secured copy tools. The mic runtime libraries such as libiomp5.so for OpenMP runtime are installed under Composer XE install directories `<install_dir>\compiler\lib\mic`.

You can debug the native applications from VS using procedures similar to those used for a remote Linux target.[4]

Summary

This chapter looked at the development, debug, and application profiling supports on the Windows platform for the Xeon Phi coprocessor. These procedures closely follow those for Linux-based development, and many of the concepts presented throughout this book are equally applicable for Windows-based application development and profiling.

---

[3]`http://www.putty.org/`
[4]For debugging details, see the Intel Composer XE user guide.

APPENDIX A

OpenCL on Xeon Phi

Open Computing Language (OpenCL) standardizes language and *application programming interfaces* (APIs) for programming heterogeneous parallel computing systems, such as hosts containing Xeon Phi coprocessors. This is an open standard maintained by the industry consortium, Khronos Group, and adopted by various leading companies to make the language-based applications portable across devices.[1]

The Intel *Software Development Kit* (SDK) for OpenCL Applications XE 2013 provides support for compiling and running OpenCL 1.2-compliant applications to execute on hosts containing Xeon Phi coprocessors. Xeon Phi support is available for Linux OS only. The OpenCL tool provides another way of programming and harvesting the power of the Xeon Phi coprocessor in addition to those provided by the various programming models of Intel C/C++/Fortran compilers for Xeon Phi. The SDK contains OpenCL runtime, development tools, and relevant documentation to get you started on developing applications for Xeon Phi using the OpenCL standard. You can also use Intel VTune Amplifier XE to profile the applications built with OpenCL development tools.

A single runtime supports both Intel Xeon processors and Intel Xeon Phi coprocessors. The package supports multiple Xeon Phi coprocessors.

This appendix introduces the types of tools available for building OpenCL code for Xeon Phi. It assumes that you are already familiar with the OpenCL programming concepts.

Installation

There are two packages provided for installation purposes:

- The runtime-only package, containing the runtime and the OpenCL compiler.

- The full package, which includes the runtime package and SDKs with the necessary header files for C/C++ development with OpenCL, examples, and documentation.

You can download these packages from http://software.intel.com/en-us/vcsource/tools/opencl-sdk-xe. The final download dialog will also provide a public key Intel-x-y-z.pub that you need to download as part of the package. Install the package by the following steps:

1. First import the public key Intel-x-y-z.pub where x, y, z will have various dashed symbols that are provided by your download package. For example, the version of the package I downloaded had a public key `Intel-E901-172E-EF96-900F-B8E1-4184-D7BE-0E73-xxxx-xxxx.pub`. To import the public key as a root use the command:

   ```
   rpm --import <package public key>
   ```

---

[1]http://www.khronos.org/opencl/

2. Verify integrity of the Redhat Package Manager (rpm) packages by running rpm --checksig

```
Command_prompt> rpm --checksig *.rpm
opencl-1.2-base-3.0.67279-1.x86_64.rpm: rsa sha1 (md5) pgp md5 OK
opencl-1.2-devel-3.0.67279-1.x86_64.rpm: rsa sha1 (md5) pgp md5 OK
opencl-1.2-intel-cpu-3.0.67279-1.x86_64.rpm: rsa sha1 (md5) pgp md5 OK
opencl-1.2-intel-devel-3.0.67279-1.x86_64.rpm: rsa sha1 (md5) pgp md5 OK
opencl-1.2-intel-mic-3.0.67279-1.x86_64.rpm: rsa sha1 (md5) pgp md5 OK
```

3. Install the OpenCL package by executing install-cpu+mic.sh as follows:

```
Command_prompt > sudo ./install-cpu+mic.sh
In case of failure please consult README file
Preparing...                 ########################################### [100%]
   1:opencl-1.2-base          ########################################### [ 20%]
   2:opencl-1.2-intel-cpu     ########################################### [ 40%]
   3:opencl-1.2-intel-mic     ########################################### [ 60%]
   4:opencl-1.2-intel-devel   ########################################### [ 80%]
   5:opencl-1.2-devel         ########################################### [100%]
Done.
```

The rpm packages installed are as follows:

opencl-base: Allows applications to select between different OpenCL implementations at runtime using the OpenCL installable client driver (ICD). The ICD allows the coexistence of OpenCL implementation from multiple vendors.

opencl-intel-cpu: Enables Intel Xeon and Intel Core processors as an OpenCL device. The package contains the compiler and runtime for Intel processors.

opencl-intel-mic: Enables an Intel Xeon Phi coprocessor as an OpenCL device. The MPSS must be available for this package to work.

opencl-devel: Contains OpenCL C header files for the development of opencl applications.

opencl-intel-devel : Provides Intel SDK for opencl which includes Kernel Builder which enables full offline OpenCL language compilation and analysis of OpenCl kernels.

There are other ways to install the package. Refer to readme.txt that comes with the package for a more customized installation process.

Building and Running OpenCL Application

The SDK provides the following tools to help you build and execute OpenCL applications on Xeon Phi.

Once you install OpenCL SDK on your system, the library libOpenCL.so for building and running OpenCL application is copied to the /usr/lib64 folder and the base OpenCL header files are available in the /usr/include/CL system-level folder. To build an OpenCL file, you need to invoke the compiler as follows:

1. Set C++ compiler path and environment.

2. Invoket heC ++c ompilera s

```
Command_prompt > icc test.cpp -lOpenCL -otest.out
```

where test.cpp contains OpenCL calls and includes the header file CL/cl.h to declare the OpenCL APIs.

The test.cpp will include the OpenCL kernel calls that need to run on the Xeon Phi coprocessors. The SDK itself comes with a separate KernelBuilder64 tool that allows you to check your kernel code for OpenCL syntax errors and test its correctness, look at generated *low-level virtual machine* (LLVM) and assembly code, and analyze kernel performance. Please refer to the users guide for details of the Kernel Builder tool.[2]

Intel OpenCL implementation supports shared context between the host Xeon processor and multiple Xeon Phi coprocessors. This implementation allows the sharing of memory objects and events between these heterogeneous devices for the development of workloads that run on both devices. You can also create separate contexts for the Xeon host and Xeon Phi devices to handle them separately by creating separate OpenCL buffers for each Xeon Phi and Xeon device.

Performance Optimization

Although OpenCL codes can be portable across platforms, measures should be taken to optimize OpenCL for the individual hardware it is targeted to run on. For example, Xeon Phi has certain features, such as its 512-bit vector unit and 240 hardware threads, that must be utilized to obtain best performance.

The execution order of work items within a *work group* (WG) and the execution order of WGs are implementation-specific. When launching the kernel for execution, the host code defines the global work dimensions (NDRange) and may also set the partitioning of the NDRange to the WG size. The OpenCL basic parallelism enables the kernel to execute on multiple work items. The Xeon Phi architecture supports SIMD parallelization, which enables the processing of multiple work items with SIMD as necessary to achieve high performance on Xeon Phi with OpenCL. The vectorization unit packs work items for dimension 0 of the NDRange, the innermost loop to utilize SIMD units on Xeon Phi.

On Xeon Phi, each WG is assigned one thread that loops over all the work items within the WG, with SIMD processing thus providing parallelism within the WG level. The parallelism between the WGs is implemented by threading.

Guidelines for optimizing OpenCL on Xeon Phi include the following:[3]

- *Parallelization*: It is recommended that you have at least 960 (a multiple of number of threads) WGs per NDRange with longer execution duration per WG. This allows the OpenCL runtime to utilize the 240 threads with load balancing. The long execution duration (100K clock cycles) for WGs helps reduce context switching overhead.

- *Efficient vectorization*: The Intel OpenCL compiler implicitly vectorizes the WG routines. In order for the compiler to perform its vectorization, do not vectorize the kernels. This requires extra work for the compiler to scalarize the code for later implicit vectorization. Use a workgroup size that is a multiple of 32, as that will allow the compiler to efficiently vectorize the code. The performance benefit may be lower for kernels with complicated control flows.

- *Data alignment*: For efficient data access and vectorization, use a local size that is a multiple of 32.

- *Unit stride access*: Try writing your kernel so that the innermost loop of the WG accesses memory in unit stride for low latency memory access.

- *Local shared memory*: Avoid using shared local memory on Xeon Phi architecture as this results in unnecessary data movement between the cache and GDDR memory to simulate the shared local memory model of GPU architectures.

- *Data prefetching*: Some Xeon Phi applications may benefit from using prefetch built into the kernel code. This allows you to reduce memory access latency in cases where hardware prefetch does not kick in.

- *Tiling/blocking*: Make use of Xeon Phi's cache hierarchy by maximizing intra-WG data reuse by tiling/blocking of the code.

- *Array of Structures/Structure of Arrays (AOS/SOA)*: Use AOS for sparse random access and SOAf ora ccesst oi mprovec achel ocalitya ndu sage.

---

[2]Intel® SDK for OpenCL* Applications XE 2013 User's Guide for Linux* OS. Document Number 328882-002US, Intel Corporation.
[3]Intel SDK for OpenCL Applications XE 2013, Optimization Guide for Linux OS. Document Number 326542-002US, Intel Corporation.

■ ■ ■

Virtual Shared Memory Programming on Xeon Phi

Although nonshared memory programming is widely used in developing applications for the Xeon Phi coprocessor, the Intel C/C++ compiler supports *virtual shared memory* programming. The advantage of this programming model is that it allows you to have more complex data structures shared between the host and client, removing the requirement that the data objects be bitwise copyable (such that the data can be copied using simple memcpy function) between the host and the coprocessor. With virtual shared memory constructs, the data copied between the host and coprocessor can be arbitrarily complex, including structures containing pointers such as linked list and tree data structures. The data must be placed in the shared virtual space before the offload computation can be performed on the shared virtual memory objects. In this model, the underlying software implements and maintains virtual memory that is shared between the host and the coprocessor.

Placing Data on the Virtual Shared Memory Region

In the virtual shared memory programming model, the underlying middle layer of the compiler runtime maintains memory regions that map to the same virtual address space for both the host and the coprocessor. The programming language extension by Intel C++ compiler defines a keyword _Cilk_shared that you can use to declare variables that the runtime should place in the virtual shared memory region. You can also define functions with the same keyword to indicate that these functions will be available on both the host and the coprocessor.

A variable declared with the _Cilk_shared keyword is placed in the same virtual memory address in both the host and the coprocessor, such that the pointer values are the same between the physically disjoint address spaces but give the appearance of being in the same address space. Thus, the offload code can work on non-bitwise copyable data structures such as linked list data structures. The runtime synchronizes the variables between these disjointed address spaces automatically at offload call sites.

When a variable is declared as shared, the memory is allocated dynamically for the variable by the host in the host and coprocessor virtual address spaces region that both share. As the declaration must be visible at the host compile time because the host manages the allocation of the shared variable, the declaration of such variables cannot be conditionally controlled. That is, you cannot declare such variables as follows:

```
#ifdef __MIC__
_Cilk_shared float fvar1;
#endif
```

Incorrect code is generated here because during the host compile time the code generator does not see the variable declaration, as __MIC__ macro is undefined. As such, the compiler will not allocate the shared memory address space needed by the variable in the coprocessor space. When the coprocessor tries to access the variable, an illegal access error will occur.

You can also use the _Cilk_shared keyword to declare the functions that will execute on the coprocessor. When a function is declared with a _Cilk_shared keyword, the code will generate two functions: one for the host and the other for the Xeon Phi coprocessor.

When applied to a C++ class, all of its member functions and all of the objects of that class are shared between the host and the coprocessor. You can apply the keyword to static fields of a class, assigning pointer-to-shared variables to pointer-to-nonshared variables. Other valid rules are assigning the address of a shared variable to a shared pointer. However, you cannot use _Cilk_shared on the field of a structure, on a static variable, or on variables local to a function.

For dynamic memory allocation in the virtual shared region, the compiler provides the following functions:

- void *_Offload_shared_malloc(size_t size); and void *_Offload_shared_aligned_malloc(size_t size, size_t alignment);: Allocates memory to be shared between the host and the coprocessor. This function reverts back to corresponding versions of malloc() if the coprocessor is not available or the Xeon Phi driver is not loaded.

- void *_Offload_shared_free(void *p); and void *_Offload_shared_aligned_free(void *p);: Frees the memory allocated by Offload_shared_malloc and Offload_shared_aligned_malloc. Reverts back to free if malloc is used during the allocation process, such as when the coprocessor is absent or the Xeon Phi driver was not loaded.

A third way of allocating virtual shared memory is to use the shared memory allocator defined in the Intel C++ standard library. By default, the containers provided by the standard C++ library will allocate memory from the nonshared memory space. When a standard C++ library object is declared with the _Cilk_shared keyword, its data members are allocated in the shared memory. However, these objects will use standard C++ allocators which will allocate memory in the nonshared memory space, resulting in a memory access error during the runtime as the memory space is adjusted for the object. The Intel C++ standard library provides a special allocator template for allocating memory from the shared address space declared as shared_allocator<T> defined in offload.h. For example, to be able to use a shared virtual memory space for a standard C++ library linked list class, you can define it as follows:

```
using namespace std;

typedef list <float, __offload::shared_allocator<float> > shared_list_float;

_Cilk_shared shared_list_float * _Cilk_shared L;
```

Shared Functions

You can use the keyword _Cilk_shared to declare and define the functions that will be offloaded to Xeon Phi. The compiler creates two copies of the function: one for the Xeon host and the other for the Xeon Phi coprocessor. You can declare a shared function as _Cilk_shared void f(); and define it as follows:

```
_Cilk_shared void f()
{
    x+y;
}
```

You can call these functions from host code to be offloaded to the coprocessor by using the _Cilk_offload keyword:

```
int main()
{
    _Cilk_offload f();
}
```

Some of the rules for using _Cilk_offload functions are as follows:

- The named function called by _Cilk_offload f() must be declared _Cilk_shareda nd defined extern.

- The function pointer in the _Cilk_offload indirect call must be of the type pointer-to-shared.

- A shared function whose address is taken must be defined extern.

- Pointer arguments sent to offload_function must be pointer-to-shared variables or objects.

- Global variables, pointers, and functions referenced within _Cilk_offload _Cilk_form ust have shared attributes and pointers must point to shared variables.

- Global variables referenced inside the functions declared _Cilk_sharedm ustb es hared.

The Cilk_offload keyword allows synchronous and asynchronous execution of functions and code fragments on the CPU and coprocessor. Using _Cilk_offload before a function call executes the function on the coprocessor. Using the keyword _Cilk_spawn before _Cilk_offload results in asynchronous execution on the CPU and the coprocessor. You need to use the keyword _Cilk_sync before the host can use the result of the offloaded code for the asynchronous execution.

A _Cilk_offload before a _Cilk_for loop specifies that the entire loop is to be executed on the coprocessor. The syntax for using _Cilk_offloadisa sf ollows:

```
lvalue = _Cilk_offload func (rvalue)
lvalue = _Cilk_offload_to (target-number) func (rvalue)
lvalue = _Cilk_spawn _Cilk_offload func (rvalue)
lvalue = _Cilk_spawn _Cilk_offload_to (target-number) func (rvalue)
_Cilk_offload _Cilk_for (init-expr; test-expr; incr-expr;)
_Cilk_offload_to(target-number) _Cilk_for (init-expr; test-expr; incr-expr)
```

where:

lvalue is an object assigned the return value of the offload function call.

rvalue contains the input shared variables.

func is a function name to be offloaded.

target-number is a signed integer value having following interpretations:

-1: The runtime system selects the target. If no coprocessor is available, the program fails witha ne rrorm essage.

>=0: The code will be executed on the (coprocessor number = target-number %(modulo) total number of coprocessor). For example, if you have 2 coprocessors, the number 4 will signify mic0 (4 modulo 2) or the first coprocessor enumerated by the runtime system and soo n.

init-expr, test-expr, and incr-expr are initialization, test, and increment expressions, respectively, for the for loop expression that will be offloaded to the coprocessor for execution.

Additional examples of virtual shared memory usage can be found under compiler-install-dir/Samples/en_US/C++/mic_samples/LEO_tutorial.

Synchronizing Between the Host and the Coprocessors

Memory synchronization for shared memory variables between the host and the coprocessor happens at the following points only:

1. When an offload function is called by the host code and is entering the offload function on thec oprocessor

2. When an offload function on the target returns

3. When _Cilk_sync is invoked after an asynchronous offload using _Cilk_spawn

Any simultaneous access between the host and the coprocessor outside these synchronization points will result in a race condition, and the value of the shared variables will be undefined.

It is possible for multiple host threads to execute concurrently on the host, and for one or more host threads to offload computation to the coprocessor. In this case, you cannot synchronize between the offloaded code and other threads running on the host through thread synchronization mechanisms, such as mutexes and atomics. However, if the host uses OpenMP parallelism and one or more of the OpenMP threads perform offload, the OpenMP synchronization at the end of the OpenMP parallel region is guaranteed to work. An exception cannot be generated in the coprocessor to be caught and handled on the host.

Index

■ I, J

■ K

■ L

■ M